No

where to Belong

Nowhere to Belong

Punished for the colour of her skin

Harmony Brookes
with Corinne Sweet

HODDER

Publisher's Note
Names and places have been changed throughout in order to protect the identities of individuals.

First published in Great Britain in 2009 by Hodder & Stoughton
An Hachette UK company

1

Copyright © Harmony Brookes

The right of Harmony Brookes to be identified as the
Author of the Work has been asserted by her in accordance
with the Copyright, Designs and Patents Act 1988.

All rights reserved. No part of this publication may be reproduced, stored
in a retrieval system, or transmitted, in any form or by any means without
the prior written permission of the publisher, nor be otherwise circulated
in any form of binding or cover other than that in which it is published and
without a similar condition being imposed on the subsequent purchaser.

A CIP catalogue record for this title is available from the British Library

Paperback ISBN 978 0340 977132
Trade Paperback ISBN 978 0340 977149

Typeset in Plantin Light by Hewer Text UK Ltd, Edinburgh
Printed and bound by Mackays of Chatham Ltd, Chatham, Kent

Hodder & Stoughton policy is to use papers that are natural, renewable
and recyclable products and made from wood grown in sustainable
forests. The logging and manufacturing processes are expected to
conform to the environmental regulations of the country of origin.

Hodder & Stoughton Ltd
338 Euston Road
London NW1 3BH

www.hodder.co.uk

To my two sisters
who I loved and lost

CONTENTS

ACKNOWLEDGEMENTS

My thanks to my two children who spurred me on and also to my friends who stood by me. To everyone at Hodder and to my agent, Jane Graham Maw, for her dedication and belief that my story needed to be told. And to the special friend I made along the way, co-writer Corinne Sweet.

But most of all, my thanks to Dr Brown for being the first person to see past the labels and for giving me back my life.

PROLOGUE

Toy cars. That's what they look like. I look down and feel numb. The traffic is whizzing past on the dual carriageway below at sickening speed. It's a stiflingly hot July afternoon and the stench of the car fumes fills my nose. I look down again at the roaring vehicles below: red car, juggernaut, white car, motorbike. Whiz, whiz, whiz. Everyone whizzing off somewhere. Where are they all going? Why are they all in such a hurry? It's going home time. I guess they're all going home. To families. To loved ones. Home.

Then it hits me again. I feel a pang and I decide to heave myself over. I have nowhere to go home to, nowhere to belong. I've made my way to the centre of the red brick bridge and have been peering over the parapet for God knows how long. The afternoon heat, coupled with the smell and sound of the traffic, makes my head swim. In my right hand the photo is now crumpled. I daren't look. I've only just stopped crying and I don't want to start again.

In a flash I decide. *This is it. No more battling, no more struggle.* I am weary, weary, weary. All I have to do is climb over and drop. It's that simple. But would it be better to drop onto a car, or onto the road? For a minute I hesitate. If I drop on a car, I might hurt someone. I don't want to do that. The desperation inside of me wells up at the thought of hurting someone. I know all too well what it's like to be hurt. I just want the clean, hard satisfaction of smashing myself into something; of dropping like a stone. I need to throw myself at something because the pain inside is threatening to engulf me. To destroy me. It almost has already. Why not finish the job?

OK. I just need to land between the cars. Hit the road. Then they can run me over. Over, over, over. It's all over. I don't want to feel any more. Can't think. Won't think. I have to do it now. This minute. I can't breathe. I can't go on. I'm sick of it all. All of it. I can still feel the photograph stuck fast in my gripped hand. I won't let it go.

With all my effort, all my attention, focused on this moment, I try to pull myself up on to the top of the brick parapet. All I have to do is get to the top and drop. Simple as that. I'm a bit heavy for all this, although I used to be able to run so fast. Can't run now, but I can fall. *OK. One, two, three. Heave* . . .

A strong hand lands firmly on my shoulder. *Shit!* I look sideways, to the right, where the hand is. It's a big, white hand against my black skin. There are black hairs on the back, like a giant spider. All I want to do is brush it off. Further up from the hand is a hairy arm in a white shirt, with a stocky man attached. He's looking at me with what seems to be concern. I've seen that look before. *Shit.* I pull hard against his hand, but it holds fast.

'Wait a moment,' the man's voice says urgently. 'Think about it'.

Wait a moment! What the hell does he mean, *think about it?* I've thought about it. I've thought and thought and thought 'til it's made me ill. Bugger him, what does he know ? I look away from his worried face, down back over the bridge to the road below. It's so inviting, so seductive, that hard concrete, and that endless stinking drone beneath me. It's beckoning me with its siren call: *Come on, jump. Do it. Now. Get it over with*. I can't look at the man. If I do, I am done for. I've got this far and I can't turn back.

'Nothing's worth that,' his calm voice is saying. 'Life's worth living.'

Ha! He doesn't understand. None of them do. How could he? I bet he has a family, children, a home. Someone who loves him. Someone who cares. Somewhere to belong.

God, who's that with him? Underneath my lashes I can see a woman's anxious face peeking out from behind the man. She's standing by their blue car, which has drawn up to the kerb. Her face is scrunched up with worry – or is it fear? I can't decide. She's biting her lip, her arms crossed. Other people are gathering around us now. *Shit.*

OK. It's now or never. I've got to go. I pull hard against the man, trying to wriggle from his iron grasp to hoist myself up onto the parapet. Just a few inches more and I'll be gone. I'm nearly there. I can let go. I'll be free. I'll fly, like a bird in the sky. *Get away you stupid, interfering man. Leave me alone. Let me be.*

But the hand is holding on firm. The voice is droning on and on too.

'You have something to live for.'

Suddenly I am angry. Furious. *Stupid bastard. What does he know?*

'No, I don't!' I shout. 'No I don't – there's nothing left.'

'You're wrong,' he says quietly in my ear, 'I can't let you do this.'

'Let me go!'

I want to kill him. How dare he stop me? What does he know? What does he care? Why can't he just let me go? I try to kick at his legs, but I miss. Everything I had has been taken from me. I've nothing left to live for. At twenty-five I've had enough of this life.

Out of the corner of my eye I see some figures running. *Oh no.* They're coming from the direction of the hospital, to the right of the bridge. I know what they'll do. *They can fuck off too.* I struggle harder. The man is holding on still, and he's talking quietly all the time.

'You will go on. We all have to.'

'I can't,' I shout, the hot tears coming again. 'I won't.'

Nothing to live for now; nothing. I've lost her. They've taken her.

'You don't understand.'

Suddenly, the photo in my hand drops to the pavement. *Oh God.* I panic. The woman steps forward and picks it up. She uncrumples it. I see a sweet little face, black curls, dark eyes. It's too much. She can't have her. I try to snatch the photo back, but I'm pinioned. *Bastards!*

'Come on,' coaxes the man. 'Come down, now. Nothing's that bad, believe me.'

But it is. She's been taken. *They fucking won.* Suddenly, my legs are jelly. There's another hand on my other shoulder. I turn and see a familiar face. A male nurse I know is helping the other man pull me down. Behind them, more people. They've got me, the bastards. I'm trapped. *Why can't they let me do what I want?*

'Come on, Harmony,' says the male nurse. 'Come on now.'

I've heard it all before. I know that voice, and I know that tone. They talk to me like I'm dumb. A stupid, crazy person.

In answer, I struggle and fight. I put all my effort into trying to wrench free. I wrestle, but the two hands restraining me are strong and I feel their fingers digging into my arms. I'm bruising as I pull away from them with all my might, but I don't care. I like the pain; it relieves the anger and grief. My teeth are clenched as I let out a humungous roar of despair and frustration.

'Let me go. Let me go!'

I try to bite and scratch whatever flesh I can find. I've nowhere to go. Nowhere to belong. Nothing to live for. This is the end and I want it to come. Right now. Hard and fast.

Moments later I feel a sharp prick in my buttock.

Darkness.

I

Shameful Beginnings

'... the whereabouts of father are not known ... mother lives somewhere in London, but doesn't seem to be interested in having any contact with her daughter ... the children appear well cared for by their foster parents, and are not unduly disturbed by the lack of contact with their own mother ...'
(Social worker's report).

Right from the start I had nowhere to belong. I was homeless from day one. I truly believe that every child should be a wanted child, and have loving parents, a safe home, and a strong sense of belonging. Even one loving parent is better than none. That's every child's natural birthright. Unfortunately, I had none of these things. The truth is – as far as I have been able to uncover so far – that my birth was the product of a dangerous liaison and therefore the source of immense shame to all concerned.

My father originally came from an island in the Caribbean and was a well-known and highly-respected pastor. He came to the UK in the 1960s, as did many African-Caribbean people, lured by the promise of a better life in the 'Mother Country' (as it was called back then), which openly recruited West Indians from the Commonwealth to run vital services for the predominantly white population. Handsome Jeremiah Andrews arrived off the boat in the mid-Sixties and soon fell in love and married a woman from his island whom he courted here in the UK. He worked hard, and quickly settled down in a leafy, home counties market town, a couple of hours from London. In time, the Andrews had five children. They didn't have much money, and mainly lived in council properties, but they were respectable church people, and were able to clothe, feed and educate their growing brood.

However, despite being a family man and religious leader, Jem, as he was known, was not as God-fearing as he was thought to be by his loyal Pentecostal parishioners. A vital, stocky man, he had an eye for the ladies, especially the younger ones, and apparently he wasn't above paying for his pleasures. It seems, from what I've discovered subsequently, that my own mother was a fourteen-year-old black schoolgirl in the same town with whom he had sex in exchange for a little cash.

There is a cloud of shame surrounding the whole affair, and one version I heard was that my mother was being prostituted with her own mother's knowledge – even encouragement – to bring home money for her cash-strapped family. Apparently, my grandmother was utterly furious to find out her daughter was pregnant, and subsequently more money changed hands. The outcome of their furtive, illegal union was *me*. Despite my mother's age, the police were never involved. I imagine that my grandmother – who was a tough old matriarch from the Caribbean – would not have trusted them at all. If she was complicit in her daughter's downfall, she would have avoided the police at all costs. Whatever the case, my grandmother must have been frightened about what would happen to her daughter, and worse, to her own reputation, if it all came out in the open. Being a God-fearing woman

– albeit one full of contradictions – she never considered an abortion.

Apparently, the two families – my mother's and my father's – knew each other back in the Caribbean. They'd actually been neighbours, and for all I know my father was settling an old score. Things sometimes happen like that, with feuds being worked out over generations. People had long memories back then.

It seems that back home on the island sexual behaviour was often more casual, and people started having sex younger than here in the UK. As I've heard it, it was not unusual for sexual liaisons to happen between family members, or between older men and younger women, or even for money to be exchanged. Maybe that explains why my father thought it was okay to pay for sex with a schoolgirl. Or perhaps my dad just did what came naturally to him, and figured he could get away with it because he was such a respected member of the community? He was certainly the head of the family, a strict and untouchable man, whose word was law at home. Later, however, I heard he was often called 'jerk-off Jeremiah' round our town, so maybe his reputation wasn't as squeaky clean as he'd hoped.

Whatever people might have called my father behind his back, my grandmother was not of a mind to shop him to the authorities. Besides, she had bigger things to worry about. In the 1960s, Britain was not a welcoming place for people of colour. Enoch Powell was working the nation up into a frenzy, scaremongering that immigration would eventually lead to terrible racial conflict, and Britain's streets transformed into 'rivers of blood'. This was at a time before any race relations laws existed, so people could discriminate quite openly, putting up signs saying

'No Irish, No Blacks and No Gypsies' in their windows when they rented a room. It was also a time when the civil rights movement was just beginning to stir, especially in America with the rise of Martin Luther King, the great black civil rights orator and leader. However the UK was still way behind the US in most things, including black and ethnic minority equality. Thus, their sleepy, rural, mainly white market town was a fairly hostile environment for both my grandmother and mother to have to deal with an illegitimate black baby girl, born in very dubious circumstances.

The outcome of this sorry escapade was that my birth was shrouded in mystery and shame. I was not a welcome arrival to anyone's household. I was definitely something to be hidden and scorned, a reminder of the painful difficulties that had befallen a young girl who was really still just a child herself.

Thus, on 5 December 1968, I was born into very inauspicious circumstances, with my grandmother making it absolutely clear that I would never be allowed home from the secret nursing home she sent her teenage daughter to. As far as I know, my mother was not allowed to hold me, feed me, or bond with me. In fact, she was actively encouraged to give me up and even if she had wanted to keep me, everything was stacked heavily against her. I've been told that my grandmother forced my mum to choose between being thrown out on the street with her illegitimate baby to make her way alone in the world, or to give me up, and carry on as they were before. Clearly there was no real choice for a schoolgirl of fourteen, even if she was working a regular 'night shift' for cash for the family kitty. Thus, my mother was sent off to stay with relations – probably in London, which was big enough to cloak such a shameful secret – and stayed there until I was safely 'disappeared'.

Because of my scandalous background, there seems to be scant record of the beginning of my life. I don't know how much I weighed, if I had hair, or what colour my skin or eyes were. There are no proud baby photos, no baby albums, nothing at all to note my coming into the world. In a way, this set up a pattern that was to be repeated over and over for the rest of my life. I was to be hidden. I was an embarrassment. I was something to be forgotten or 'lost'; even hated. From my very first moments I was an object of shame and, as such, was to be blamed for anything bad that happened to my mother's and grandmother's family.

It seems from my NHS records, which I eventually managed to procure, that I spent my first couple of weeks in the nursing home. The notes are very brief and impersonal. Nobody writes anything much about me, as an individual.

After that, I was handed on to a temporary foster carer, a GP and her family who took pity on my situation, while a longer-term solution was found through Social Services. Although the records are poor, I think Social Services were desperate to place me as soon as possible. The temporary foster home I was in terminated very quickly when, sadly, my foster mother suddenly had a heart attack and died. There must have been a lot of confusion and upset, and I would have been handed around again, a bit like an unwanted package. I must have been bottle-fed by a series of strangers – nurses, social workers, GPs, midwives, indeed anyone who was around. Finally, a local white couple stepped forward to foster me. Social Services must have looked at their files and noticed this pair had fostered before and that there were apparently no complaints. Plus they were willing to take a 'coloured' child (as I would have been called back then), something most people in my home community would have thought twice about. This was an era when newspapers were crammed full of stories about the imminent swamping of the UK by a flood of black immigrants. There was a real sense of fear about what might happen to (literally) change the complexion of English life, and our town seemed to be doing its best to resist that change.

The Stabards, a middle-aged couple, had three children who had already grown up and left home by the time I entered their household, around Easter 1969. When the social workers brought me in my regulation Social Services carrycot, with no clothes or toys of my own, the only other child in the house was another foster daughter. Faith was also black, and three years older than myself. She was thought to be a 'difficult' child to place with a family, since she was sickly, with a drooping right eyelid, and it was also believed that she was somewhat 'educationally subnormal' (the term used at the time for 'learning difficulties'). Faith had absolutely no family, so was more or less a permanent placement with the Stabards.

The house that the social workers entered had a neat, magnolia-painted hall and lounge, with an orangey, chintzy sofa and two armchairs, floral wallpaper and curtains, white paint and burgundy-coloured, patterned carpet. The overall effect would have been of a family home; lived-in but tidy. Mr and Mrs Stabard would have seemed a dowdy but solid middle-aged couple. As they sat on the comfy 'best' sofa, with me gurgling in my carrycot sandwiched in between, they would have probably seemed the perfect pair to take care of a waif and stray with murky beginnings. The social worker might well have left the house feeling satisfied that, at last, another 'difficult' child had been placed with people whom the local authority could really trust to put a child's interests first.

Faith, who was watching the new arrival quietly, would have probably been dressed in a neat pale blue dress and white cardigan, with a big white bow in her short curly hair – a testament to how well looked after a black foster child could be. This was her Sunday best. Although shy and a little slow, Faith would have looked like a sweet little 'piccaninny' to an outsider, with her shiny black patent shoes and clean white socks. She would probably have watched the proceedings very quietly, with wide eyes, and may have sucked her two fingers for comfort, but would not have made a fuss or have spoken unless she'd been spoken to. She would not have shown any feelings – she knew better. Social Services would probably have made an official report noting that she was clean and well cared for, just as they usually did about the children in our house. What they didn't know was that the neat living room and the Sunday best were a show to distract them from delving into the mess beyond.

Memory is a strange thing. Most people can remember faces and places, time and dates, whereas my earliest memories are of smells, feelings, looks and strange visual images. When I think back to my early childhood the main memory I have is of fear and darkness, and immense feelings of claustrophobia and dread. My memories are like a string of snapshots – like flashed-up images on a screen – and it is often difficult to remember all the bits in between. My flashes of memory have many horrible feelings attached, which make me shiver to remember them. In fact, they're so painful, I've tried to shut them out, or shut them down, for most of my life.

... I am lying waiting. It's cold, dark and I'm hungry and wet. I just know I've been waiting a long time, and there's a horrible feeling that no-one will ever come. A small brown face appears above me and disappears. This happens several times. I think I'm in a small dark room, and there is another girl in there. I can hear crying. I'm hungry, hungry, hungry and I feel cold, wet and scared. No-one comes and the room gets darker and then light and then dark again. I remember crying till I couldn't cry any more, and yet no-one comes, except the little brown face which looks at me and goes away again ...

... I am on a cold floor in a very dark, scary place. It smells of wood, of dampness. It's freezing cold and there's lots of spiders. I feel things running over my legs and arms, and I'm wet and cold, hungry and frightened. It's dark, but I can hear the other girl there and she comes over and I see her brown face in the shadows as she picks me up. She hauls me up by my arms, which hurts, and then I'm on her lap, sitting on something softer, which feels nice. I'm warm and comforted. I put two fingers in my mouth and suck them. They taste warm. She's humming in my ear, holding me tight, and I feel a bit calmer, although she smells of wee and poo. I forget I feel so hungry as she strokes my hair and hums. She rocks me back and forth and I feel a bit calmer, although I somehow know we can't get out of where we are ...

... Back in the small, dark, boxy bedroom, I'm in a cot with wooden bars crying – I don't know what about – when suddenly a white-haired man's ruddy face appears above mine with stinky breath and a hairy arm grabs me by the hair while

another arm pulls me out of my cot by my arm. I scream and I feel a slap of a big hand sting across my face. I'm half-pulled, half-carried up on the man's shoulder and he's really pongy. My eyes sting and my face is burning and I'm still crying. I can feel he's very angry. He's shouting something, and I feel the force of his strength as he goes quickly from my room to the next one, opens a door in the corner and suddenly I'm thrown on the floor in the dark. Slam. The door is shut tight. It's stifling, pitch black. I scream my head off, terrified. I want to get out. Right now. But I can't. I'm next to something big and padded which is hard and boiling hot. I put my fingers through the padding and scream in pain when I touch something which burns my fingers. I can hear the man shouting outside and telling me to 'shut up and stay there till you're told.' I know I can't move. I'm crying and shaking and my wee comes and the floor is wet when I touch the puddle under me with my fingers. Then I put my hands up and there's something hard and wooden over my head – a shelf. The crack of light under the door gradually goes dark as hours go by. I'm starving hungry, and now cold and wet, but I know I can't get out or the man will shout at me and slap me even more. I feel terrified, hopeless and completely alone . . .

. . . I am walking along the road, dressed in my Sunday best, holding the hand of Mrs Stabard. I like walking holding her hand, but she walks fast and doesn't look down at me. My hair is tightly curled and I have a big bow on the side – it hurts where it's clipped in. My shoes are too tight and I've been told I mustn't get my white socks and cardigan dirty. I am aware that people are stopping and staring at me; at us. Everyone we pass, as we go by gates and houses, gapes at us, open-mouthed. I wonder if I haven't done my dress up properly. Then we're in a big booming place with everyone standing in rows, singing and sitting with their heads down, and I have to be very quiet.

I peek out from under my lashes and catch Faith's eye as she is looking up too. I have to stifle a giggle – I bite my tongue. Faith looks away, but I sense she's smiling . . .

. . . I am back in the familiar damp, dark place: the shed in the garden. It smells of dank wood, earth, wee. Light comes in through a high slit in the wall. Faith's there too, sitting in an old chair, rocking herself back and forth, singing and then humming. Humming and singing all the time, over and over. I watch her and feel things crawling up my legs as I sit on the cold hard floor. Outside I can hear children's voices, laughing, shouting. I get up on unsteady legs and toddle over to the gap in the wall. If I pull myself up on tiptoe, and hold onto the slit, through it I can see children running around on the grass outside, kicking a ball, laughing and rolling on the ground, throwing things at each other. There are loads of coloured things they are playing with – toys and bikes. I look back over at Faith in the old brown armchair, but it's too dark to see much. Her face is a blur. I'm cold and hungry and I can see sun coming in under a big door, which I know is locked. I feel hopeless, scared, and angry that I can't get out to where the other children are on the grass outside. My nappy feels full and heavy hanging down between my legs, which are chapped and sore on the inside. It's hard seeing the other children running and laughing outside – why am I in this stinky place, and not having fun with them? Why can't I go out? I want to go out, now! I know it's hopeless and I start crying, feeling numb inside . . .

. . . It's pitch black. Freezing cold. I'm exhausted, wet and starving. I've been asleep on the ground. All around I can smell wee and poo. Faith is asleep in the chair, but I can't see her. Suddenly, the door of the shed bursts open and a woman's face framed with grey hair appears. 'Wake up, come on, hurry up,' she snaps. The light flooding in the door suddenly makes me blink. Faith moans.

The woman strides in and pulls me up roughly by the arm, and then shakes Faith awake, and we are pulled outside. It's dark and drizzling. We are pulled roughly upstairs to bed in the dark. I have no idea how long we've been in the shed, but it's been hours and we've had no food. It feels very late. As we go upstairs I can see a door, and through it a man's legs stretched out in an armchair. He is snoring, a glass in his hand ...

... It's winter, and a little baby appears in our box bedroom. I am now big enough to be in the bottom bunk, so the baby is in my old cot, crying its head off. It's night. I get out of bed and the other girl, Faith, is there, hanging over the cot. We look at each other. The baby's face is screwed up and she is screaming, tears running down her face. It's dark and cold and I can feel the rough wooden floorboards under my bare feet. We can't put the light on as there's no bulb overhead. We open the net curtains a bit to see better. We've no idea where the baby has come from, and Faith and I look at each other in wonder and shrug. What are we to do with it?

The baby is loud and agitated, and its crying goes on and on. Eventually Faith leans over and picks it up. She hugs the baby and it quietens down. I'm relieved that it's quietening down, but still can't understand what it's doing in our room. I watch Faith hugging the baby and shushing her, and I feel a pang of envy: I want someone to pick me up, to hug me and make me feel good too. I longed for someone to love me and make me feel safe. At that moment I'm jealous of the baby for taking Faith away from me ...

I found out much later that the baby – Hope – was my half-sister. My mother, wherever she was, had clearly fallen pregnant again, and somehow this baby had found its way to our house. I was stunned for a while, in a childish sort of way, that my mother was still alive. I think I'd come to think that she must be dead by now, otherwise why would she not visit me or take me home with her? To think she had had another baby, and had given it away as well, seemed very strange and I remember feeling very gloomy as I sat in the shed day after day. Why didn't she want me? What had I done? Was this why I was in the shed – because I was so bad? And why didn't she want her other baby? What was wrong with us both?

 I couldn't think about it very logically as I was so young, but I felt her absence as a deep ache in my guts. Every day I ached for my mummy to come and love me; to make everything different. But my mummy never came, and bit by bit I began to forget about her again.

 Anyway, I was pleased to have a half-sister, but she was a little, crying baby, and it took some time before we began to develop any real kind of relationship. At first Mrs Stabard kept Hope in the kitchen in the daytime in a cot, but once she got a bit bigger and started sitting up and moving, she ended up in the shed with us every day. We would all be locked in there, and it was expected that Faith and I would look after her. This was difficult for us, as we were small too, and I sometimes resented Hope being there. Other times it felt nice, especially when the three of us huddled on the smelly armchair and fell asleep, or made up stories, or sang songs to keep us going during the long hours in the dark.

Around this time, when I'm about three years old, my memories become sharper and more focused. I know there were three of us girls living in a box room at the top of the stairs in the Stabards' house, over the porch: the black foster kids' room. This box room was tiny – just about big enough to cram in a single bunk bed. Our bunks had just one thin orange blanket and dark sheets, which were seldom changed. We all had one plain cream winceyette nightie – but no slippers or dressing gown, so we were cold a lot of the time.

The walls had been stripped at some point, but had never been papered or painted. They were bare, chipped brownish plaster and very grotty. The windows were covered with flimsy black curtains and some dirty grey nets. There was no carpet on the floor – just scuzzy bare floorboards with nails sticking up out of them. I learned fairly early on to be careful not to rip my bare feet on their jagged edges. Most bizarre of all, there was no light bulb. The Stabards had not seen fit to put one in, for some reason. I don't know if they were saving money, or deliberately keeping us in the dark, but if they came into our room at night time, they'd bring a bulb with them. Otherwise, we huddled together in the dark, trying not to be scared.

Since we didn't have any toys we were very bored most of the time. We weren't allowed books, dolls, teddies or board games. What made it worse is that we knew that there were loads of toys under the stairs, which we longed to play with. However, we learned very quickly that these were not for the likes of us. We had to make do with amusing ourselves as best we could without anything to stimulate our minds. Sometimes we made up songs and weird games, but a lot of the time we were silent, hardly moving or speaking. Other times, when our foster parents were there, we caught each others' eyes, and somehow understood each other without words.

In our room there was a built-in hanging wardrobe containing a few second-hand clothes. These were the total of our worldly goods. The box room was exactly that – a cold, empty box. However, the rest of the upstairs was completely different. The Stabards had a big double bedroom at the back, looking out over the garden, with pink flowery curtains and a big comfy double bed. Their wallpaper was white with big orange flowers on it and they had fitted carpet and wardrobes. It looked like a palace to us at the time, although we were not allowed in. There wasn't any central heating in the house, and the Stabards' bedroom had the only bar fire – a real necessity on cold winter nights. Next door to their bedroom there was a bathroom with black and white lino tiles, and a separate, old-fashioned chain-pull toilet with a dirty grey floor.

Between our front box room and their bedroom at the back, was a large bedroom, with pale blue walls, three single divans in it and more fitted carpet. This was the Stabards' own children's room (they had three), and as they'd left home, it was now kept for when their grandchildren came to stay. Each bed had crisp white sheets, several thick blankets and a fancy candlewick cover. The room was much nicer and cosier than ours, and there were fitted cupboards, a dressing table with a heart-shaped mirror and pretty flowery curtains. This room was bright and clean and felt like a proper bedroom. However, we were completely forbidden from entering this luxurious room, even though it lay empty most of the time, because it wasn't 'ours'. The Stabards didn't think we deserved a room like that.

Our home wasn't in the house at all, but in the garden shed. Looking out the back kitchen window to the left, next to the neighbours' fence and high hedge, there was a red brick shed with a plastic see-through corrugated roof. The shed was about five foot high, six foot long and rectangular, with a narrow slit of a window, about a foot long and six inches deep, along the underside of the roof, facing the lawn. It had a slanting roof which was higher at the fence side, like a lean-to. The shed itself was accessed through a high, black wrought iron gate, which had a big padlock. Between the shed door and the gate, there was a small paved courtyard, about four square feet deep. I think the shed might have been a coal-bunker in earlier times, with a wooden roof or covered chute, where the coal was poured in. In fact, I can remember a coalman coming round selling sacks of potatoes, so there must have been a coal round in the area, not too long ago.

We were put in the shed because we weren't supposed to be in the house, because it wasn't 'ours'. This was the place we girls had to live in every day, come rain or shine, except on Sundays when the Stabards dressed us in our best Sunday clothes and took us to church. And, indeed, we called the shed 'our home'. In fact, the shed was the home of any black foster children passing through the house.

From as far back as I remember we would be taken out of the house in the morning and were told, coldly and firmly, to stay in the shed, behave and be quiet. Then the outer wrought iron gate was locked with a padlock – *clunk*. The shed was dark and smelly, which we hated. It had no lighting, except for the sunlight coming in through the slit window and the dingy corrugated roof. It had big spiders, which absolutely terrified me. Since there was no heating it was freezing in winter. Of course it had no toilet – which probably explains why I was kept in nappies until the age of five. We didn't have anyone to change us, so we weed and pooed all day into the same nappy, which became sodden and heavy by bedtime. When we were too old for nappies, we simply went to the toilet on the floor in the corner of the shed, as there was no way we could get out of there without being let out by one of the Stabards. Since we couldn't wash ourselves, or our hands, we were always filthy, and I expect we stank.

The shed had a rickety, falling-apart table, a ripped, smelly, brown armchair and a peeling, upright kitchen chair. We would cuddle on the armchair together for warmth or we'd just stand around. Sometimes we'd sit or lie on the concrete floor, but it could be ice-cold, especially in winter. There was no food in the shed, but there was water. They put an old white plastic water bottle in there with us and we could swig out of it when we were thirsty. But if it ran out, which it often did when it was hot, there was absolutely nothing we could do about it. We could shout and call to Mrs Stabard, but if she heard us she usually ignored us.

If we were especially 'good' and didn't make too much noise in the shed, Mrs Stabard would come and open the shed door and let us go out in the little paved courtyard between the shed door and the wrought iron gate. This was our reward. But sometimes we'd get a bit too bold and start shaking the bars of the iron gate. It was so tempting being only inches from the lawn. We could see all that space to run around in, and beyond the garden the freedom of the hills seemed to be beckoning to us.

Sometimes it was just too hard to control ourselves. We'd need the loo so we'd shake the bars, and the padlock would rattle. Sometimes we'd jump up and down, with our fingers in our mouths, shouting, 'Ya, ya! Ya, ya!' as a kind of protest. I think we just felt very fed up at being caged and sometimes it all boiled over, especially on summer afternoons when the sun was out and the sky was blue. We just wanted fresh air, exercise and freedom. And as we were hungry all the time, some food too. But whenever we made a noise Mrs Stabard would be furious with us. She'd come marching out with an expressionless face and push us back into the shed, slamming the door shut. By the time night came and we were allowed back into the house, we were exhausted, cold and shut down. Without a word we'd head straight to our dark, cramped bedroom.

2

The Odd Couple

'... they appear well cared for by their foster parents ... they seem very happy in their present home ...' (Social worker's report)

The Stabards were a well-respected, highly religious, local couple, who had a long track record of fostering children, especially those who were difficult to place: those who were black, Asian or disabled. They had been married just after the Second World War, where they met in the forces, and were now in their fifties. Our town was an old farming community, with old-fashioned values and traditions. The Stabards were typical, and would dress up in their Sunday best for church. During the week Leonard Stabard worked full-time as a maintenance engineer in a local factory, while his wife, Prudence, ran their 1940s council house and looked after their three children, Bernard, Jemima and Petula.

The Stabards lived in a quiet cul-de-sac on the edge of town, overlooking a small circular green. The surrounding council houses around 97 Forestlane Way were respectable red-brick homes, with trimmed hedges and neat lawns. There were not many cars, as most people used the buses, or walked or cycled into town. By the time I went to live with them in their end-of-terrace semi, their children had left home and they were already very set in their ways.

Although we passed the neighbours when we went to church, or saw them through the hedge in the back garden, we never spoke to them. Mr and Mrs Stabard would say 'hello' and seem friendly enough, but they never invited the neighbours in and kept a careful distance. The outside world was completely alien and unknown to us. We didn't go to nursery or pre-school, or to other children's houses or parties, and we never went swimming, to the park or out to any of the local shops or cinemas. Our world was tiny: our shed, our room and whatever we saw on the weekly ten minute walk to the Baptist church.

Despite being devoted church-goers, the Stabards were a very odd couple. Thinking about it now, I don't ever remember seeing them kiss or hug, or show any real warmth or affection towards each other. I don't know if she was happy with him or whether they loved each other. She seemed a bit trapped and down sometimes, like she just had to make the best of things. They didn't really seem like a married couple, but more like a brother and sister living in the same house. I think she kept him at arm's length physically and was actually a little bit scared of him. Only once did I really see them row, when he raised his hand and hit her across the face. I was shocked, but all she did was turn and scuttle off without a word. I never saw him hit her again after that, but he was definitely the dominant partner.

Mrs Stabard was a short, round woman who seldom smiled. She had long, grey hair pulled into a severe bun and wore very plain, conservative clothes. Most days she wore either a grey or navy top and skirt, or a white blouse and grey skirt. She'd always wear one of those old-fashioned housewives' pinnies, with little flowers all over it and a big pocket at the front. She never wore make-up or perfume, and rarely sported jewellery. The only exception would be a simple silver or gold brooch pinned to the lapel of her navy Sunday suit. On her feet she usually wore schoolmistressy, black brogues and pinkish stockings. I remember her legs always being 'bad', and her wearing bandages round them. She was a cold, odd woman who always kept her distance – even from her husband – and stayed inside most of the time.

Mr Stabard was about six inches taller, with a florid complexion and cold blue eyes. He had white hair and a streak of grey through the top. Mr Stabard was quite a strong man, with muscly arms and large hands, which were covered with dark hairs. He was stocky, yet clearly had been quite fit in his military years. He wore old-fashioned dark tweedy trousers with braces, and a white shirt with the sleeves rolled up. His one personal luxury was Brut aftershave, which he splashed on liberally. He was often out of breath, and wheezed, although he didn't smoke. However, he did drink a great deal, especially Guinness, whisky and gin, and I was used to the heady smell of alcohol on his breath mixing with the Brut aftershave. He often went out to the local British Legion club to drink with ex-forces mates after work, leaving his wife at home alone with us. I never saw Mrs Stabard drink herself, although she didn't seem to mind it when her husband came home drunk. Instead, she liked her tea and cakes, which she'd consume in great quantities.

By the time I came to live with them, all of the Stabards' natural children had married and Jemima, the eldest girl, had a boy, Basil; Bernard, the middle son, had two boys, Arnold and Brian; and Petula, the youngest, had three girls, Doreen, Sandra and Vivien (she went on to have three more boys, Derek, Kevin and David, making six in all).

Thus, several small grandchildren would visit the house a couple of times a week and have lots of fun with all the toys and games that were usually hidden away in the cupboard under the stairs. The Stabards prided themselves on being good with children – in fact Pru Stabard had worked as a nanny before she had married and had her own brood.

I heard much later that they had both actually worked as volunteers in a notorious residential children's home in our area earlier in their marriage, and were very friendly with the chief officer. Later this children's home was closed down, and the chief officer was convicted for crimes against children, including sexual abuse and child cruelty. I'm not sure what they learned from working there, but it certainly didn't improve their fostering skills.

At the time, of course, I had no clear idea of what foster parents were supposed to be like. I'd never been in anyone else's home and I suppose I thought what I was experiencing was normal. However, it did hurt to see Mrs Stabard being warm and friendly to her own children and grandchildren. It's the only time I ever saw her round, bland face break into a weak little smile.

. . . I'm standing in the penned-in area, in front of our shed. It's a warm day, and I'm watching the cats play fight on the lawn. I hear voices and can see a little boy being hugged by Mrs Stabard in the kitchen. I'm looking through the back door, which is open, and I feel pain in my tummy as I watch her give him a big hug and ruffle his hair. Mrs Stabard goes to a kitchen cupboard, and gets out a lollipop and gives it to the little boy, bending over towards him and smiling. I feel tears sting my eyes.

Later, Mrs Stabard is bent over, doing up my buckle shoes. I look at the top of her grey head and long for a hug. I want her to look at me warmly, and smile like she did to the little boy. My legs are dangling over the chair sides and she roughly drops my foot with the shoe on, snatches up the other one, and pushes on the shoe. 'Sit still!' she snaps in a hard voice. She's so cold and distant that I feel like crying. Why doesn't she like me? When the job is done she straightens up and turns away. No smile. No hugs. I put my fingers in my mouth and suck. I start swinging my legs to make me feel happier. Mrs Stabard turns round and says sharply, 'Stop that. Sit still and be quiet.' She talks to me like I'm the dog, but not one that she likes. I sit there sucking my fingers, feeling very lonely and hopeless. It's not fair . . .

As I got older, I noticed that my foster mother had two sides to her personality: a strict, cold one that she'd show to Faith, Hope and me, and a warm, tender one she saved for her real family. Even so I still felt very attached to her and desperately wanted her to love me. I hoped that if I tried hard enough to get everything right she would treat me like her grandchild one day. If I did whatever she and her husband wanted, she might finally give me a hug, or be kind and warm. It was unbearable to think that her coldness would go on and on for ever, so I did everything I could to win her approval.

It was Mr Stabard who seemed to really hate us foster kids. He was much more aggressive than Mrs Stabard, who may have been cold, but wasn't as deliberately cruel. She seemed under his thumb most of the time. She barely spoke to us; instead she'd point with her arm to tell us to go upstairs or out the shed. I don't know if she thought it was beneath her to talk to us, or whether she thought we were so thick we couldn't understand English.

Mr Stabard, on the other hand, would bark orders. He was quite militaristic, and would shout at us to get tea or supper, and would then come and check we had done it. If we hadn't cut the bread right, or peeled the onions correctly, he would bark at us like a sergeant major. We'd have to stand to attention until he'd finished, and then do it all again until he was satisfied. He liked it when he made us jump with fear. It would make him laugh. He had a dry, nasty, sarcastic laugh, which we'd come at first to loathe and then later, utterly fear and detest.

The uncomfortable truth was that both Mr and Mrs Stabard really hated black people, and black children in particular. For them, fostering was simply an easy way of earning money.

From the start we were told that we should be very grateful that we were being fostered. We were obviously very lucky. Not everybody would take in the likes of us, and clearly nobody else wanted us. The Stabards told us over and over that they put us in the shed because we were 'bad, dirty children'. In their twisted minds, black skin clearly equated with evil and filth. We were not, therefore, worthy to go into all the areas of the house that the little white grandchildren could go into, such as the lounge or the nice bedroom upstairs. We would only spoil them. Since we were not allowed to play in the garden, we could only watch the grandchildren kicking a ball about as we peered through the slit window in the shed wall. When they left their toys scattered carelessly on the lawn, we had to tread past them, careful not to touch them in case we contaminated them with our evil. It was all very confusing and upsetting. What was wrong with us?

Strangely, the Stabards loved animals (certainly more than little black children) and had a small menagerie of pets. They had seven cats, of various colours and varieties, four dogs, and four rabbits, plus hamsters and guinea pigs in wooden hutches. There was also an aviary sporting zebra finches, quails, cockatiels, budgies and canaries. Geese and ducks sat on the small, stagnant pond in the back garden, near the rockery and old greenhouse. They even had three brown, fluffy chickens and a tethered white goat. I really loved one of the geese, and used to tell her all my worries. She was white and waddled around after me and I loved her very much. Unlike her human owners, she didn't care about the colour of my skin.

It was important to the Stabards that they try to purify our souls because we were black, and therefore evil. So every week we'd be marched to church, dressed up smartly in our Sunday best. They'd do our hair, pulling it taut in big white ribbons, Minnie-Mouse-style. Out would come our pale blue dresses with matching blue jackets or little white cardigans. We'd wear our too-tight black patent squeaky shoes and little white socks, or tights in winter. Hand in hand we'd walk along the road, in complete silence, following Mrs Stabard, like three little black ducklings bobbing along behind big white mamma duck.

Since there were virtually no black faces at all in our neighbourhood, we three, in our silly white ribbons, were a total oddity. People trimming their hedges would stop mid-clip to gawp at us in our church finery. Mrs Stabard would be in her plain navy suit and a navy hat, and Mr Stabard would be in his dark tweedy suit and shiny black shoes. We'd look very respectable, but people would still goggle at us as we passed. I felt so self-conscious and awkward then, and very aware that having black skin made us different from everyone else. This was drummed in at home, when Mrs Stabard would tell us sharply to come away from the window in case someone saw us. It was like she felt embarrassed to have the likes of us seen in her house. Even when we were walking to church, looking very prim and sweet, but unmistakably black-skinned, I could sense Mrs Stabard's tension as she met other people.

The Stabards were a different couple once they were out of the house together. He became friendly and chatty, and she smiled at people and talked to them. I looked at her, wondering, 'Why doesn't she talk to us like that?' and 'Why doesn't she smile at me that way?' At home Mr Stabard was a very silent, secretive man (except when he was drunk, or lost his temper), so it was so weird to see him being all jolly and talking to other church-goers. It was like a different man had emerged into the daylight. He'd even take our hands to cross the road and part of me would think: 'Ooh, maybe he's changed. Maybe he likes us now. Maybe they'll love us when we get home?' Then we would go home and the minute we crossed the threshold he would revert instantly to the old regime.

Then one day something happened that was very strange indeed. It was a weekday, and we were expecting to go into the shed as usual. Mrs Stabard came up to our box room. She stood in the door awkwardly for a moment, then gestured to the wardrobe and said, 'Put on your Sunday outfits.' It was a Wednesday, but we did as we were told, of course, although we were very confused as to what was happening. Mrs Stabard pointed to the stairs and said, 'Front room, now.' Since she seldom spoke to us, it was all very unusual. We filed downstairs and stood in a little row at the bottom. Mrs Stabard walked past us, and opened the lounge door. *The lounge*. I had never been in there to my knowledge since arriving in the house, but today I was going in. When we walked in we saw a pile of bright objects, gleaming on the burgundy carpet. *Toys!* We looked up at Mrs Stabard's flat, motionless face and she pointed at the toys. Amazed, we three girls looked at each other for reassurance, and then back at her, but then when nothing untoward happened we shot towards the toys and started playing. I chose a big pink dolly and I started brushing her hair and moving her long eyelashes up and down. She made a 'waaa' sound when I tilted her. I couldn't believe it. I'd seen the grandchildren playing with her before and it had always been my wildest dream to hold her myself – and now I really was. It was a fantastic feeling, something I'd never experienced before.

All of a sudden the doorbell went *ding dong*. We never had visitors. All three of us looked up with big eyes open wide, curious and alert, just in time to see Mrs Stabard disappear and come back in with a tall, fair women in a dark suit. She sat down in one of the chintzy chairs and Mrs Stabard sat in the other. The visitor got out a clipboard and started writing something. The two women talked in whispers so we couldn't really hear. Anyway, we were sitting on the floor, each so engrossed in the toys, we didn't really care, and every so often we would look up at each other and grin secretively. We were having the time of our lives. Faith and I were completely ecstatic, and little Hope was sitting on her bottom, putting toy after toy in her mouth.

Suddenly, we heard the door click. We looked up and the visitor was gone. We'd been so absorbed we hadn't noticed. Mrs Stabard rushed towards us, a strange look on her face, yanked us up, and pulled us out of the room. The toys went flying and I had to drop my dolly, which made me distraught, and I strained to pick her up again. I started crying loudly, which I knew my foster mother hated. Faith and Hope joined in. I was thinking, 'She's *my* dolly now.'

I didn't want to let her go. Mrs Stabard kicked the doll out of reach and pulled me out of the room. Then we were pushed upstairs, all sobbing loudly, and ordered to take off our best clothes. After that we were frog-marched outside to the shed and briskly locked in, with absolutely no explanation whatsoever.

It was only much, much later, after this scenario was repeated again and again over the years, that I realised that this had been one of our first visits from Social Services. The authorities would write to the Stabards, giving them two weeks' warning, so they had time to stage-manage the whole event. Mrs Stabard knew that they never looked beyond the front hall and the lounge, so she felt safe. I guess the officials assumed it was as nice everywhere else and took the Stabards at face value. The whole scene of us playing happily with toys, dressed in our Sunday best, was literally staged for their visit. At no other time did we ever have access to the grandchildren's toys. Social Services never came upstairs to see where we slept, and they never went out to the scuzzy kitchen, and had absolutely no idea about the shed. What's more, they didn't ever come near us. They never spoke to us, or examined us. We were observed from across the room, as the social worker ticked the boxes on her clipboard, sipping tea with Mrs Stabard who was almost nice to us for once. The officials would talk to her about us over our heads, but never asked us anything directly. If they looked at our bodies at all, they did so with our clothes on, so they never found anything untoward.

Of course, what the social worker did not know was that something was happening beneath the surface at the Stabards', which was far from savoury or normal, despite appearances to the contrary. It was something so profound that it would shape my life – and that of every other foster child who entered their house, over the next twenty-three years. It was something that no visitor would have picked up on sitting in the neat, cosy living room, sipping tea with Mrs Stabard, or even sharing a glass of Guinness with Mr Stabard. However, once the act for the social worker was over, life returned to 'normal'. And that 'normal' was the most abnormal life anyone could possibly imagine for three small children, supposedly 'in care'. Especially as we three kids were really the Stabards' domestic house slaves.

3

House Slaves

'Harmony enjoys the company of her sister and the other child at the foster home. She has normal interests for a girl of her age ... and continues to enjoy good health ... ' (Social worker's report)

We three foster children had to 'earn' our place in the house, and we had to do that by doing all the chores. Behind the 'respectable' façade of the house was a different world altogether. While the hallway and the front lounge were presentable public areas, fairly clean and tidy, the rear of the house was a completely different story. The kitchen was filthy, the red-tiled floor permanently grimy and covered with animal faeces. The cats, dogs, even the geese and ducks, could wander in and out at will and deposit their droppings wherever they wanted. The kitchen was large, cold and old-fashioned, with tatty, brown-painted cupboard units, and a huge wooden table down the centre of the room with eight wooden chairs. The kitchen windows looked out over 100ft of scrubby garden, to the aviary and the brick wall at the back. The kitchen was fairly primitive and low on mod-cons and was greasy most of the time. We foster kids were expected to prepare all the meals for the Stabards.

... I'm being picked up roughly under the armpits by Mr Stabard and made to stand on a chair at the sink. He puts a

thing in my hand, and with his hand over mine, makes me pull off the skin of a potato. I can feel my legs wobbling on the chair, and the water is cold, but he makes me take all the skin off, then start on the next potato. There is a whole pot of potatoes on the sink. 'Do that lot now,' he barks. 'Cut them like this.' He cuts the potato in half and although I try, I can't do it, and the potato skids off the sink onto the floor. Now he's angry, and he makes me get down to get the potato, then up again. I'm scared I'll get it wrong and the more scared I become the worse it gets. Then the carrots have to be cut in a special way, getting it just right. I cut the carrots in half instead of in slices (they're too hard and slippery) and suddenly I feel a sharp jab in my stomach. I look down and there's a knife. Mr Stabard is poking me in the side and laughing his dry 'ha ha ha' laugh. Then he chucks some carrots on the floor and makes me jump down and pick them up for him – it seems to amuse him to see me scrabbling about for them. Afterwards, when I look, there are red marks on my body, like little slashes . . .

Although we were taught to prepare the meals, we weren't allowed to eat with the Stabards. The deal was this: we got their breakfast, or lunch, or tea, and then we went to the shed and waited. We had to get up before them every morning, whether it was the week or the weekend, and go down and put the kettle on for tea, and lay out the breakfast. We had to cut the bread for toast, or, when we were older and going to school, make a fry-up, which Mr Stabard liked a lot. However, on no account were we allowed to eat anything ourselves. We would be punched if we did or slapped round the face. Our job – it was made absolutely clear – was to prepare the food as quickly and quietly as we could, and then we had to toddle out to the shed while they came in, sat down at the kitchen table in silence and ate it. The same was true for lunch, for supper and for Sunday roast lunch. We had to do this every day before we went to school and after we came home from school – no excuses.

Back in 'Our Home' (the shed) we'd peer out of our slit window, watching them eat the food through the house's kitchen window. Of course, we'd be starving by then, drooling with hunger. Our bellies would ache and our empty tummies would rattle, but we'd have to be patient. And silent. It did us no good to complain. When I was younger, I remember us shouting out, crying, screaming, stamping our feet, even swearing (copying Mr Stabard, whose language was often colourful). Mrs Stabard appeared at the shed door at these times, and would look furious with us and tell us to be quiet. The neighbours also complained because we made a noise and they would come round to the front door and tell Mr and Mrs Stabard to make us quieten down. On these occasions we had to skip a meal, even if we'd been up very early or late at night preparing it all.

So we learned to be quiet. To wait. To control our hunger. To suck our fingers in a vain attempt to assuage the pain in our bellies. We couldn't eat until the Stabards were finished, and they would take all the time they wanted to, and eat as much as they wanted, until they were ready for us to eat their leftovers. Then one of them would come to the iron gate, unlock the padlock, and the shed door would swing open. We'd be allowed to go from the shed, across the paving area, through the iron gate and into the kitchen where the half-chewed leftovers would be on the floor either on the Stabards' own plates, or in dog bowls.

We had to go on all fours on the floor and eat the leftover food, like dogs. Mr and Mrs Stabard would sit at the table and watch, silently amused by our plight, or would go out of the room, and leave us to it. Any quality food would be locked away so we couldn't get to it. The food we ate was disgusting. Even worse, sometimes, was when Mrs Stabard's eldest daughter, Jemima, was there. It amused her to walk through the plate of food I was trying to eat on the floor with her shoes on. She would literally put her foot right in it, and walk past, then turn and smirk, watching to see if I would go on eating. She seemed to like to see me get upset – and I often felt very angry with her, although I tried my best to suppress it. I had to learn to control my emotions, to bottle them up. I didn't want to give her the satisfaction of seeing me upset, so I would eat the disgusting, trodden-on leftovers. I was outraged, but more than that I was hungry, and I knew that if I didn't eat this slop there wouldn't be anything else. So I ate it all; I swallowed my pride, and with it, swallowed the food, footprints and all.

After we'd eaten whatever we could scrounge, we had to clear up and do the washing-up. Sometimes we were made to wash up before we could eat, which was torture. We'd have to stand on chairs at the sink and scrub the pans, knowing our food was cold and being sniffed at on the floor, or even licked, by passing dogs and cats. When we had done our chores, we had to go back in the shed. There was no playtime in the garden, no watching TV in the lounge, no drawing on paper with coloured pens at the kitchen table or playing with toys – all the things we saw the grandchildren do when they came round. No, we would be marched back to 'Our Home' and locked in until bedtime.

The Stabards' kids and grandkids really hated us, and I think it gave them immense pleasure to ridicule and humiliate us whenever they could. Jemima's behaviour was a signal to her children to treat us badly, and I even saw one of them spit in my food once before it was handed to me on the floor. I had no option but to eat it. I couldn't complain, as this was all I knew, and there was obviously no-one to tell. There were more of them than us and they knew it. I was so hungry that I'd eat what I was given, whether it was disgusting or not.

Another horrible aspect of everyday kitchen life was the leashes on the doors. The Stabards had dog leads hanging from the door handles and from time to time they would chain us up to one of them. They would put the leather collar bit round our wrists, and we would be tethered like a dog, having to watch them eat when we were starving hungry. They did this particularly when they had parties for their grandchildren. Of course, it goes without saying that they didn't celebrate our birthdays – none of us ever had a birthday cake, a present or a card. But when it was any of their grandchildren's birthdays, there would be a party – and we, their house slaves, had to do the preparation as usual. We would have to prepare trifles, jellies, cakes, sandwiches, little sausages and cheese and pineapple on sticks. There'd be Twiglets, crisps, peanuts . . . all those amazing, yummy things we'd never eaten before. As we got older we would sometimes try to sneak a bit of something and put it in our mouths or pockets, while no-one was looking. But they usually were, so we had to prepare their birthday feast while trying not to drool, and with our tummies rumbling with hunger, before being tied up to the door and made to watch the other little children have their fun.

It was part of the grandkids' birthday party fun to throw food at us to see if we could catch it. We were so hungry that we really tried hard to catch it with our mouths, but we often missed, causing even more laughter from our 'audience'. Sometimes it was just one of us in the room being humiliated, while the other two were in the shed, watching vigilantly through the window. Sometimes it was all of us. The grandchildren would pull faces at me, stick out their tongues, shout, 'Here doggy!' or 'Catch wog!' and throw a sausage at my face, seeing if I could catch it in my teeth. All the kids would take it in turns to laugh at us, and if I got upset they enjoyed it even more. I often took the bait and got angry, then wished afterwards that I'd stayed calm. I guess the children had watched their parents treating us like slaves, worse than animals, and took their cue from them. They saw their parents treading in our food, and believed we were not human. The hate was passed down from grandparent, to parent, to child.

Even when no-one was teasing us we still had to eat off a floor littered with animal droppings. The Stabards' pets would poo all over the place, especially the dogs, and, whether by accident or design, it wasn't uncommon for us to find dog or cat faeces in our food. It's no understatement to say that the kitchen was a literal 'shit hole' and a total health hazard.

Of course, over time, we eventually learned to fight back. We learned subterfuge and guerrilla tactics to survive. We were always scared of the Stabards (especially Mr Stabard), but we began to take our revenge. Doctoring the food was just one way we began to do it. Just as we had seen them spit in our food, we also started to do it, while we were preparing their meals. They didn't seem to notice. Then we would be bolder and we would find some dog or cat faeces in the kitchen and add it to a casserole or stew. Nothing was mentioned, and they seemed to eat it quite happily. As we got older we even cut up worms and added them to their spaghetti. Again, not a word. The only time Mr Stabard was sick was when we put Kit-e-Kat in his sandwiches. He often ate these late, after a night out drinking, so didn't notice anything was wrong until he started throwing up the next morning.

By the time it got to the leftovers we would be starving, and by then, we didn't care, so we would eat what was given to us, even though we knew what we'd put in it. We realised instinctively, I think, that if we didn't eat it, we wouldn't survive, so we had no choice. However, we had the quiet satisfaction of knowing that they'd eaten something disgusting without knowing it, and it gave us a tiny twinge of power in a terribly powerless situation. Sometimes one of them would have indigestion or a tummy ache, especially if they'd eaten a lot of doctored food, and we'd be thrilled.

Over the years we three girls had learned to communicate largely in silence with each other. We'd been taught not to speak, or to even make much eye contact. If one of us had an idea, such as putting some green mouldy cheese in a sandwich, a look would pass between us very quickly – a tiny flash of a smile, or a twitch of the cheek, like a little electric current running between us – and we knew we were on the same course of action. It was almost like telepathic communication. We were deeply connected in our misery and suffering and we learned to take any power, no matter how small, wherever and whenever we could.

In fact, looking back, it seems to me that the Stabards felt they had got themselves some handy house slaves. We did all the chores for them, and they were earning a pretty penny for each of us every week. They spent our support money on clothing, heating, travel, holidays and toys – none of which we ever benefitted from. Mrs Stabard never really seemed to do anything in the house. She had ulcerated legs, and we had to change her bandages every morning – they really stank. The ulcers were weepy and smelly, and made me feel sick, but we had to put on thick white cream, then lint, and then re-bandage them before breakfast. Perhaps she figured that with her bad legs it was best to leave all the housework to us.

The worst was the cleaning. We'd be taken from the shed and set down on the kitchen floor with wooden nailbrushes and a bucket of soapy water and we'd have to scrub. It was disgusting. It would take us hours to go from one side of the very long kitchen to the other, scouring every inch of the way with our nailbrushes. The floor was hard and cold, with red quarry tiles encrusted with every kind of poo, mud, and dirt. We'd scrub, scrub, scrub until our little hands were red and raw. We had to clean the bathroom and toilet floors, then clean the sink, bath and loo with bleach that made our eyes sting.

Although we cleaned the bath, the sinks and the toilet, we weren't permitted to really use them. We heard the grandchildren having baths when they came to stay – bubble baths, with ducks and toys to play with – but we weren't allowed that. We stayed filthy. We must have really stunk, especially because of our dirty nappies, living in the shed all day and having so few changes of clean clothes, but we weren't allowed to wash properly. I really think they thought we'd contaminate the bathroom and the toilet somehow, like having black skin meant we were dirty. Even the animals were cleaner than us, as we had to muck out the hutches and bird cages in the garden. It was a filthy job which took ages to do; the only recompense being that it was in the open air, and gave us a bit of time out of the shed.

Then there was the washing. We had to wash our own clothes and bedding, such as they were, as well as the rest of the household's, from as far back as I can remember. In the kitchen Mrs Stabard had an old fashioned twin-tub and we had to spend hours pushing washing in with wooden tongs, boiling it, stirring the scalding hot water, and then transferring a heavy, tangled load from one side tub to the other to rinse and spin. Then we had to hand wash and scrub clothes, then rinse them in the sink and hang them out to dry on the line, before scuttling back into the shed for the rest of the day. When the clothes were dry, we had to do piles and piles of ironing, often burning ourselves as we did it.

We little house slaves did all the dirty work, lived on a humiliating starvation diet, and were only allowed in the 'servants quarters': the shed and the poky box room. We were told the house was not 'ours' so we were not free to wander round it. The message was loud and clear: we were second, if not third-class citizens. In many ways we ranked lower than their animals (who had more freedom), and we should be grateful for any crumb that was thrown to us, even though we had slaved hard for the Stabards all day. We were told continually from day one that we were 'bad', and that we had to be continually punished to be purified.

4

And He Shall Purify

' ... the foster parents are well-established and experienced, especially with handling difficult placements ... I believe the foster parents wish to give the children their full support ... '
(Social worker's report)

Right from the start Mr Stabard was rough with us. Apart from the incident with the vegetables and the kitchen knife, he always seemed to manhandle us somehow. There was definitely no tenderness or care in any of his encounters with us. Mr Stabard never missed any opportunity to call me 'ugly', 'fat', or 'hideous'. He hated how I looked, and always referred to me as 'wog' or 'nigger'. My hair was wiry and when it grew it would sit on my head in tight, thick curls. Mr Stabard used to coil his finger round a curl in my hair and pull me along by it – it felt like my brain was being pulled out. He would use this method to yank me upstairs, or into another room, or to get me to go wherever he wanted me to go. I felt like a dog being pulled on a lead, except it was also agony. He did it to all of us, without a word, and I'd see Hope and Faith being yanked around by their hair too, which would make my blood boil. He'd laugh his sinister little laugh, amused that he'd hurt us.

Having yanked us into place, he would stand me on a chair to cut my hair, fiercely, with a pair of kitchen scissors. Chop, chop, chop. Since he had no idea at all how to cut black hair he'd hack at it randomly, sometimes digging into my scalp and cutting me. Of course, he never would have taken us to a hairdresser, because it would have meant spending money on us, and we clearly weren't worth it. I doubt whether our town would have had someone who knew what to do with black hair either, at that time. Even if there was a specialist salon, he wouldn't have wanted to go there – he would have hated being surrounded by black people. However, he liked my hair short, so short it was. He'd grab all us by the head, one by one, and shear us like sheep, making sure he left just enough hair to tie a big Minnie Mouse bow to when we were paraded at church on Sunday like prize piccaninnies.

In our household violence was normal: Mr Stabard sometimes whacked us across the legs or arms or face. It hurt like hell. He'd suddenly lash out, just like I'd seen him do to Mrs Stabard. But at times he could also be oddly playful with us. He liked to enact a particular 'game' with us.

Two hands pulling me up high onto his knee. I want to sit there, it's nice as it feels like a cuddle, like I'm getting a hug. I don't want Hope on his knee first, because it's my treat. I want to be the one today. I want a hug, a kiss, a cuddle, anything...I like it when he smiles, looks pleased with me. I want him to smile, want to make him pleased. I like the warm feeling, being up there, special. He's nice now, not shouty. I don't like him angry, red faced. Now he's smiling, his eyes are looking nicely at me.

...then I am sitting on his lap (the other one, or two, are standing or sitting on the floor, watching, wide-eyed), and he's pulled my legs either side of his legs, sort of moving my legs round his body, like they're round his waist. Then he bounces me up and down, up and down on his lap. It's fun and I get giggly. It feels nice to giggle. The other two watching giggle

too — we don't often laugh so it's nice. We feel it's fun, funny. We go 'ha, ha' and so does he. Then he tickles me on his lap, his fingers on my legs, under my arms, round my tummy, and we all laugh more. We all laugh, because it's fun. All the while I'm bouncing up and down, up and down, up and down. Then it begins to feel strange. His eyes glaze and he starts panting and I can feel something hard, like a lump, in his lap, under his trousers, just under my bum. I don't know what it is, but it makes me feel strange, unsafe.

Then he holds on to me very tight, squeezing the breath out of me, and pushes me down harder and harder onto his lap, on to the hard thing there, with both his strong hands. The feeling of being close is nice, but I also feel very uncomfortable, like something's wrong, and he's out of control. He's gripping me hard now. I can hardly breathe as he's squeezing me, pushing me down, so tight. He's now wide-eyed, sort of glazed over, and he is pushing his lumpy bit hard into my bum, and he moans 'mmmmm' or 'aaaah'. His cold blue eyes stare through me in a trance.

Then it stops. Suddenly. Just like that. He pushes me off, and I fall in a heap on the floor. He stands up, adjusts his trousers, and then barks at us all to stand up. I sit on the ground, looking up, very confused. He doesn't like us again now and I feel like crying. Then I'm marched through the lounge, down the hall, through the kitchen, out to the garden, through the iron gate and thrown into the shed. Slam. He's distant and cold now, and bangs the door shut and that's that. Game over, fun all gone . . . and I feel so sad, so confused, so numb . . .

We didn't understand what the 'game' was, exactly, but we knew it was 'our secret'. When it happened the curtains would be drawn, Mrs Stabard would be out, and we knew, instinctively, it was something just between Mr Stabard and ourselves. Even between us girls we never talked about it. There was a strange kind of rivalry for his attention, and it made us feel uncomfortable with each other if he seemed to have a 'favourite' – which actually was often me. I guess we felt it was too weird to talk about, that there was too much to lose if we fell out with each other. We needed each other to survive.

These days we had even more to worry about. Faith was often poorly. She was quite a sickly child but now she seemed to be going to the doctor, then to hospital, more and more frequently. It was eventually diagnosed that she had *'lookeema'*, which I didn't understand at all. This meant that she was off for long periods in hospital and we wouldn't see her for weeks. When she came home, she would be very pale and weak. However, she still continued to be part of the shed regime, and didn't have any special treatment. Despite being ill there was no lying in bed or watching TV on the sofa for her. Hard times continued.

Faith's illness did nothing to alter the Stabards' conviction that we were completely 'evil' and that they had to 'purify' us. We soon found out that Mr Stabard had his own special method of trying to purify our souls that would leave us totally terrified and hurt in body and mind.

From as early as I can remember, Mr Stabard talked to us seriously about our 'sin'. I don't know whether he felt that because we were black we were more tainted and sinful than anyone else; or whether because we were unwanted (due to our shameful origins) he felt there was something about us that needed purifying. Either way, he came up with his own bizarre way of cleansing our sins which involved a further extension of the 'game' he played with us on his lap, whenever Mrs Stabard was out of the house.

... It's early evening, getting dark, when he suddenly appears in the doorway of 'Our Home' with a brown canvas holdall in his hand. We're sitting on the floor in a daze – bored and shut-down, as we often are – when we're startled by him. We're very scared of our foster father, as we never know whether he's going to be nice or nasty. Rather than take any chances all three of us girls run over to the battered armchair in the corner of the shed, fling ourselves in it, and cling onto each other, peeking out at him. Usually, he comes to punish us in some way – which could just be shouting, but can also be a slap or a beating – but today he obviously has something else in mind. He can hardly stand up in the shed, as it's so low. He comes in and plonks down his holdall on the shelf that runs along the back wall and then unzips the bag. We watch him carefully as he rummages in the bag, and then he brings out something strange: a purple and silver long thing. We sit together, wide-eyed, watching him carefully as he takes it out of the bag and puts it in his trouser pocket.

Mr Stabard says nothing, but points at me. I don't move, just huddle closer in to the girls. I'm in the middle of Hope and Faith, holding on tight to both of them. With Faith sick, and Hope so little, I feel like it's up to me to protect them.

Since I don't move, Mr Stabard comes over, winds his finger into a curl on my head and pulls me over to the rickety table in the middle of the shed. He puts his big hands either side of my waist and lifts me up and plonks me back down, so I'm sitting on the end of the table, facing him, my legs hanging down over the edge. My heart's racing and my mouth's dry – I've no idea what he's going to do next. Suddenly, he pushes me backwards and I end up flat on my back, with a whack to the back of my head. My knees are still over the edge of the table, legs hanging down. He stares intently as he bends over me, and I can smell beery, stinky breath. I get a waft of his pungent aftershave and I'm only inches from his cold blue eyes which bore into mine. His knee comes up and suddenly I can feel the heavy weight of it on my chest. I panic and wriggle, trying to push him off, but he holds me down. All the time the other two girls are watching this. I can hear one of them begin to whimper quietly. It's probably Faith, and I hope she'll stop, or things might get worse.

They do. Suddenly, with a swift movement, Mr Stabard rips off my nappy. It's very wet and smelly, as I've had it on all day. He's pulling it down and drops it on the floor: 'thunk'. Then he gets the purple and silver thing and puts it up to his mouth, ripping the shiny paper with his teeth. Something long and brown appears. I recognise the smell of chocolate. Is he going to give us a treat?

'If you make a noise, I'll hurt you.'

I'm terrified now and my heart flutters wildly with fear. What's he doing? I stare at his glinting, blue eyes, but they're dead and empty.

'This is to purify you, to let the evil spirits out ... '

Then I feel a searing, ripping pain between my legs. I gasp, then shriek and try to sit up, to wriggle away. But his knee's still on my chest, and his other hand's now clamped over my mouth, pushing my head back hard on the table. I can't breathe. All I can feel is a burning, stabbing pain where my wee comes out. Mr Stabard's other hand begins to move in and out between my legs, and I feel something hard stabbing into my body down there.

'I'm going to make you pure ... this is to make you clean.'

His eyes bore into me – the pain is agonising. Tears run

down my cheeks, but his hand is over my mouth, I can hardly breathe or cry out. I can't move, or get away, and he works the brown thing roughly in and out, ripping the flesh in my wee place, for what seems like hours, but for what is maybe a few minutes. All the time, he's whispering, hoarsely, that he's purifying me, that I needed cleansing.

'I'm doing God's work,' he hisses, through his teeth. 'Otherwise, you'll have to be locked up – in prison, or a home somewhere . . . you're that evil . . . '

Then he stops for a second and half stands up. I try to scramble away, but he grabs me with his free hand, and flattens me down again, whispering a prayer we hear in church each week, which begins:

'Father above in Heaven, hear my prayer . . . '

As he mumbles the prayer, he continues to push and pull the thing in and out, in and out of my raw flesh. His voice begins to rise in a fever as he does it. My head is swimming and I can't see properly now. I feel split open and sick with pain.

Suddenly he stops. He rips the brown thing out of me, as fast as he's pushed it in and I scream under his hand. He goes to the holdall and drops it inside. I lay there blinking, confused, agonised, my legs akimbo on the table, tears running down my cheeks. Suddenly, his face appears two inches above mine, and he holds me down with his hand.

'If you tell anyone about this,' he spits, 'you'll be locked up, I'll be sad, and then I'll have to kill myself. Do you understand?'

I blink. I can't speak. I can't cry. I'm absolutely shocked.

And then he's gone. Slam. It's dark. I feel numb, wet, confused. I feel I'm weeing and pooing uncontrollably. I lie there until the other two come over to me. Faith helps me put on my nappy again. It's the old one, filthy and stinking. I hurt between my legs. When I look, later, there's red stuff in the nappy. What is it? Mr Stabard said I mustn't tell anybody, so I can't show Mrs Stabard, can I? There's no-one else to tell.

Afterwards I hurt badly, can hardly walk or sit down, and it burns terribly to wee. If I sleep I have nightmares. We girls never talk about it. It's happened in front of them, and yet we all pretend it hasn't really happened ...

What I didn't know the first time my foster father 'purified' me was that this was to become a regular evening ritual, and that it would happen more and more frequently. Mr Stabard would appear once or twice a week at the shed door. He always had the same brown holdall which I understood eventually was full of sweets and chocolate bars. Sometimes we hoped that he would just give us some and leave. We even thought we might be rewarded with some of the sweets in the holdall after being 'cleansed'. Not so. He always did the same thing. He chose a different one of us each time, so the other two had to sit in the chair, or hide behind it, trying not to witness his sickening chocolate bar ritual with that evening's chosen victim.

Sometimes he would insert the chocolate bar into my poo hole, which hurt like hell. I could feel myself rip open and for hours, even days, afterwards, I would have red stuff in my nappy. As I got older I realised it was blood. I bled every time I pooed, and I would lie awake wondering if he had broken something inside my bottom. Mostly he inserted it into the front hole, which he seemed to prefer. All the time he would be chanting religious verses, even praying, saying he was 'driving out the devil' and making me 'pure'.

Sometimes he would come into the shed and say, 'We're nearly there, girls, you're nearly pure. Just one more time.'

For a split second I would believe him and think if we went through the humiliating, painful ritual just once more, we might be 'cured' of being so evil. I even volunteered sometimes, not only to save my sisters from the pain, but because I felt it might get me purified quicker. I offered myself. In a twisted way he made me believe that the more I did it, the more I would get better. That was the trick of his mind games with us. But, of course, it didn't work. Mr Stabard just kept doing it, and doing it, and doing it, and we never seemed to get any nearer to being purified. It went on until I was four or five I think. I learned not to fidget and not to fight him once on the table. At first, because it was agony, I would wriggle and twist, trying to get away, and tears would spring to my eyes. But I could sense he relished my pain, so I began to shut down. I learned to lie very still and blank out my feelings. That way I could get through it. I looked at the ceiling and counted plastic ridges. I learned to suffer and to put up with it in silence, hoping against hope that it would be over soon and I would be pure.

When he saw that he'd made us bleed − he could hardly miss it − he told us that the blood was a sign we were really being purified. The bleeding was a cleansing thing, he said. He never cleaned us up afterwards, and he always left us naked and battered on the table. We had to sort ourselves out, put the dirty nappy back on, without washing ourselves or cleaning up the mess. It was totally and utterly humiliating and it left us battered and bruised, shocked and degraded. Sometimes my nappy wouldn't do up again, as the tags had snapped, and I'd panic as I was smelly and there was smeared chocolate and blood mixed with wee and poo on my legs and body. It was disgusting.

Sometimes he would come to us in the shed to purify

us after church on a Sunday. It might be after lunch or later in the day, and he'd often be drunk. He was much more violent then. I don't know whether going to church had worked him up into some kind of frenzy, or whether having a few drinks got him going, but he would grab one of us and throw us violently on the table, pull off our nappy, and shove two of his enormous sausage-like fingers into us. This would hurt much more than the chocolate bar. He'd push them in and out roughly, snarling all the time that the evil part of us was coming out.

Once the blood began to flow he'd say, 'See, there's the evil coming out of you. You're being purified.'

The chocolate bar in the shed routine continued for years and every day towards evening we would begin to get agitated, sensing that he might soon descend on us. But what could we do? We were locked in there, unable to escape. He just came and hurt us and we were powerless to stop him.

5

Night Duty

'I view Mr and Mrs Stabard as a safe pair of hands, with years of experience, which Harmony can benefit from . . .'
(Social worker's report)

One vivid memory stands out for me: my fifth birthday. We never celebrated our birthdays, or had any fuss, but still I remember this one – probably because it was the opposite of what any child would ever want their birthday to be like. I was actually allowed a bath that day, which was a rare treat. I remember I was sitting in the bath, with about six inches of warm water – I knew hot baths were expensive and a luxury – when Mr Stabard came in. I froze. I'd been expecting Mrs Stabard, not her husband. But here he was in the bathroom, leaning over me being very nice. He seemed, for the first time ever, to really care about me, and I remember thinking: 'It's my birthday, so maybe he's decided to love me, after all.' Then he whispered hoarsely, 'Stand up.'

I stood up, dripping, and started shivering in the cold bathroom. The water was only up to my mid-calves and was rapidly cooling down.

'I'm sorry I have to do this,' he said mysteriously. 'Be very quiet.'

With a quick movement he had a chocolate bar between my legs and up inside of me. I gasped as he ripped into me.

He looked very fierce, but I grasped onto him involuntarily, feeling my head swim and knees buckle.

'Ssh! I have to do this, to purify you . . . you wicked girl.'

My feet were slipping in the water, I felt giddy and sick, as though I was going to fall under the water and drown. Suddenly I was down on my bottom, the water splashing round my waist, but he was still stooping over me, thrusting the chocolate bar in and out of me with a crazed look on his face. My head was going round and round. I was seeing stars, feeling nauseous and terrified. I felt ripped apart and wanted to get away, but his grip on my upper arm was like a vice, his fingers digging in me, still holding me half-upright.

Then the blood came. It was flowing into the water. I wanted to cry, but he pressed his face right up to mine.

'Don't cry, don't say a word. This is the evil coming out . . .'

I felt like I was dying, but I just stared at him, which he hated. I stared and stared. I felt I was just an object in the bath; not a girl, not human, just a thing. He went on moving the chocolate up and down, up and down as I slipped in and out of consciousness.

'All that dirty stuff is coming out of you,' he hissed. 'See!'

He started chanting one of his favourite prayers and I wanted to slip under the water and sink without a trace. *Please make it stop.* Everything was going black, when he suddenly pulled the bar out very abruptly. It was over. He let out his dry, harsh laugh – the filthy old man's chuckle he always did. At that moment I absolutely hated him with all my being. But I was too weak to do anything and now the bath was streaky red.

Suddenly, Hope's head popped round the bathroom door. Her eyes widened. 'Why's the bath red?' she asked.

None of us ever spoke without being spoken to, but Hope was often bolder and braver than me, and would say things we'd only think. I'd hate her for it sometimes, because I feared he'd punish us even more.

'It's the evil stuff coming out, Lord be praised,' whispered Mr Stabard. Then he flung open the door, knocking Hope sideways, and disappeared, leaving me appalled in my red-streaked bath.

Hope helped me creep to our box room, and I snuck into my bunk bed – something I was never allowed to do usually. I preferred the top bunk, but I just crawled in the bottom, wrapped in an old towel, and lay there. I didn't move for a very long time. *I must be very evil*, I thought, *for him to do that to me.*

Luckily, Mr and Mrs Stabard didn't come and I got a bit of time to lie down and close my eyes and wish it would all go away forever and ever. There was a bottle of rat poison on the shelf in our shed, and I had a fantasy about putting this in Mr Stabard's food or beer – he'd never notice. I comforted myself with magicking him away in my fantasies and managed to drift off to sleep eventually. What a happy birthday present he'd given me – I certainly never forgot the day I turned five. The bath treatment also began to be an occasional part of his gruesome purifying routine from then on.

When Mr Stabard hurt me, like he did in the shed, and now in the bath, I felt he absolutely hated me, and hated my blackness in particular. I used to stare him in the eyes at these times because I also despised him for what he was doing to me and my sisters. It was my only weapon. If I was on the table and I stared at him, it unnerved him, and he would slap my face to stop me looking. I concentrated all my hate in my stare and eventually he'd have to look away. My sisters didn't meet his eyes, but I always did. I wanted him to know, somehow, that I was there, watching him, while he hurt my child's body. I would lay still, telling him with my eyes how much I loathed him and how much pain he was causing me. Meanwhile, the rest of my body would be on shutdown. I controlled my emotions while he did whatever nasty thing he felt he had the right to do in God's name. What I didn't know was that Mr Stabard had plans to 'purify' us evil black children in ways which would be even more frightening and painful.

It wasn't long after the bath incident that Mr Stabard began to want to play a new game at night. It especially seemed to happen when he'd drunk a lot that evening. After work he would either go to his club, the British Legion, or he'd come home and open a beer, then have whisky or gin. As the years went by, he seemed to drink more and more, sometimes even having a drink in the morning. This was never good news for us.

. . .The first time he comes into us at night he's pretty drunk. We three now sleep together in a bunk bed meant for two, and take turns for two of us to sleep together on the bottom bunk, top to toe, with the other one on the top. The best place is on your own on the top bunk, so we rotate who can sleep there, to be fair. This night I'm on top and the other two are on the bottom, fast asleep. The room's pitch black as it's late at night – probably midnight or one in the morning. I suddenly become aware that someone's in the room. I'm awake, bolt upright, sitting up in my bed. I'm scared, hearing our foster father's unmistakable heavy breathing, and can instantly smell his horrible breath and aftershave.

Suddenly the light goes on.

Mr Stabard has come upstairs with a light bulb and has put it in. The other two wake up then, and we all jump out of bed and stand to attention. It's very strange to think how much he has trained us by then, but we knew if he comes up to our room, which he often does when he wants a fry-up or cup of tea late at night, then we have to jump to it. He's like a sergeant major commanding his troops — even if we're three young children, and it's the middle of a dark, winter's night. I remember it's absolutely freezing cold. Our nighties are thin, and the windows drafty, as we stand barefoot, waiting for his orders. He's swaying a bit and looks quite bleary, so we know not to move or say anything until he's ready.

I'm shivering like a leaf; my heart's racing and I know we'll have to obey him, whatever he wants us to do. The chocolate game is being played a lot in the shed and bath these days, and it crosses my mind he might want that, but he doesn't have the brown holdall with him. Every time he comes in to us in the shed, or pulls us by the hair into the lounge for a lap game, I hope against hope that he'll tell me I'm now pure and it is all over. But he never does. Purification seems further away than ever, especially on this bitterly cold January night.

Mr Stabard stands there a moment, scrutinising us woozily, like he's sizing us up.

'You're evil, you know that don't you?' he slurs in a hoarse whisper. 'You're sick . . . sick and evil . . . '

Instinctively we crowd closer together and hold hands, sensing a new threat. I feel something really awful is about to happen, and I want to protect the other two at all costs. Faith starts whimpering and I squeeze her hand hard, willing her to stop. He hates crying, or any sign of weakness — it just makes him lash out.

'It's God's job to purify your souls. It's His Will to make you pure . . . ' He sounds like he is working up to something. 'And

*he wants me to continue His great work. He wants me to purify
your evil, wicked ways . . . '*

*My knees are shaking as he takes a big, lurching step forward.
He's towering over us, like a monster, looking dishevelled and
red-faced. We look up at him, blinking against the light bulb
which swings just above his head, casting a weird halo of light
around his white hair.*

*Mr Stabard bends over us even closer, and I get a whiff of
sickening boozy breath as he points with his thick sausage-like
finger to each of us in turn:*

> *'Eeeny, meeny, miny mo,*
> *Catch a nigger by his toe . . .*
> *If he hollers let him go,*
> *Eeeny, meeny, miny, mo . . . '*

*'Ha, ha, ha' goes his dry little laugh, as he amuses himself with
his ditty, he grabs me roughly by the shoulder and pulls me
towards him. The other two hang onto my hands for a second,
but he jerks me away so they have to let go. Without a word, he
rolls up my nightie and looks at my body. His eyes look hungry
and he licks his lips. I feel shy as the other two scuttle up the bunk
bed ladder, and hide on top, holding each other. As Mr Stabard
grabs me to him hard with both hands, Faith whimpers. I glance
quickly at the door, which he's closed behind him, calculating
whether I can push past and escape – no way. Faith's snivelling
gets louder and Mr Stabard shouts up at the top bunk, with a
fierce look, 'Shut that noise up and get down here, you two.'*

*Obediently, Hope and Faith crawl down the ladder again
and stand just behind him. I can see them shaking, with their
arms round each other. Oh my God, what's he going to do this
time? My mouth's dry and I feel sick. I want to cry, but I bite
my lip – I have to control myself.*

Roughly, he pushes me backwards and I fall hard across the bottom bunk. He moves swiftly towards me, and pulls my arms down by my sides. I stare at him, which I know he hates but he just looks over my head. Then, he's on top of me. I can't breathe. A fifty-year-old man on top of a five-year-old child. His whole weight is on my chest and my body's squished. I'm frightened I'm being crushed to death. Brut, mixed with sweat and alcohol, fills my nose as he puffs and blows on top of me. My throat's closing, I can't get air, so I wriggle, trying to get free, trying to breathe, trying to get him off.

'Lie still,' he snaps, 'or it'll get worse.'

He lifts himself off me slightly and I can breathe a bit better. There's some fumbling and a zipping sound while he moves my legs apart with his free hand. All the time, my heart's racing, and I'm thinking: I've got to get away. Get me away! My mind whirls. I hold my breath in sheer terror. Help me. Then I feel his scaly fingers digging into my private parts; poke, poke, poke. He starts moaning and I try to close my legs, to protect myself. He isn't having it. Ignoring my struggles he yanks them open and pulls himself back on top of me again, his full weight pinning me down to the bed.

Somewhere behind him are the girls but I can't see them over his hulk. I will them to get help. Go and tell! But Mr Stabard is focused completely on what he wants. It seems like I'm dying, like I'll be flattened out and crushed under him. I have pins and needles in my legs. Are my bones snapping? I want to scream out. Then I feel it. Something hurts me, something very big, very hard. I feel I am being split open with a log. A sickening, searing pain, like I've never felt before; like my guts are being ripped open. I want to wee and poo at the same time – maybe I am weeing and pooing – but I can't tell really what's happening because his whole weight is heavy and sweaty on me.

He starts moving on top of me, grunting. This is much worse than the chocolate thing, and he is groaning and half laughing. He shifts up and down on me; up feels like I'll split, down feels like I'll rip. He's gouging my insides out. I'm not breathing any more. He moves faster and faster, gets heavier and heavier, and pushes down on me hard until I feel my whole little body might crack.

Then he stops. It's over – whatever it was. Without looking at me or saying a word, he pulls himself out, and I think my insides will come out too. He gets off me, shoves a floppy pink thing back in his pants and zips up, then goes to the door, flicks off the light and disappears. Just like that he's gone. There's a moment of strange silence in the dark, as I'm lying flattened out on the bed, legs open and shaking uncontrollably. The other two, I now see, are sat crouched against the wall, arms around their heads and faces turned away from the bed. The door flings open and he's back. My heart stops and I play dead. He shuffles over to the light bulb and takes it out; then I hear him go out the door again. I wait for ages. I hardly dare breathe until I'm sure he's really gone this time.

Even when I know he's not coming back I just lie there in the cold, dark room. Sweat is like ice on my body. I'm still spread out on the bed, half naked. I can't move. I can't cry. I feel something slimy oozing between my legs, and I shiver. All I feel is sick and numb. I lie there completely still for what seems like hours, not moving. I don't sleep. I'm in total shock. I don't understand what has just happened, but I do know it's utterly horrible, like nothing I ever imagined was possible. I expect to see a hole in my body, with my insides spilling out. I don't look. In the end, I somehow roll myself sideways and pull the sheet and blanket over me. I lie on my side, with my hands between my legs, eyes open, watchful. I hardly breathe. I'm too scared to feel myself 'down there'. I'm too frightened to move, or shut my eyes or think or speak. I keep seeing him grunting, sweating, pressing on top of me. The other two girls are back on the top bunk. I can hear them breathing rhythmically like they're asleep, but I'm sure I'll never sleep again. I can't take my eyes off the door.

Finally, in the grey morning light, I see there's blood. Lots of it. And poo, and wee, all over the bed clothes. I'm used to seeing blood coming out of me after the chocolate game, but this is lots of blood, which really scares me. I go to the bathroom and wash off the mess and wipe myself with toilet roll. I'm terrified what Mrs Stabard will say if she sees the sheets, so I bundle them up and although it's painful to walk down the stairs, I stuff all the bedding in the washing machine. I'm scared she'll ask me what's happened as I know it's something very bad. I must be a very wicked girl, otherwise this wouldn't happen to me. Maybe being black is bad, after all? Maybe he's right? It must all be my fault.

He's gone to work already when I get up and I feel relieved not to see him. I'm still in shock as I try to go and make breakfast with the other two. It hurts to walk, it hurts to sit, it hurts to wee or stand, and my legs are like jellies.

I'm bending down to bandage Mrs Stabard's stinky legs, just as always, and I wonder if I can say something to her? There's no 'hello' or 'good morning', and she doesn't look at me. I give up; I don't exist. I don't speak to the other two. I don't look at anyone's faces. I don't cry. All day I'm locked in the shed as usual, but I'm not playing or singing. In the armchair I hold myself and rock backwards and forwards, over and over, humming quietly. I don't want to feel what he has done to me. I can tell that the other two don't know what to do. We don't talk about anything; we never do. I can't talk about it anyway. There's no-one else to tell, no-one to go to get help from . . .

From that first night onwards, from when I was just five until I was twenty-three, Mr Stabard came and played his 'eeny, meeny, miny, mo' game with us three girls on a regular basis. It was always late at night, and always after he had been drinking. Because Faith was often in hospital the choice was usually between Hope and me, and he alternated between us. Whoever his chosen girl was for the night, the others had to watch. It was part of his sick game. He hated it if we cried and would start slapping us about until we stopped. Faith often cried more and I willed her to be quiet. I learned to bite my lip and clench my teeth. I learned to pinch myself and dig my nails into my own flesh to try and shut down my feelings.

Mr Stabard would chant a prayer from the Bible, or say we were 'wicked' and needed 'purifying' before every sordid ordeal began. I wanted to protect the other two from him, so as time went on I actually volunteered when he came into the room, to save the others from pain and humiliation. I said things like, 'I'll be your special girl tonight,' which made me feel sick. I thought I might get cleansed quicker and then he'd stop hurting us all – his constant brainwashing was working. But no matter what any of us did he just kept coming back.

Only very occasionally, when the other two were asleep and the house was quiet, did I feel safe to let go for a short while. Then I'd put my head under my pillow and cry. Even then I'd keep it brief, because I was always vigilant; always listening out, just in case he came back, or the others woke up. I was bottling up oceans of pain, masses of bad feelings, and there was nowhere to put them. I took on a mothering role for the other two, so I had to be strong for them. It felt like a great responsibility, but in some ways it also kept me alive, by forcing me to be stronger and braver for them. Of course I didn't always feel it, but I knew I couldn't give up. Only much later did my feelings begin to come out, and when they did it was like unleashing a torrent of pent-up fury stored over those years and years of horrendous abuse.

Once Mr Stabard had got the taste for us at night, there was no stopping him. I wondered for a long time if Mrs Stabard had any idea what her husband was up to. Did she know what he was doing to us? Surely she noticed when he got out of bed in the middle of the night? I fantasised about telling her everything, and throwing myself on her mercy. That hope died one night, when she came into our room very late, and went over to where I was sleeping. Without a word she made me sit up, then she took off my nightie and laid me back down on the bottom bunk. My foster mother spread my legs apart and seconds later her husband came into the room. I lay there, horrified, not knowing what to do. Mrs Stabard silently turned and went out of the room, leaving her husband to unzip himself, then throw his heavy bulk on top of me.

This pattern of behaviour continued until well into my late teens. Mrs Stabard would come in and lay one of us out for him. She'd stand there in her bulky dressing gown and slippers, not speaking or making eye contact with us, until her husband arrived, and then she would leave him to his nasty night work. At first this happened once a week, but as I got older, it happened twice or three times, sometimes more.

Mrs Stabard not only knew what he was doing to us, but she was part of it. She helped him; in fact she seemed to endorse it. This shocked me to the core and meant there was no-one I could turn to. Sometimes it also made me feel like I was crazy, like what was going on was a nightmare and I would wake up one day and find out that it was all a bad dream. Unhappily, it wasn't. It was reality – our reality – one that no-one could have guessed at by looking at the God-fearing Stabards or at the respectable white front door of 97 Forestlane Way.

6

Fighting Back Backfires

' . . . Harmony is lucky to have such caring, experienced foster parents as she is such a moody, difficult child to deal with.'
(Social worker's report)

Even though Mr Stabard was 'purifying' us two or three nights a week, life in the house still went on as if nothing had happened. We still had to do all the household chores, and still had to be locked in the shed, while the Stabards and their family lived a seemingly 'normal' life. Faith was sickly, and getting worse, but she still had to do what we did. Except when she was able to escape to hospital, she was given no special treatment.

In fact, the Stabards made sure we had as little contact with the outside world as possible, even if we were sick. We were taken to see a local doctor and dentist from time to time, but Mrs Stabard would talk for us and we were totally silent throughout. We were scrubbed up for visits, so we didn't look as dirty and smelly as usual. I suffered from chest infections a great deal, which the damp shed and our freezing box bedroom didn't help. I had to see the doctor quite a lot, as I often couldn't breathe properly. However, even then I didn't speak to the doctor directly, and sometimes I was even sent out of the room – so I had no idea what the doctor and Mrs Stabard were really saying about me.

Sometimes we were taken to a local hospital, where we had to do some exercises. We were never told why. We had to hold onto wall-bars and stretch, perhaps to make us breathe better or stand more straight – we didn't get much exercise in the shed all day, after all. Again, we never spoke to the medical staff about anything, we just quietly got on with whatever we were told to do. Even if we were ill we weren't allowed to rest; we were still shoved out into the shed all day, and we'd still have to do the chores, regardless. I remember we girls had a little bit of cloth we used as a comforter – a scrap from an old dress – and we used to sniff it under our noses, and cuddle it, especially when we were sick. We'd also suck our middle and index fingers, and stroke our own hair. I think we did this to comfort ourselves. After all, no-one was else was giving us a hug, or snuggling us up when we were poorly. We just had to do what we could for ourselves, without parents or teddy bears to keep us happy.

Another strange thing was that we were always given pills to take. I had no idea what they were, but the Stabards would hand them out every day, little white and pink ones. They weren't multivitamins, since they came in brown medicine bottles. Every day we would be lined up, and made to take our pills. As we got older, the number of pills increased – sometimes we were taking ten or more a day each. I have no idea what they were for, or even if they were prescribed for us, but looking back I wonder if they were actually giving us some kind of tranquilliser to keep us quiet in the shed. We always had to take them, and they got furious if we didn't.

Apart from keeping us docile, the most important thing to the Stabards, I believe, was to not to leave us alone with anyone. We might have started talking about what was going on at home, and they did not want us to give the game away. Mr Stabard was never there when Social Services came, or when we went to the doctor – I felt he hid from the authorities. However, he'd already frightened us so much that we wouldn't have said anything, even if someone had asked us directly. I think we were too scared of the consequences.

Mr Stabard had told us over and over that if we told anyone about his nocturnal activities he would have to kill himself. As much as we hated him, and hated what he did to us, we didn't want to be responsible for him dying. Also, if he did die, where would we go? Who would look after us? Not only did we have no idea what was 'out there' beyond the Stabards' house, but we didn't feel we belonged anywhere else and we desperately wanted to stay together as the three of us had become a real family by then.

Something we began to do, however, to keep us sane, and to make ourselves feel a bit better in a hopeless situation, was to get our own back. We only did fairly little things, but it made us laugh and therefore made us feel more powerful, even if just for a few moments. We often acted out a scene in the shed about giving Mr Stabard rat poison we found on the shelf.

Me (playing it up as Mr Stabard): Gulp. Oh, I've swallowed something . . . aaagh, I feel so ill. I'm dying. Help me!

(Faith is watching, smiling, from the chair as I fall to the ground, writhing, clutching my stomach and groaning)

Faith (innocently, as me): Oh dear, Mr Stabard, you look very sick. What's wrong?

Me: I drank something. I think it's poison! I'm
dying ... help me, please help me! I need help ...
Aaaaaagh!

Faith (stepping over his writhing body): Oh dear.
Sorry, I can't help. No way. Never. Bye.

We'd all fall apart giggling at this point, and then we'd re-
enact it, this time with Hope as the one who walks away,
and me as Mr Stabard. We loved getting to the bit where
we said 'NO' to him, and this would reduce us to fits of
helpless laughter. The very thought of leaving him in agony
made us feel a whole lot better about our hopeless plight.

Mr Stabard was obviously our main focus, and there
were times when he was absolutely paralytically drunk,
when he rolled home from the British Legion and carried
on drinking beer from the crate in the larder. He would fall
asleep in his favourite armchair in the front lounge – in our
forbidden territory. It would be late at night and very quiet
in the house, except for the sound of his drunken snoring.
We would muster up all our courage, tiptoe barefooted
downstairs into the lounge, and tie his shoelaces together.
Later we'd hear an enormous thud, followed by incoherent
shouting, and we'd be back up in our box room bunks,
giggling helplessly under our thin covers. It was a brilliant
moment; to think of him falling over and banging his head,
completely confused because he was too out of his skull to
know what was happening. We tied his shoelaces together
many times, and it always gave us a thrill. These moments
made us stronger, made us laugh and feel happier and
allowed us to develop a sense of humour together, which I
believe, was one of the things that kept me going. We were
being naughty little girls, but in a tiny way we were also
managing to fight back.

We didn't get our own back on Mrs Stabard very often, as we felt she probably had no choice but to help her husband hurt us. However, we knew she was terrified of mice so one day we nicked her grandson's toy mouse and put it in her slipper. We were preparing tea that evening, and there was suddenly an enormous shriek from behind us. Mrs Stabard had put her slipper on, found the mouse and thinking it was a real one had thrown the shoe across the room and nearly fainted with shock. We were helpless with silent laughter, but just had to carry on peeling spuds and carrots at the sink. She didn't say anything, but I know she was angry about it as she sulked for ages with us afterwards.

Of course, we were still being creative with our cooking, and were still adding some 'interesting' extras to their food. Every time we did this, it would be a thrill. We'd all peer out the shed slit window at them eating our doctored food, which we could see through the kitchen window. We'd be waiting for adverse reactions to worms in their spaghetti or dog poo in their casserole, but it gave us a sense of victory just to see them scoffing it all down and we'd giggle together in the dark. Also when Mr Stabard was drunk at night, and got us up to make him food, we'd take our revenge by making Kit-e-Kat sandwiches or adding laxatives to his food. It really felt like we were getting one over on him at last, especially when he was up in the toilet all night afterwards, and complained of tummy ache next day. We also put wee in the roast potatoes and enjoyed seeing them eat them with relish, even though we knew we'd be dished up the remains in our dog bowls later.

However, the place where we showed our greatest revenge was against the grandchildren's toys. It seemed so unfair that they had loads of toys stuffed under the stairs and we had none. Christmas was the worst time, as they would be unwrapping masses of lovely, brightly coloured things, and we would be left out of the celebrations: no stockings, no decorations in our room, nothing. While preparing the Christmas lunch we'd hear the kids ripping open their toys and shrieking with delight at what they found. It felt so unfair.

So one year, while they went in to eat the Christmas lunch that we had prepared for them, we snuck into the lounge, where all the grandchildren's presents lay carelessly strewn amongst the ripped Christmas paper. I remember there was an amazing wooden train set and boxes of Lego, but my favourite thing of all was a baby doll that had a mouth that opened, eyes that fluttered, and tummy button that made noises. I was fascinated by the fact that you could feed her with a bottle made of gluey stuff and she would wee in her nappy, and you'd have to change her.

The three of us secretly had a quick play with the toys, and then a look passed between us. Without a word, we started ripping things up. I remember smashing the boxes, ripping the train set apart, damaging as much as I could, as quickly as I could. It felt absolutely wonderful, especially as the grandchildren taunted us so much and behaved as if they were so superior to us. We all worked hard and fast, and then ran upstairs to the box room. After lunch, the grandchildren went back into the living room and we waited at the bedroom door, holding our breath and waiting for their reaction. When we heard the shrieks and screams of upset, we hugged each other. Triumph! There was a sense of victory, of momentary joy, because, as we saw it, we had got our own back on the spoiled little brats who made our lives a living hell. Inevitably, we were dragged out of our room, beaten and slapped, and shoved into the airing cupboard as punishment, without even having our Christmas leftovers. But whatever they did to us the shrieks of the grandkids were still ringing in our ears, and I have to say, we savoured the sense of revenge. Of course, the Stabards just bought them mountains of replacement toys, but we realised that we could always sneak under the stairs and smash them up again. It was war.

I'm sure that our revenge-filled antics convinced the Stabards that the devil was at work in the house. If anything, our behaviour justified their mistreatment of us even more – we were clearly wicked black children who needed to be purified. Since what they had done to us so far was clearly not working, they had to find some other way to 'teach us a proper lesson'. They were grown-ups with all the power, but we felt we were fighting for our freedom, for our lives, so we weren't going to give up.

Most weekends were interminably boring for us. We'd be locked in 'Our Home' and have to listen to the grandchildren playing tag or hide-and-seek outside on the lawn. We'd hear the neighbours talking and cutting their hedges next to the shed, but inside the hours seemed to drag on and on.

Then one Saturday, when I must have been about seven or eight, something different happened. Mrs Stabard appeared at the wrought iron gate while it was still light and unlocked the padlock. It wasn't time to prepare supper yet, so we looked at each other, a bit confused. We crowded to the slit window to see what was up. The door was flung open and she pointed that we should come out and follow her. As usual nothing was said to us. Did she think we were too stupid to understand words? Or did she think we were mere animals, to be herded? Like the mute, dumb creatures she thought we were, so without a word, we did as she indicated, and trotted obediently out of the shed, stretching and yawning in the dimming light, and then through the hall and, amazingly, into the lounge. The lounge was usually so out-of-bounds that I couldn't work out at all why we were going in there. Was it a visit from a social worker? If so, we would have been scrubbed up for it. It wasn't Christmas ... that had just passed. It wasn't a lap game with Mr Stabard, as he only did that when his wife was out of the house.

And then we saw them. It was a total shock. There were four people we recognised from church standing and sitting in the lounge, waiting for us, with weird expressions on their faces. What was going on? Our immediate reaction was to shrink back towards the door and cling to each other, as they seemed far from friendly. The atmosphere was tense, and I felt a real tingle of fear rush up my spine. This didn't look good. Not at all. The assembled people were quite old. All were white, and one, I remember, had a woolly hat on. There were two women and two men. Mr Stabard was standing by the ceramic fireplace, with the fierce expression that I recognised so well. Mrs Stabard stood between us and the door. I suddenly felt very trapped, like something really bad was about to happen. Without a word, Mrs Stabard pushed me in the back and I stumbled forward a little. I looked round at her, and she was pointing to the centre of the room, to the dark red carpet, between the sofa and the two armchairs.

Mr Stabard snapped at us, in his usual military tone: 'Come here. On the carpet. Here. All of you. Now.'

The three of us shuffled over to the spot where his fat finger was indicating. The other adults stood up and sort of surrounded us. *Oh my God, what's going on*? We girls darted looks of sheer panic at each other. What were they going to do? What was going to happen now? Were they going to kill us? As they approached all I felt was dread.

One of the grown-ups got out a piece of paper and showed it to Mr Stabard, who nodded. He said to the people there, 'We're here to drive out the devil, as you know,' and then said something that sounded like 'xisms'. I was utterly terrified as the man holding up the paper started chanting the words out loud in an eerie voice, like he was half-shouting:

'Oh most Glorious Prince of the Heavenly Armies, St Michael the Archangel, defend us in the battle . . . and in our wrestling against principalities and powers, against the rulers of the world of this darkness, against the spirits of wickedness in the high places . . . '

We three girls were holding onto each other tightly, shaking, while the grown-ups moved in on us. We didn't understand the words or what was going on. The adults started walking round and round us in a circle, with their left arms raised over our heads, like they were playing some kind of bizarre adult game. Mr and Mrs Stabard joined in, looking very solemn, and we soon had six adults circling round us, their hands joined above our heads, with us, dizzy and terrified, in the middle.

The voice continued to boom out, getting wilder and scarier:

' . . . Beseech the God of Peace to crush Satan under our feet . . . cast into hell Satan and all the other evil spirits who prowl throughout the world, seeking the ruin of souls . . . '

The man went on and on, getting louder and more urgent, until suddenly one of the old women fell on the floor and started shaking and screaming. It looked like she was having a fit – she was writhing and moaning and practically frothing at the mouth. We girls hid our faces and clung on even tighter to each other, but the old woman continued to scream and shout, and peeking out, I could see her arms and legs thrashing about. It was completely bizarre and very frightening, since I still had no idea what was going on. While the woman was rolling about on the carpet, the man was still reading out the chant over and over and his voice was getting louder and louder and stranger and stranger, like it was reaching a frenzied pitch. I wondered again, for a moment, if they were going to kill us in some sort of ritual. The woman's legs were kicking out and she just kept screaming. It was terrifying.

Then all of a sudden the man stopped chanting and the woman quietened down. She lay on her back panting at first, and then closed her eyes and lay still, and I wondered if she was asleep or even unconscious. One of the men bent over and pulled her up to her feet. She was flushed and sweaty, and looked very dazed, so the others fussed over her. Meanwhile, nobody said a word to us about what had just happened. Then Mrs Stabard came up to us and pointed to the door, and, just like that, we were shunted back out to the shed.

Once there, we huddled on the dirty old armchair, and cuddled each other. We said not a word to each other; it all seemed too scary to speak about. This kind of spooky ritual happened several more times over the years and I eventually came to understand that the Stabards were 'casting out the devil' that they thought resided in us, through an exorcism of sorts. It was another kind of purification which they really must have believed was necessary to cleanse our blackened souls, or maybe to whiten our skins. Our wrecking of toys and naughty tricks around the house must have exasperated them to the point where they thought they had to teach us a lesson we would never, ever forget. They were right – we wouldn't forget, but it wouldn't make us give up fighting back either.

7

The Aliens have Landed

'Harmony is of low average intelligence, appears emotionally immature, but gets on well with most of the girls at school ...'
(Social worker's report)

When I was sent to primary school at five and three-quarters, it was a total shock. I'd never really been out of the house, except to go to church or the doctors, and then only with the Stabards in tow, so I had no idea what life outside was all about. Not surprisingly, Mrs Stabard didn't prepare me for it. I was simply walked to an enormous grey stone building, which had loads of children running around in the playground outside, who all stopped and stared at me, open-mouthed. Everybody else was white, and my arrival was the source of much amazement and amusement, it was as if the aliens had landed: I was an alien come to earth. And it was a bumpy ride.

After the silence of the shed, the school seemed wild to me. Children were running around screaming, playing, shouting and I'd jump when they went past. I was actually scared of other people, especially after the horrible church people had come to our home to 'purify' us, so I didn't really understand where I was at all. I felt really terrified of the kids, and I think they sensed it, because they started picking on me from day one. They would shout 'wog' or 'blackie' right in my face, or say

I was a 'fat, ugly, black bitch'. I felt like a misfit from
the start, especially as the parents of the children weren't
happy that I was there either. We three children were
some of the first black children that had ever come to
the school as we were a minority in our village. When the
parents saw me coming in through the school gate they
would put their heads down and hurry past, pulling their
children along behind them. Or they'd cross the road,
so they didn't have to look at me or talk to Mrs Stabard,
who took me there at first. Was I so alien? Obviously, to
them I was.

Three things stick out in my mind about first going to
school. Right from the beginning there were objections
to me using the same things as the other children –
simply because I was black. The parents put pressure on
the headmaster, Mr Harrow, not to let me use the same
facilities as their children because they believed I would
contaminate them in some way. Unbelievably, I had to
bring in my own cutlery, plastic beaker and plate in a
plastic bag for mealtimes and sit at a separate table. Faith
was already at the school by then, although she was away
a lot, through illness, and wasn't there the day I started.
Hope joined the year after, and we three eventually ended
up sitting together, at a small table to the side of the dining
hall – again a little isolated group of three. As I got older,
I began to feel Mr Harrow should have stood up for us
more, and let us use the cutlery and eat at the same table
as the other kids, but I became fearful about eating in front
of white people after that.

Secondly, I wasn't allowed to drink out of the water
fountains in the playground. There was a rumour put
around the playground that if I – or any of us three – drank
from the fountain the other kids would catch something. In

fact, I did sneak a drink a few times as I was thirsty and I got rapped over the knuckles with a ruler by my strict form teacher, Mrs Brookfield, which I thought was very unfair.

The third thing – and this one really hurt – was that I was not allowed to go swimming with the other children. There was actually a swimming pool in the school grounds which all the kids learned to swim in – except Faith, Hope and me. The school would simply not allow us to go swimming. Maybe it was the parents bringing pressure on the school to keep us out of the water. There was this great fear around that we were carrying some awful disease, or that we would contaminate the children, and nobody wanted to be near us, let alone allow us to share the swimming pool water with them. This really upset me, especially on hot summer days, when everybody excitedly went off to swim. Of course, the Stabards didn't fight for us – in fact since we didn't confide in them they probably didn't even know. What's more, given that they were still keeping us in the shed at home, they probably would have agreed with the parents that we were to be kept separate from everybody else. After all, they were doing it too.

To be fair, I actually think the headmaster, Mr Harrow, felt quite bad about what he was doing. He was actually quite nice to me personally – and to the other two – and he would say things like, 'I'm sorry, but my hands are tied,' when he told us we couldn't go swimming or use the water fountain. He was probably the first adult who had been warm towards me, and it meant a lot, even though the outcome was unpleasant. What was important was that he talked to me like a person; something I had seldom experienced before.

I think the parents were scared of us because not only were we black, but we were also quite dirty. There was no way we were as clean as the other kids, and we must have smelled quite badly because we weren't properly looked after.

One really embarrassing incident sticks out in my mind. Just after I'd started primary school I was bleeding heavily from a nasty night attack by Mr Stabard. I remember it so well: my knickers were full of blood from where he had 'hurt' me (I always thought of it as 'hurt', it was the only way I could describe it), and I was supposed to do PE. I didn't have any PE kit, so I had to borrow a pair of shorts from the teacher, who kept some spare shorts at the back of the class in case kids forgot them. Of course, after the lesson, the shorts were covered with blood as well, and I was terrified. I didn't know what to do, or how to manage the situation, so I stuck them in my bag and took them home. I hid them at home, and hoped they'd disappear somehow and she'd forget all about it.

About a week later the PE teacher called me to the front and asked me about the shorts. I didn't know what to say. How could I explain it? I couldn't. What did I have to say for myself? I had nothing to say. She told me, in front of everyone, that she was very disappointed in me. I felt so humiliated, but even more so when a girl piped up, 'That black girl, over there, she's stolen the shorts. She's a thief.' I couldn't say, 'Actually, I've hidden the shorts because they're covered with blood,' or explain how that blood got to be there in the first place. So I said nothing, and they thought the worst of me. I was labelled 'dishonest'. But what did they expect from black foster kids, after all? In their eyes, I was obviously behaving true to form.

What made things worse was that the Stabards never acted as proper parents, or supported us in any way at school. They never sat down with us and helped us with our homework, or talked to us about what had happened at school that day – they simply weren't interested. Instead I talked to my favourite goose, who roamed the garden and the house, if I needed to confide in someone. I told her all my worries and wildest dreams. However, I'm convinced Mr Stabard wrung her neck pretty quickly once he saw she was my favourite confidante. The Stabards had no real idea what went on with us once we left the house. Although we walked to school unsupervised it never occurred to us to run away. I guess even though I desperately wanted to get away, the world 'out there' seemed just as hostile and unwelcoming as the world 'in there', at home.

When there were school trips, we didn't go on them. I don't know whether that was because we weren't invited, or whether the Stabards refused to fork out the money for us to go. I remember the rest of my class going to the zoo, and us being left out. I remember there being another big trip to an ice rink I really wanted to go to, but again, we were left behind. I was probably six by then, going on seven. When parents' evenings happened, the Stabards didn't attend. Mrs Stabard usually made an excuse and I had to take a note in. I think we simply were not important enough.

The irony was that although school didn't like me because of the colour of my skin, I actually liked school. Not the environment, particularly, or the other children, but I loved the lessons, and I loved learning. My favourite thing was reading. At home I managed to sneak the odd *Daily Mirror*, which Mr Stabard read every day and then dumped in the waste bin. I'd fish it out of the bin and smuggle it into the shed to read by the streetlight at night to pass the time. I still remember the thrill of first beginning to make out letters and then some words; it felt so exciting to be able to read.

Needless to say, neither of them had ever sat down with us and read a book or even pointed out letters. So reading at school was a fantastic experience. I adored the books, and I loved beginning to learn some French. I liked maths as well, and found I had quite a facility for it. But reading especially fascinated me. I wanted to know what signs meant at school or in church, or on advertising hoardings on the way to school, and wanted to be able to understand all the things around me. Now I was at school, there were things to read everywhere and I started to pick it up fast. I continued to fish out the old *Daily Mirror* at home and practise, and even began to make out whole stories, which was very satisfying to do.

In time I was able to piece together the outraged letters to the editor of the local paper about the influx of black children lowering standards at the local primary school. Given it was such a tight, rural community, I wondered if Mr and Mrs Stabard were getting letters and phone calls from parents who objected to us going to the school altogether. It was felt locally that we were somehow invading, that we were taking over the school, and that we should be sent back to whatever planet we came from. I remember people shouting out things to us on the street when we were walking to church together. I'd hear, 'Go home wog!' or 'Dirty black bastards!' and the Stabards wouldn't react at all. I also remember a parent coming to our front door complaining about us playing with their children at school and Mrs Stabard, just saying meekly, 'Oh, I'm very sorry, it won't happen again.' She didn't stand up for us, so she just seemed to agree that we shouldn't be mixing with the local white children – and I guess it suited her to keep us isolated.

Even though we were at school during the day, our lives

didn't improve any at home. Mr Stabard continued to come in to us at night, and his wife continued to make us do the chores – and if we didn't do them well enough, we'd have to start again from scratch. Meanwhile, back at school, I discovered I was very good at running. I think all that time pent-up in the shed, not running around like other kids, meant I was utterly thrilled when I was finally allowed to stretch my legs. I was a good athlete and even went on to represent the school in athletic races. It was really the only thing I was allowed to do, and I excelled at it. The PE teachers pushed me and I enjoyed winning all sorts of medals and trophies for the school. It was the only place I was allowed to succeed, and I guess they thought it was OK for black kids to be sporty, as that was an acceptable thing for us to be good at in a racist society. I didn't get any praise from the Stabards however, who never commented on my success.

The one aspect of PE I didn't like was when I was told to take the skipping ropes back to the PE cupboard, which meant I had to cross the playground, holding a huge bundle of ropes. Once, I remember I was cornered by a gang of white kids, who stripped me down to my underwear and then tied me to the football goalposts. I was there for ages until a teacher came and untied me. When they asked who had done it, I didn't give the names away. I knew it would only make things worse if I told on them. I was just told to go and get dressed, and no one was ever told off.

From the start I was very isolated at school. I didn't really make friends with the white kids, and we three black children (or two when Faith was away in hospital) were very much left to ourselves. Later on there were more ethnic minority children at school – when the Stabards fostered more black and Asian children themselves and some more families arrived in the area – but we all had a hard time, and the school didn't really integrate us at all well. The main thing was parental opposition to our being there. I remember when I did very well in a reading test, and came top of the class, one of the parents actually made a big fuss and said it was impossible for me to be able to read better than her daughter, who had always been top until then. I was embarrassed and upset as I'd really tried hard to improve my reading by myself. I think this parent made such a big hoo-ha with the headmaster that I was eventually marked down to keep the peace. That really hurt, although I kept it to myself, as always. There wasn't even the goose for me to go home and talk to anymore, so I just had to bottle things up.

Of course I did try to make friends. Sometimes I made myself into a playground donkey, giving other kids piggy-back rides. I think I wanted to please them, to buy their friendship. I was quite a bit bigger than other children of my age, and I tried to make them laugh and give them a good time. It would work to some extent, in that they would play with me at playtimes, but only if I remained their donkey. I made myself useful in a clownish kind of way. I wanted to be liked, I needed to join in, and it was all I could think of doing. Other times I could be disruptive, and not sit down or get on with anything. I was told off, and I would want to sulk or misbehave, to get my own back. I didn't take it too far, but the teachers weren't as scary as Mr Stabard, so I think I was trying them out.

Few of the other children wanted to talk to me, or be seen to be talking to me. However, one girl, Tanya, did invite me to her house one day for a play. I was very excited about this, as it was the first time it had happened. I must have been about eight by then but I had never been inside anyone else's house before, and I had no idea how other people lived. I guess I must have thought everyone lived like we did. When I got to Tanya's house, we just got our coats off – her mum was actually quite friendly although I was painfully shy – and were beginning to play, when Mr Stabard arrived at the door. Within ten minutes I was pulled out of her house. It was very embarrassing. He literally grabbed me, without explaining anything, and I was dragged home. After that, Tanya avoided me and I was never invited back again. Looking back I guess he was terrified that either I would spill the beans, or I would see how a 'normal' family lived and it would make me rebel. Instead he nipped my flowering friendship well and truly in the bud.

Christmas at primary school was fun as we had parties for the first time. We'd be given sweets and presents and Santa would come and visit, which was utterly wonderful. When we got our sweets and stuff, we'd gobble them all up on the way home, else they'd be confiscated the minute we got back. One trick we learned over the years was to hide anything we wanted to keep under one of the wonky floorboards in our bedroom. If we got a bit of cake or a book, we'd hide them there, and then bring them out on Christmas Day – and that would be our Christmas presents to ourselves. Even if the cake was stale, we'd eat it, as it was like precious buried treasure. A couple of times, however, Mr Stabard found things I had hidden – a book, and some sweets – and he ripped the book up in front of me, and threw away the sweets.

One thing though about Christmas at school was that I was never picked for any of the main parts in the nativity play, even though I liked acting things out and had plenty of practice, thanks to the endless imaginary games we played to keep ourselves sane in the shed. Even so, I was either backstage, or I'd be a tree or the end of a donkey or something hidden well out of sight. The same was true of Hope, who was much more outgoing and mouthier than me, and Faith, who was shy and poorly, but nonetheless could play-act and sing. We were always pushed to the back, and I felt we were never picked for anything important. However, even if we had been, neither of our foster parents would have come to see us perform as they never appeared at a single school concert or play. We never had someone in the audience to look out for, to smile at and wave to. It obviously hurt like hell to see other parents looking proud, or cooing over their kids in the play, while ours were totally absent as usual – but that's just the way it was.

I also remember that I loved doing woodwork in primary school, and one day, I brought back a little table I'd made in class. I'd spent all term working on it, and although it was crude and simple I was very proud of it, and thought it was the bee's knees. It was childish, but I was so pleased to be able to show Mr Stabard because I knew he liked doing woodwork himself. When he came over to the shed eventually at bedtime, I couldn't wait to show him and blurted out, 'Look, I made this.' He had an odd look on his face when he saw it, but said nothing, just turned around and disappeared. A few minutes later he returned with a hammer in his hand, and smashed it to pieces in front of me. I couldn't believe it, but I didn't cry – I knew better than to cry, as he would then lay into me and call me weak. I saved my tears for much later, when I was finally alone in bed and everyone was asleep.

All this time at school Mr Stabard was still playing his purification games with us at home. I never thought for a moment that I could tell anyone about it and it felt like

I was living in two completely different worlds at home and at school. Social Services used to come and check us over at home before each school year started. We would be brought into the lounge – a rare treat – and they would peer at us and talk to Mrs Stabard over our head, who would be watching us like a hawk. We'd also be dragged to the surgery for a check-over, but although I had loads of urinary infections, nothing was ever picked up about what Mr Stabard was doing to us at night. I might have had blood in my pants, but the doctor wouldn't have known as he didn't look, and I couldn't have told him. When I did urine tests, Mrs Stabard came to the toilet with me, and peered at my sample, probably checking it was clear of streaks, and then took the bottle back to the doctor, making sure I didn't get a chance to say a word. Anyway, I don't think doctors thought about those things back then, and I was convinced that if I said anything they would have thought I was making all those horrible things up. And always the Stabards would be with us, watching us carefully.

It seemed for a moment like things might be getting better when we were taken to join the Brownies (what a fitting name for us!) when I was about seven. Most of the girls in my class were in the Brownies and for some reason Mrs Stabard agreed to take us to a meeting. We were standing in a queue, the three of us, amid the white children. The Brown Owl was sitting there with a register, and she let in the three white girls before us in the queue. But when she got to us she looked at Mrs Stabard, then at us, very po-faced, and looked down at her register and tutted. Then she simply said that she was sorry, but there was no more room for new kids. Mrs Stabard just accepted it at face value, and we walked away, crushed, although as

I looked back I saw the white girls behind us in the queue being let in, no question. I never said a word to the other two, but we knew deep down, without saying anything, that unfairness was the score. The most painful aspect of it all was Mrs Stabard not standing up for us – she wouldn't have thrown water over us if we'd been on fire.

8

Wildflower Woods

'Mrs Stabard is concerned about Harmony's fits of temper and wants help in controlling these – but otherwise Harmony seems to cope fairly well with the foster home ... ' (Social worker's report)

One night Mr Stabard was particularly brutal with me. I don't know why, but he was in a very bad mood and also quite drunk when he came to our room late that night. He shouted at us all to get up – Mrs Stabard must have heard it – and he put the light bulb in, swaying on his feet. Faith wasn't well at the time, and I pleaded with him to let her alone, but he started on his 'eeny, meeny, miny, mo' thing, and then chose Faith. I found my voice somehow and said, 'No, leave her alone,' and he turned on me, furious. You never, ever answered him back: that was the rule. He grabbed me and threw me down on the bottom bunk bed and barked at the other two to watch – he nearly always said this. I was fuming with a mixture of fear and rage and I glared at him. I seldom spoke – I knew what I had said meant I had already gone too far. You never ever talked back to him, and I never had until then. He was cursing me all the time, saying I was evil and needed teaching a lesson, as he prepared to throw himself on top of me for the usual degradation. All the while, I was glaring at him, trying to make him feel the fury I felt inside, channelling

it through my eyes. They were my only weapons in this
sordid war.

All of a sudden he fumbled in his trouser pocket, and
out came a roll of something. I only had a moment to
try and work out what it was before I heard a ripping
sound, and suddenly he was pulling Sellotape across my
eyes. I put my hands up instinctively to pull it off, but
he slapped them away, and then wound the tape around
my head a couple of times, very roughly. The pressure
on my face felt unbearable. Satisfied I wouldn't glare at
him anymore, he proceeded to push himself into me very
brutally, and I just switched off and lay there, totally inert
and numb, eyes stuck closed, Sellotape cutting into my
face, counting the minutes in my head until it was over. It
seemed even more revolting now I couldn't see a thing or
stare my protest at him.

Then he pulled out roughly– job done – and I could
hear him stumbling around the room, fumbling with the
light bulb, and it all went dark again. I lay there for some
time until Hope and Faith crept over and helped me get
the tape off my head, taking with it clumps of my hair
and pulling out loads of eyelashes. After this ordeal, we
didn't say anything to each other, but I felt really desperate
that night. What had happened felt like a step further
into something horribly dark and violent. I did wonder
sometimes if Mr Stabard would suddenly produce a knife
and kill me one day. I think he was capable of it, because
in those moments when he was drunk, and full of hatred
towards me, I really felt I was just an object to him, just a
piece of meat to be skewered on the spit.

In the silence of the early hours I made my way over
to the window. There were old grey nets and some dark
material curtains hanging there. I pulled them to one side

and looked up through the smudgy glass at the wonder of the stars. It was something I had done several times, late at night. I just loved looking up at the space in the sky, looking at the inky black and the twinkling lights, and imagining the vast space out there. It was magical to me, so fabulous that it made me relax inside. I felt so utterly trapped in our room, in the shed, in the house, and at school, but the sky offered something fantastic, far beyond things made by the humans who always seemed to hurt me.

I imagined flying up to a star and sitting on it, looking down at all the little people going about their daily business, and feeling they were not that important any more. I'd love to be able to fly like a bird, or like a fairy, up to the heavens. To be free, to have wings, to fly.

While I looked out in my reverie, the other two had crept to my side and were looking out too. I have no idea why I did what I did next, but it was going to change our lives forever. I must have been only around six and a half, or seven, but I opened the window. We could smell the sweet night air rush into our stifling, soulless room, and it felt good. Beneath our window was a small grey flat roof which was the porch over the front door. I looked down at it for a few minutes and for the first time I realised that either side of the porch there was a trellis with shrubs. Without further ado I got up onto the window ledge and popped my legs over the sill and onto the cold, gritty flat roof. I had to drop down a couple of feet, but suddenly I was standing on the roof in my bare feet and nightie. I looked back and the other two were hanging out of the window, with huge eyes, looking terrified.

I don't know what made me do it, but I was filled with an urge to escape. The Sellotape over the eyes was like the last, degrading straw, and now I needed to break free.

I turned, and started climbing down the trellis on the right side of the porch. I stopped and looked up at the other two and beckoned them to follow. Without a word, Hope hopped over the windowsill, crept to the edge of the porch roof and anxiously watched me go down. I hit the floor and grinned – turns out it was really fun climbing down. I beckoned to her furiously and she started to follow. However Faith, who was much weaker than us, was still half hanging out the window looking scared. I gestured wildly for her to follow, but she shook her head. 'Come on!' I hissed, and beckoned again; as did Hope, who was now nearly at the bottom of the trellis. Suddenly Faith decided, and she was out the window, on the roof and feeling her way carefully down the trellis. She was clearly scared she was going to fall, but probably more scared of being left behind, so she gathered all her courage up and joined in. What a trooper!

When all three of us were at the bottom we stood for a moment in the front garden, wondering what to do next. All we had on was our nighties and bare feet, and it was chilly. I was hurting a lot between my legs, and I must have been bleeding, but I didn't care. The fresh air was like nectar, and the night breeze felt fantastic, so, without a word, we turned right, crept past the house, and then padded through the alleyway, past the shed, and up to the tall back fence. The sky was clear shades of indigo with clouds scudding by, and we could still see the stars sparkling like diamonds above. We never spoke to each other, or discussed what we were doing, but I started climbing the back fence and the other two quickly followed. Suddenly I dropped down – what seemed like a very long way – onto a gravelly path that was actually a narrow back lane running behind the house. The other two dropped down beside me. Faith was shaking with fear, but I could see her eyes were shining with excitement too.

If Mr Stabard had woken up and put on a light in his bedroom, or shone a torch out onto the back fence, he would have seen three ghostly little bare-footed figures making a bid for freedom. Our antics would have been discovered and our one chance of escape would have been ruined forever. However, luckily, he didn't wake up. No doubt he was snoring away, deep in his drunken sleep, worn out from hurting me.

Free, for once, we padded happily down the lane in the dark, which led out into some fields. We could hear animals snuffling in the darkness, but we weren't frightened. The wind was rustling in the trees overhead, and we could hear an owl hooting somewhere quite near. But still we weren't scared. It felt fantastic to be outside, free, alone and untethered; just going where we wanted to go. We came to cornfields and we started walking along them, then through them, past bungalows and the backs of houses, where I imagined families were fast asleep, with no idea that we were trotting past outside. I could feel my lungs expanding – for once, I could breathe good fresh night air. I could hear cicadas making their night noises, and I felt so light-hearted. We picked up stalks of corn each, and chewed them, which was fun. We walked along, not talking, but chewing on our corn, feeling the hard, dried mud between our toes and the wind on our faces.

Next we came to a narrow path that started leading upwards through some woods. We all looked at each other – not in fear, but in a sort of question – but I was determined to go on. I wanted to know where the path led to, so I started walking, pushing aside the brambles. The woods got denser and denser, and the tree branches met in an arch over our heads. It was pitch black in places, the darkest we had ever experienced, even in the shed or airing cupboard, and we clutched each others' bramble-scratched hands. We walked in a little crocodile, scrambling our way up an incline on a narrow, woody path. The smells and sounds were amazing; we could hear all sorts of rustlings and buzzings, and even the odd bird. We didn't know much about nature, but we felt like we were right in the middle of it, and it felt like it was protecting us, somehow.

Eventually we came to the top of a hill. We had a view of the valley below, of yellow street lights and dotted house lights. The stars were burning bright overhead and we could see clumps of trees on the top of the hill, and then sweeping, rolling curves, with bushes and hedges lining the surrounding fields. It was utterly glorious, and I started running as fast as I possibly could downhill. From top to bottom, in the open space, I could feel the soft dewy grass between my toes, and I could smell those wonderful, damp, new-mown smells as they wafted up to me as I ran.

At the bottom we found a sort of dip, covered with fallen leaves. We worked out it was some kind of bunker or hideaway that ivy and branches had grown over. We chased each other round the base of the huge trees, giggling quietly. We played catch, like we'd seen the kids do at school. We mimicked people we knew – the Stabards, their grandchildren (particularly the ones who swore at us), nasty parents we'd met, the teachers, church people – and fell about laughing till our sides ached. Up until this moment we had never been free. We'd never had the experience of running around with the wind in our hair, free to choose what we did next. We'd never climbed trees, or explored our neighbourhood. We'd never been allowed to dig the garden or go out on bikes. This was our very first taste of being out in nature and enjoying its beauty entirely for ourselves.

To my amazement I wasn't scared of the dark here in the way I would have been at home. It didn't feel menacing; it didn't feel like it was out to get me and do me harm. It wasn't stifling or demeaning. I felt I could be myself, and that I belonged, finally, to the world.

We looked up at the sky between the gaps in the branches, and we spotted stars and gave them names between the spaces in the bushes. We could see the moon as it rose, and it was a honey-coloured wonder. We could make out the face of the man in the moon, and he looked very kind and calm. The moon seemed to follow us as we explored through the undergrowth, putting our toes into all sorts of squishy wet things. It didn't matter at all, we just laughed and giggled, ran and breathed deeply, and jumped and whooped for joy. We looked to see if the moon was peeking out over the branches at us, like a wise old thing. We hid behind ivy-clad trees and played hide-and-seek with each other. We made up songs and dances and looned around. It was wonderful. We jumped off rocks and rolled around in the dirt. We had fun.

Eventually, when the light began to change, we realised that dawn was breaking. Without saying a word, we turned together and started walking home. I was able to remember how we'd got there, although it was about half an hour's walk. We walked back in total silence. We were exhausted, but very happy. The birdies were tweeting wildly around us, and I'd had no idea how much they sing in the early hours until that moment, as the day came up. Once we got to the house it was quite light and we managed to get up the trellis again fairly easily (although Faith struggled a bit) and then fell through the window back into our room. After pulling it shut we collapsed into bed.

It was a school day, and we had to get up only a couple of hours later, but oddly I felt energised. I was very tired, but I felt something very special indeed had happened to us. The three of us made our way down to make breakfast, and then on to school, with lighter hearts. That place, Wildflower Woods, was our great, secret escape.

From then on, we went to the woods as often as we could. We always went after he had hurt us at night, usually once or twice a week. It was our special place. We called it 'Wildflower Woods' because there were loads of wonderful wild flowers there that we didn't know the names of. We had no idea what the names of trees or animals or plants were, so we made them up.

Over the next few years our trips to Wildflower saved our sanity. It became our real home, the place where we celebrated our lives and performed all sorts of wonderful rituals. For instance, on our birthdays we never had presents from the Stabards. It used to upset us deeply. Now we had a place to celebrate, and we would use leaves, twigs and stones to create cakes and presents for each other. We'd sing 'Happy Birthday' and have all sorts of birthday ceremonies for each other. As we got older we got clever at stealing some food to bring with us. I remember we sometimes filled a sock with the dog's Winalot biscuits, and we'd eat them for a treat. They actually weren't that bad – very crunchy – and at least we weren't starving hungry, like we were most of the time at home. If we were lucky, we would manage to get some cheese or bread and we'd have a real party. If we had anything left we'd hide it under a stone, wrapped in paper or foil. We even managed to take a tablecloth there, a red and white checked one, which we'd spread on the floor for our picnics and parties. It was brilliant. We would have imaginary toys, or a baby, which we'd feed. At Christmas, we'd nick some Christmas cake and have a Christmas party. Sometimes we'd argue as to whose turn it was to have a birthday party, and one of us would say, 'Oh, she had hers last time,' and then we'd giggle, because it didn't matter really who had it last time, as we all enjoyed it.

We were acting out all those things we'd never ever had at home. And also all those things that we'd seen the grandchildren have, which we knew we weren't allowed. We would sometimes have a tea party, where we had to talk in very posh voices to each other, and stick our little fingers out while we pretended to drink tea. We'd ask to pass the sauce or the potatoes, and we'd giggle at being so refined. Sometimes we'd even have real potatoes or a piece of pie we'd squirreled away, and then it was a real picnic and we revelled in it.

Sometimes we'd play at swapping roles and pretend we were the Stabards, and they were the slaves and we were the bosses – we particularly liked this game, as we got to tell them what to do all the time. I would point at my bare feet and command Hope, playing Mrs Stabard, to 'lick my boots' and she'd have to do it. We'd point to everything, and issue commands to each other, and fall about laughing endlessly as it seemed so absurd. We never played out the 'eeny meeny' game, as we didn't ever mention that to each other. We avoided that completely; it felt too dangerous to go near, too painful and humiliating. Instead, we danced, sang and frolicked to our hearts' content. Sometimes we'd just lie on our backs, hands under our heads, and gaze at the stars and moon, watching the clouds wander past and call out what we thought they were shaped like: animals, cakes, anything that caught our fancy. It was our earthly paradise out there in the woods, and it was utterly fantastic.

We went to Wildflower Woods whatever the weather. We went in wind, in rain, in snow, in storms. We didn't care. One time I actually burnt my foot on snow when it was freezing cold. I guess it was some sort of frostbite. Luckily Mrs Stabard didn't notice; she never paid much attention to me. It was really painful and hurt for a very long time, but I didn't mind. It was worth every inch of pain to have the freedom that going out to the woods gave us. It was our reward for being hurt – the release from the pain and constant humiliation, mistreatment and slavery. The only problem was we would be very tired in the daytime. As we went more and more, we got more and more tired and I'm sure it affected my ability to concentrate at school.

I was the leader of the pack when it came to going up to Wildflower, and helped develop all sorts of other ideas over time, such as taking a black bin bag with us and a watering can filled with water. We would climb carefully to the top of the hill, wet the underside of a bin bag, and slide all the way down on one of the long chalk markings. It was an amazing instant slide. Sometimes we would burn the back of our nighties or our legs, but it didn't matter. We did the washing and ironing, so we could hide any holes and scrub off any marks ourselves. We even went to the woods when there were other foster children living in the box room with us. We would simply wait until Mr Stabard had played his 'game', and the other children were asleep, and then we'd silently signal to each other, and we'd be off to the woods. I don't know if any of the other children found out we'd gone, but if they did, they never said anything.

When we went to Wildflower, we were desperate. When we trotted back, exhausted and spent, we always felt better. We still knew that we were evil, and had to be purified further, but somehow the long journey to purification seemed more bearable if we could escape at night and be free to be children, far away from the constant, critical gaze of the Stabards. We were different people up there; we were like real children, not the vigilant, silent slaves we were at home. We were sometimes vicious to each other at the Stabards', hitting each other out of sheer frustration, or getting jealous of each other over something trivial. But up at the woods, we felt united again. I could be generous, loving and kind, and we would put our arms round each other and dance a happy, carefree dance, the likes of which we could never, ever do in the prison that was 97 Forestland Way.

9

First Bitter Pills

'Harmony and the other foster children seem very happy in their present home' (Social worker's report)

When I was nine I started to develop breasts. I had no idea what the bumps on my chest were at all. I thought they were 'evil lumps', that the evil in me was coming out in these growths. Mr Stabard noticed, and kept grabbing them and trying to hold them, making me feel even more embarrassed and uncomfortable. None of the other girls in my class had a chest like mine, and I felt very self-conscious about my changing body. I hunched my shoulders over, trying to hide them, because I didn't want anyone to see how evil I obviously was.

Then one day I was sitting on a step at school and noticed that blood was pouring out of me. It was different from the blood that came after my foster father hurt me, this was bright red and was really dripping out. I was terrified that everyone would think I was really wicked – I had been so convinced by Mr Stabard that any time I bled it was actually the pure evil coming out. As I got off the step, I could see a red patch left behind, and my dress was sodden. I didn't know what to do, so I went to my classroom and the teacher sent me to the medical room. I was hysterical, I felt so ashamed and also terrified about what they would do to me at home, now I was bleeding in public. My 'evil' was now in the open for all to see.

To my amazement Mr Harrow took me home in his car: he was very nice to me, and spoke kindly and quietly. I remember it was summer, as he had the roof open. I was very worried about spoiling his seat as my dress was bright red at the back, but he quietly put a newspaper on the seat and said nothing about it. I'd never met with such kindness from an adult. When we got home Mr Stabard was there, which was unusual. I think Mrs Stabard must have called him at work, but I didn't know why. I could see from his face, as he stood on the doorstep, that he was terrified. I think he thought I'd given the game away, and all the blood pouring out was because he had hurt me the night before – and so I'd finally told on him. Mr Harrow was very kind and spoke softly to the Stabards, but all the while I could see the hatred in Mr Stabard's face and I felt very scared.

Even though I tried to tell them what had happened, the minute the door was shut I was pulled upstairs by my hair by an absolutely livid Mr Stabard. I thought he was really going to kill me this time, but he just dragged me up the stairs and stuffed me in the airing cupboard and jammed the door shut. I was stuck in there for two, maybe three, days after that. I was being punished for bleeding in public. I just sat there, with terrible tummy pain, very hungry, thirsty and afraid. I had no idea what on earth was happening to me or my body, and it was terrifying. I missed school, which really upset me. The other two were not allowed to come near me. I was bleeding all the time, and blood was pouring out, not just leaking a bit, like it did after he hurt me. I wasn't given anything to put in my knickers, no toilet paper or fresh pants, so when I was eventually let out, the cupboard was awash with blood, and it stank. Dried blood was all over the floor, all over me, my clothes, the boiler cladding and the pile of towels. My punishment was to get down on my knees and scrub everything clean, but by then it was all brown and crusty, and it took forever. I had no idea what was happening to me at all, or why, all I knew was this was a life of hell, and I was evil and was in big trouble with my foster parents, yet again.

The bleeding stopped after a week, and then a month went by and I got pains in my tummy and it started all over again. This time Mrs Stabard gave me a packet of sanitary pads and an elastic belt to wear round my waist and told me this would be happening once a month from now on. She didn't explain any more than that, but she said each month I should go to her and she would give me the pads. Now I understood it was going to be a regular thing, and that the evil was going to pour out of me each month, I felt even more miserable and confused. The other two girls didn't seem to have this problem, and they also didn't have the lumps on their chests like me.

Faith had been pretty poorly over the past months and had been in hospital having treatment. Mrs Stabard didn't really explain very much and we weren't taken in to see her. I had no idea what 'leukaemia' meant, but when Faith came home she was very frail. Nonetheless, Mrs Stabard expected her to go to school, stay in the shed, and to do her chores, just like always. On the days she was too poorly to go, she would lie in bed all day, but I don't think she got any special looking-after from Mrs Stabard. Mr Stabard continued to come in to 'purify' us at night, and on the night Faith came home from the hospital he chose her in his 'eeny meeny' game. She was lying in the bottom bunk, hardly able to move, when he came in. He looked at all three of us, deciding which one he'd go for, and then he lurched at Faith. He grabbed her, then threw her back on the bed, snapping at her to spread her legs properly for him. I was on the top bunk but I jumped off and said, 'No, no, take me! Take me! She's too sick.' I watched helplessly as he ripped the nightie off Faith. She didn't have the energy to resist, to cry, to do anything but lie there, emotionless and blank, while he 'purified' her.

I wanted to kill him. I suddenly felt this enormous rage in me and I didn't know what to do with it. I always tried to protect both Faith and Hope, and usually I could get Mr Stabard to choose me over them, especially now I had my evil lumps. I don't know why he insisted on going for Faith this time; perhaps it was because she was really poorly and it gave him some strange pleasure to hurt her when she was really down? Or maybe he just couldn't bear the fact that I had challenged him? However, once he was gone, the two girls turned on me, as if it was all my fault. Faith wouldn't speak to me, and neither would Hope. I think they were so upset they didn't know what to do with their feelings, so they took them out on me. We often did that – when there was no-one else to blame or be angry at, we got angry with each other. I'd myself been cross with them in the past, when really I was maddened by the Stabards and their treatment of all of us.

This night everything came to the boil. I had done my best to save Faith and our foster father had just ignored me. I realised it wasn't my fault. But I also felt really guilty because I knew how ill Faith was, and I thought he really might kill her in the end. As far as I was concerned I had let my sisters down terribly, they now hated me, and I couldn't take it any more.

Without a word I went downstairs, into the kitchen and inside the walk-in larder where I knew the Stabards kept our pills. There were painkillers there too. I found a bottle and started taking tablets. I was only nine years old, but there I was, barefoot in the dark, desperately trying to swallow down tablet after tablet with the help of a mug of water. Although they were hard to get down I carried on swallowing the bitter pills until the bottle was half empty – I was like a little robot.

Then, to my horror, Mr Stabard was suddenly there behind me, breathing heavily, smelling of drink and looking furious. I thought he would beat the living daylights out of me. He started swearing at me, saying I was an ungrateful bitch, that I was evil and deserved to die. He grabbed the bottle of pills from me, poured some into his huge hand, and started stuffing the pills down my throat. I gagged. He kept pushing them into my mouth, one after the other until I retched. He had hold of me by the back of the neck and was towering over me, forcing me to swallow pill after pill until I could hardly breathe. His hand hurt my neck, and all I could see was him staring at me with his hate-filled eyes and snarling as he crammed more tablets into me with his fat fingers.

The next thing I knew I was coming round in hospital. I was in a bed, which had clean, crisp white sheets. I thought I'd died and gone to heaven at first, especially when I saw the walls were light and bright. The staff seemed to float by on clouds and were very kind to me, just like I imagined angels would be. A nurse came and stood by me, took my right wrist and looked at her watch. She bent over me and stroked my head, and said I had had my stomach pumped. I didn't understand what that meant at all. She asked me how I felt and I didn't know what to say. My throat felt very sore, so I just nodded.

I was amazed by the day or two I spent in hospital. The nurses came and plumped my pillows, fed me hot food and helped me wash. They talked to me, and smiled and even stroked my hair. I didn't have to go out in the cold; I could stay nice and warm and I slept a lot in my warm, clean, comfy bed. The nurses smoothed the sheets and tidied things up. People spoke kindly to me, and no-one was angry. I thought I'd get into big trouble for taking pills, but I didn't. I didn't tell anyone what Mr Stabard had done with the pills, I didn't dare.

At the end of the first whole day in hospital, the nurse came and said my parents were outside. For a moment I didn't know who they meant. Then she said 'your foster parents', and I understood. She leant towards me and said, 'They were really devastated they might lose you,' and I felt really confused. Surely she didn't mean the Stabards, who were only too keen to get rid of me – especially Mr Stabard, who had just tried to kill me with the tablets? However, the door opened and they came in together. I saw them walk down the ward towards me, looking very concerned. They both came to one side of my bed, and in front of the nurse, Mrs Stabard took my hand and looked softly at me. Usually she was an ice-cold lady, but now she seemed to be caring for me at last. Then her husband leant forward and kissed me on the forehead. I didn't know what to make of it. *What on earth was going on?* The nurse watched all this and smiled, and the Stabards stood by my bedside making me feel that I was a little princess and that they really cared about me. Despite everything, I couldn't help thinking: 'Maybe they've changed? Maybe they see now how miserable I've been and now they'll really love me?' I really felt that things might change for the better. I hoped they had finally seen the light and I actually slept peacefully that night for the first time in years.

The next day they took me home. The minute we got in through the front door everything reverted to how it always was. We were back to the old routine: out to the shed, then up to the box room after cooking the supper and doing the cleaning. Nothing had changed. Faith and Hope were glad to see me though and hugged me close to them. Faith looked weaker than ever and was soon back in hospital. That night, however, Mr Stabard came to our room and he was more vicious with me than I could ever remember him being before. He even slapped me around before 'purifying' me, so I ended up with bruises and cuts. Absolutely nothing had changed. Not a single thing.

During this time, when I was nine going on ten, the Stabards had quite a few other foster children to stay. Some were very short-term – just a few weeks or so. It was expected that we three girls would look after them at night, and during the day at the weekends. The babies would be in a cot in our room, and we'd have to get them up, feed them, change their nappies, and give them their bottles. It was hard not to resent them crowding into the small space with us. We were short of sleep as it was. The room next door still stood empty most of the time, with three nice divans and clean bedding; but it was out of bounds to the likes of us. At one time there were ten of us in that room, and I had to sleep on the bare floor to let the little ones have the bunks. There were three children in each bunk, sometimes four – it was completely ridiculous. They would also shut be in the shed with us in the day, so it was all very over-crowded. When it was hot, it was unbearable. I don't know how the Stabards got away with it.

As well as the babies our foster parents took on a couple of Asian children, Raj and Prathi, who lived with us for three and a half years. Mr Stabard took a particular liking to the young boy, and he would hurt him at night – usually around one or two in the morning – and get him to do things to him in front of us. I would see him strip Raj and touch his little boy's willy. Then, he would make the boy touch his own willy. Mr Stabard even made Raj put Mr Stabard's disgusting thing in his mouth, by pushing Raj's head onto it. Raj absolutely hated it and would choke and cry and try to resist, but Mr Stabard would slap him and make him do it, calling him 'evil' too. It was totally disgusting. I would feel completely sick and powerless to help Raj, who was only about four or five at the time. I would feel so revolted afterwards I wouldn't be able to sleep. Instead Hope and I would climb out the window to Wildflower Woods, and try to run, sing and dance it all out of our systems in the fresh early morning air.

During this time things were not going too well at school. The horrors of home meant that I was getting to school exhausted and found it hard to concentrate. To make matters worse, there were zero expectations of me. As I was nearing eleven, it was decided that I was not fit to go to the local comprehensive along with the other children, but that I should go to a special school for the 'educationally sub-normal' – the nice term they used to use for kids with learning difficulties. Amazingly the same decision was made for Faith, who had missed a lot of school through her sickness, and also for bright, bubbly Hope. All three of us black foster children ended up labelled ESN while the white kids – even the very naughty ones who got up to no good and never did their homework – ended up going on to the local comprehensive.

At the time I had no idea what 'ESN' meant, but I knew it sounded bad. However, just before I was to leave and start this new 'special' education, something else happened that would take my mind off school altogether.

10

Backstreet Hell

'... *Mrs Stabard cares for this difficult child very well* ...'
(Social worker's report)

I had just started at my new ESN school – which I didn't
like very much. There was a special minibus that picked
us up from round the corner that the local kids used to
jeer and spit at. Once we got there, I was usually put in a
classroom with children with all sorts of disabilities and
problems, to build towers of bricks. That's all we seemed to
do, day after day: build bricks, sort bricks, play with bricks
and stack bricks. They liked bricks there a lot. Meanwhile,
I was longing for a book to read, and the boredom was
driving me mad. I was now just eleven, and wondering
if school was ever going to get any better. The only good
thing was that Faith was out of hospital, and at the same
school as me. There were quite a few other black and Asian
children at the school, too, so we didn't feel as alien as we
had at our primary school.

Meanwhile, I had continued to bleed every month, and
hadn't really taken much notice when I missed a month.
I was too busy settling in to my new school and getting
used to the new teachers and endless brick building. In
fact, I'd been relieved that the blood hadn't come as I
found it very unpleasant to deal with each month. It was
nice to have a break.

Then one morning, after I had got breakfast with Hope and Faith and cleared away the dishes, Mrs Stabard pointed for me to go upstairs to my room. The other two went off to school as normal, and I headed up to the box room, wondering what was going on. Mrs Stabard walked in, went over to the wardrobe and pointed to my Sunday clothes. She told me to put them on and went out of the room again. I did as I was told, and when I came downstairs she was waiting for me, with a small navy holdall. She handed me the holdall but I didn't look in it – I knew better than to do something like that without being told to.

We sat in the kitchen, and she didn't say a word to me. It was very unusual for us to sit together like this, and I really couldn't understand what was going on. Suddenly the doorbell went, and Mrs Stabard stood up and pointed to me to get up and go down the hall. At this point, Mr Stabard arrived at the front door from upstairs, and my heart sank; I'd thought he'd gone to work already. I hated being in the same room as him and I didn't fancy going anywhere with him, that was for sure. However I had no choice in the matter, and I went out the door sandwiched between my foster parents. Where were we going? What on earth was going on? Of course, they didn't tell me; they never did.

Outside there was a taxi waiting. We got in the cab, and I sat beside Mrs Stabard in the back in total silence, while Mr Stabard got in the front seat and spoke to the driver. The Stabards had a car, but we weren't allowed in it – hence, I guess, the taxi.

Mrs Stabard didn't open her lips for the full half an hour journey. Once Mr Stabard had given the directions to the driver, he fell into silence too. Meanwhile, I just looked out the window and wondered at this new, fascinating experience. It felt very luxurious to be gliding along in the back of a big, silver car. Maybe they were going to take me for a treat? I didn't understand why I was getting special treatment. After all these years of walking I now knew what it was like to sit in a big car like this, and I imagined I was a royal princess going to the palace for tea.

My daydream was broken when we finally arrived at a big old house. It wasn't a fairy tale palace, however. In fact it was one of those gothic Victorian houses; more like something out of a horror film than a daydream. Mr Stabard paid the taxi driver while his wife pulled me up to the front door. I didn't like the look of the place at all.

We stood on the step and the big black door opened. Standing in front of us was a plump middle-aged woman, quite official looking, in a green suit, with her dark brown hair in a bun. She didn't smile. Instead she shook Mr Stabard's hand and asked, 'Is this her?' nodding her head at me curtly.

'Yes', he replied sharply, not looking at me.

I thought, by now, that I was being sent away because I was evil. The Stabards had often threatened it when we misbehaved. This was clearly a new step-mother or a care home for naughty children; my new carer looked very cruel and nasty to me. Maybe it was a kind of prison, and I was going to be locked up? Mr Stabard had threatened me many times with putting me away somewhere – like a dungeon, or a prison – where I'd have to stay until I rotted because I was so bad. As I was thinking this he turned to me and said, in front of the woman, 'We're here because you've been naughty. You know you've been evil, don't you? Well you're going to be punished for what you've done.'

I was now utterly terrified. I was hardly breathing, hardly able to stand. They half-pulled me in through the front door and we were in a large, cold hallway. It was clean, but had an echoing black and white tiled floor, and felt very sterile, like some sort of clinic. There was a medical smell to the place, like disinfectant. I was ushered into a side room and told to get undressed. I didn't know what on earth was going on. Maybe they were going to kill me?

I remember that Mrs Stabard came in with me as I undressed and so I looked to her for reassurance. I pleaded with her with my eyes, feeling desperate and shaky, but she just turned away. She pointed to my holdall and, to my surprise, there was a new nightie inside, not my old shredded one. I put the nightie on, and then a white towelling gown that was draped on a chair in the room. My knees were really shaking now, and I was panting with fear.

The woman came back in and looked at me sternly. She suddenly moved forwards and pulled open my dressing gown. I shrank back, but Mrs Stabard pushed me forward. Then the woman pulled up my nightie and saw that I still had my knickers on underneath.

'You must take those off,' was all she said, in a very strict voice.

I stood transfixed. I couldn't move – I could barely breathe – so she leant forwards and with both hands she yanked my pants down. I stepped out of them, dazed.

The woman then told me to follow her and very reluctantly I went with her into another room, while Mrs Stabard stayed behind in the changing room. In the room the woman led me to there was a long bench covered in white paper towel, and a small table with silver equipment on the side. I wondered if she was some kind of dentist, as I'd seen similar things before in the dentist's room. There was a big bright light over the bed. The woman put on a white coat, and told me to lay down. She said nothing to me, but leant over, picked up my wrist and looked at her watch, just like the nurse had done in hospital. I lay there, blinking in the blinding light. I couldn't understand what was happening at all. Then, without a word, the woman turned around and fiddled with something. I heard a loud hissing sound and then she turned back, with a big black rubbery thing in her hand which was connected to a long metal tube going to a big bottle. She clamped the rubber thing hard over my face. It filled my nose and mouth with this hissy, terrible-smelling gas, and I thought I was going to choke. I tried to struggle but my legs and arms felt like they were made of lead. I didn't want to breathe in, but I had to and suddenly my mind whooshed off uncontrollably down a long dark tunnel.

The next thing I knew was waking up in severe pain. My tummy felt like someone had scooped out the insides with a vegetable peeler. I was back home, inside the airing cupboard, in a heap in the dark. When I felt myself 'down there' I realised I had a sanitary towel on, although I hadn't been bleeding before I went to see the horrible woman in the big house. I felt completely bewildered. As I sat there, crouched over in pain, I had flashbacks of coming out of the big house, being held up between Mr and Mrs Stabard, half-awake, half-asleep. As far as I could remember they'd half-dragged, half-pulled me to a car and bundled me into the back.

Now there was lots and lots of blood, and it started to seep out and down my legs and pool on the floor. I could feel it trickling down the inside of my thighs. I felt giddy and sick and worried that I might die. I was in absolute agony. I'd never felt pain like it: huge, engulfing cramps. Even when Mr Stabard was vicious with me, and hurt me lots, it was never like this. I cried and cried, just wanting to get out, but knowing I couldn't. I was also starving hungry and very thirsty. I was used to going without food, but this hunger was unbearable. I was utterly miserable and deeply in pain, and I just didn't know how I was going to get through it.

When they finally opened the door, two days later, there were no explanations. Mrs Stabard pointed to the mess on the floor, and I had to do the usual scrubbing and mopping before I could clean myself up. I was absolutely starving, but I still had to wait until after their mealtime was over before I had anything to eat or drink. All the time I was so utterly mixed-up.

Back in our room, I insisted on going to Wildflower that very night. I needed to get away – to get out and feel fresh air on my face – even though I was weak and still bleeding. In fact I bled heavily for days afterwards. Out in the freedom of the woods Hope and Faith just played games with me, and danced and sang, and I didn't ever tell them what had happened. We never really went into the gory details of what the Stabards did to us, although we did speak more to each other outside in the woods than we ever did in the house, where we were mostly silent. I just needed to see the stars and moon and be reassured that they were still there. They were my friends, as was the wood, with all its wild night sounds and movements and smells. I was soothed by feeling the wind on my face and seeing the clouds flitting by. I had no idea what had just happened to me. All I knew was it was the worst experience of my life so far, and it felt like the blue touchpaper had been lit and was about to go off.

About this time a new TV show started called *Roots*. It was about how the slaves had come to America, and was on during the week, in the evening. Strangely, the Stabards sat we three children down in the lounge and watched the show with us. We had never been allowed to watch TV in the past, and we'd never done anything recreational with the Stabards before. If they watched TV in the evening, we were either in the shed or the box room, so I was taken aback that we were watching the show together. Were they involving us in their family life at last? Maybe they were changing their ways?

I soon understood why they wanted us to watch the show. It told the story of how the Africans were taken forcibly from their homeland and transported as slaves to America. The Stabards were trying to tell us something: we were slaves, this was our heritage. In fact, I can remember that one of their daughters – Petula, the one who particularly hated us – came and watched the show with us sometimes. Although it seemed like a treat at first, I found watching the programme very painful indeed. It was hard to see the black people being brutally treated as slaves; I hated seeing them being stolen, chained, whipped and horribly mistreated.

It wasn't just the programme that was disturbing. After the show was finished, the Stabards would make us get on all fours and go round the armchairs on our hands and knees in a circle, just like in the chain gang. They thought it was very funny. They would laugh and tell us to speed up, so we would, and then we'd fall over each other, just like the slaves on the telly, and then they'd laugh even harder. Mr Stabard would take off his belt off and start whipping us with it, laughing his dry, little cackle, then Petula would kick us as we passed, and they would all laugh like hyenas. Mrs Stabard would just sit and watch, not saying a word. I don't know what she thought, but she didn't stop them doing it. I got kicked in the stomach, whacked on the legs and arms. Hope, Faith and I went round and round on all fours, until they had had enough fun getting us to re-enact scenes from the show. They thought it was hysterical, nudging each other and saying, 'Look at 'em go!'

The Stabards took the real meaning of the programme and twisted it round completely so they could use it against us. Instead of seeing it as a way of telling the terrible story of the enslavement of black people from Africa, they actually saw it as a prompt to treat us like slaves – worse than animals. I felt ashamed watching the show, but even more ashamed of being kicked and punched, without being able to fight back. Under our clothes we were bruised everywhere.

By this time I was furious: beyond anger, beyond rage. Everything was getting mixed-up together and I was coming to the point where it was all going to boil over and I would no longer be able to hold my anger back. I was more angry than I could possibly express, more angry than I could ever explain. My feelings were off the scale. I knew that the way we were treated was utterly appalling and inhuman, and I wasn't sure how much more I could take. The accumulation of nearly twelve years of being treated like slaves – of being starved, beaten, shut in the shed, humiliated, deprived of food and love, 'purified' at night – was building up inside me into a massive ball of unstoppable rage. After years of suffering I was now poised on the brink of rebellion – whatever the consequences might be.

11

Crazy

'Harmony is a helpful, but still a very difficult teenager to live with ... ' (Social worker's report)

I was eleven years old and without warning I found myself wanting to trash everything and anything I could get my hands on. I was tired of being a silent, obedient slave. I'd been hauled along to that strange medical woman in the big house, gassed, and then locked up in the airing cupboard for days as punishment. I didn't understand what I'd been through, but I knew it was it was an abuse too far. When I was older I realised that I must have been pregnant with Mr Stabard's baby – or at least Mrs Stabard must have been scared that I was, since I'd missed my monthly bleed. I'd only just found out from an older girl at the ESN school that my monthly bleeding was a 'period' which meant I could have babies, but it was obvious that Mrs Stabard knew exactly when I was bleeding and kept track of it all. If I missed a period, she knew full well what it meant. She laid us out ready for her husband, after all, so she knew exactly what was at stake.

It was as if I had been sitting on a mountain of anger all my life, which was now growing into a huge volcano, which threatened to blow any second. I didn't feel I could hold on any more. I felt out of control. I was angry all the time, and because of that, destructive, manipulative and rude. I didn't care. For a start, I was in a school I hated. Faith had been moved to another school and Hope was in the year below me and I felt extremely isolated. There was no-one there I connected with, no-one to talk to, and I missed my sisters. Many of the kids around me at school were severely disabled – unable to talk or walk, or do anything very much – and I felt like we were all treated like hopeless cases. The teachers acted like I was stupid – like I was obviously a freak of nature, who wasn't worth bothering with.

Mr Stabard was still coming in at night and he was getting more violent. I think he sensed I was beginning to resist. After the forced pill-swallowing incident, which had scared me witless, I had begun to be more rebellious, especially when I realised their show of affection in hospital was just that – *a show*. They were still play-acting *Roots* with us; now not only the Stabards' kids, but the grandchildren were joining in the abusive game as well. We were taunted, we were called 'wog' and 'nigger' and we were kicked about – anything to ridicule us. It was beginning to rile me all the time. It was like a sport to them; they seemed to enjoy goading me to the point I lost my temper just like I'd seen the slaves do onscreen.

I'd seen one of the slave girls in *Roots* being 'hurt' by a slave master like Mr Stabard hurt me, and it was called 'rape'. I often remembered her crying, and him beating her. And I began to see that Mr Stabard thought he had us for himself, that he owned us, like the imprisoned slaves on the plantations, and he could rape us whenever he wanted to. All these years that's exactly what he had been doing – imprisoning us and raping us – and he was getting away with it. How was he allowed to do that? I found it unbearable as I began to understand more about what had really been happening to us. Why didn't somebody do something about it? How could the Stabards call themselves good foster parents? And how could they be proper church members when they treated us worse than their household animals?

There were days when we didn't even bother to go to school now. School became meaningless for children like us. After a night with no sleep we'd be exhausted. I would lie there all night in the pitch black, waiting for the noise of him coming in to our room. I'd keep myself awake, fearful he might arrive, without me knowing in advance. I was on watch, so I would be able to cope with him when he lurched in stinking of drink. Of course, he didn't come every night, so I had many nights of broken sleep, lying listening out fearfully for the creak of a floorboard or the flush of the toilet. If I dropped off, I would snap awake terrified that he was there. It was like being alert for the Bogey Man who wanted to come and get me. It was very stressful all the time. Then, when he did come in, the whole ghastly ritual would begin. Afterwards, we'd rush to the window in silence, climb out and traipse to Wildflower to recover. It was a necessary release, but it meant we'd have even less sleep. Sometimes, when he hurt one of us too much, we couldn't even go out, because we couldn't walk or we were too exhausted, which made it all even harder to bear.

On days home from school, I would just lie in bed all day, feeling very numb and shut down. For us the box room was like a prison. I almost preferred the shed to the box room because Mr Stabard was coming to hurt us so often upstairs at night now. Mrs Stabard would let us lie in bed if we were off 'sick' but she wouldn't look after us. Some days I would feel paralysed when I woke up and I'd roll over and face the wall, not bothering to get up. There would be no food, no books, no treats, no drinks or amusements, no extra blankets. Certainly no hugs, cuddles or comfort. Of course our foster mother wouldn't call the doctor, and we wouldn't have friends to visit. Instead we would be totally ignored. If we were hungry, we'd have to tiptoe downstairs and steal some food and often lived on Winalot and water. We'd stuff a sock full of it when we did the washing and then hide it under the wonky floorboard in our room for the next 'Winalot party' in the woods. However, on our days in bed, it was often the only food we had.

Mrs Stabard must have known full well that we were 'sick' because of her husband's horrendous night visits, but she did nothing about it. She was a very shut-off person, like a zombie a lot of the time, very emotionless unless her grandchildren were around. I couldn't understand why she was so nice to them and then so horrible to us. I began to feel the Stabards just kept us there in the poxy box room to meet his sexual needs and to do the housework for her. We really were their slaves.

I also knew that they claimed all sorts of things for us, as foster children, which we never benefitted from. I saw Mrs Stabard filling in forms on the kitchen table for money from Social Services. I could see they claimed for trips away, holidays, household items, clothes, shoes, special equipment, you name it. When there were ten of us in the room at one time, they must have been getting an allowance for each child for food, heating, clothing. That was a lot of money – running into thousands of pounds a year. Yet we all had a starvation diet, we had no real clothes or bedding, or toys, and certainly no treats. Where was all the money going? Who was getting the benefit of it? Mr Stabard was working full-time, until he retired when I was about eleven, so what did they do with the money? They didn't live a luxurious lifestyle, and I never saw them go on holiday themselves, although later Mrs Stabard would go and stay for weekends with her married children. They only ran one car (which we never went in), and they lived in a council house. They never threw a party or had friends round for a meal. So what did they do with all the cash? And why didn't Social Services check-up to see if it was being spent on us properly? I guess they were saving it for their pension, or perhaps he spent it on drink – he always had loads in the house.

As I was getting older, and understanding more, I began to feel even more trapped and outraged than I had before. These questions were emerging in my brain and I had no-one to ask, no-one to turn to. I was never alone with the Social Services visitors, the doctor or dentist. Now I'd left primary school, I didn't know Mr Harrow any more, and my new teachers treated me like I was an idiot, so I couldn't talk to them. The people I knew at church I'd never spoken to, and the ones who 'cast out the devil' with us weren't people I'd ever want to trust. I didn't know any grown-ups I could actually talk to, and I so desperately wanted to ask someone, 'Is this normal?' or 'Can they do this?' or even just, 'Is this right?'

It made me absolutely livid to think about the whole situation and I felt most furious with Mrs Stabard. She had been a nanny before she married and had brought up children herself; how would she have liked it if her own daughters or son had been treated this way? The answer was that she didn't see us in the same category as her own children, just like the masters in *Roots* didn't see the slaves as people. We weren't human, so we didn't count. This thought also made me fly into a rage. All I ever wanted was one hug, one tender moment; for her to say, just once, that she cared about me. The tragedy was, I would have done anything for her. I wanted her to love me, so I did everything she wanted in the hope of getting one loving smile or embrace. Yet every time I thought I'd earned her love, she would turn away and leave me to her husband's horrible clutches. That made me scream inside with such pain and rage that I thought I would simply melt down.

Even worse (and I loathed to admit this to myself) as much as I feared Mr Stabard and hated how he hurt me, I wanted him to love me too. I didn't want to feel all this pain and confusion. I thought, after all these years of doing these things to us, that he must love us, really, somewhere deep down. I felt very attached to him – I'm ashamed and confused to say – even though he hurt me all the time. Sometimes he would be a bit more gentle, such as at Christmas, which was confusing. But then he'd be brutal and he'd hit us. He was sometimes even more violent to the other two girls, which I thought was almost a twisted sign that he loved me more. Surely he must, after all this time? If either of them cried after he'd raped them he'd smack them around even more ruthlessly, as he hated tears or any sign of weakness. I would be pleading with him to stop, wanting him to just turn around and say sorry and give us all hugs and tenderness. But, of course, he never did. He'd just go away and leave us all in tatters.

Unfortunately, I was now getting so angry and bitter that I began to distance myself even from my sisters. At times I got angry with them, and even picked up a knife and threatened Hope with it one day, when I felt my temper was going to overflow. I didn't always want to be the protector for the two other girls – I wanted them to protect me for a change. I was utterly sick of looking after everyone else – what about me? After one night, when he raped all of us, one after the other, and we'd had to watch helplessly, I went crazy at the other two girls. Why didn't we all fight back? That's what they tried to do in *Roots* – although I knew they seldom won. Faith and Hope just looked at me, like they were frightened of me as well as him. I think I was beginning to frighten myself. It was like I had a demon inside of me – maybe the very demon the Stabards had told me all these years was actually in me. Well, if they thought I was evil, then I would be evil. I didn't care any more; something was going to give.

It wasn't just me who was starting to rebel. There were times when Hope challenged Mr Stabard, and then I was scared for her, and for us. One day, he told us to pick up a cup of coffee he had dropped on the floor, and clear up the mess. Usually we would scurry to do it but this time, for some reason, Hope was riled. She stood in the kitchen, hands on her hips and just glared. Mr Stabard was confused. He was also a bit drunk and he stormed over.

'Clear that up.'

'No.'

I couldn't believe what I was hearing . . .

'I said, clear it up.'

'Why should I? You dropped it'.

Mr Stabard's eyes bulged with fury and I could see he was about to lash out at her. I tried to will Hope to stop, but it was clear she was going to stand her ground. In two strides Mr Stabard came over and slapped her face – whack.

'I will not have disobedience in my house. Clear it up when I tell you.'

He was red and sweaty, and by this point Hope knew she was defeated, but she took her time clearing up so I joined in, terrified of what had just happened. Something had got into Hope and I had noticed her becoming increasingly mouthier around that time. It worried me as I felt it put us all at risk.

However, I was becoming more explosive too and sometimes it was my turn to suddenly flip. Occasionally Hope and I sniped at each other, but mainly we were fighting Mr Stabard.

Another day I trashed everything I could get my hands on. I remember going berserk and smashing up all the grandchildren's toys. Over the years we had always focused on them, because we had absolutely nothing and the grandkids had everything. On this occasion I was in the kitchen with the other two girls, I was preparing supper as usual, when one of the grandchildren was calling me 'wog', over and over. He had gone to the toy cupboard and got out some toys and was taunting me with them. That was it: I just lost my temper. I dropped my vegetable peeler in the sink and went storming into the hall, straight into the toy cupboard, and started stamping on the toys. I started ripping up board games with my bare hands, pulling toys apart. I got a doll and put my fingers in her eyes, and ripped her hair out. I got their teddies and soft toys and pulled off their legs and arms. In my rage I had enormous strength, and I kept trashing and ripping until every last toy was broken.

Afterwards, I was absolutely shaking with fury. It was like an uncontrollable stream of energy, and I even sent myself to the shed to try to cool down. I sat in the shed, supper half-prepared, and waited to hear the grandchildren's pained reactions. I heard a shriek and crying, and, I admit, it was satisfying. It felt like I'd finally got my own back, like they'd now know a little about what it felt like to be bullied. I had never thought of myself as a nasty kind of person, but now I sometimes worried I was becoming one because I had pleasure in these spoilt children's pain. As I sat there, shaking with fury, I thought that we weren't living a life that kids lived; we were living an adult's life, doing all the cooking, washing, cleaning and being Mr Stabard's sex slaves. Why shouldn't I get my own back? Ripping things up and hurting the grandkids' toys were really the only weapons I had.

After I'd smashed up the toys big time, Mr Stabard just replaced them and I was so livid that I smashed them up again. It was war. I started losing my temper all the time now. Anything could set me off. I didn't care any more. It was like the genie was finally out of the bottle, and I couldn't put it back. The more I lost my temper and trashed things, swore and shouted at the Stabards, the more my foster father would taunt me that I was 'crazy', which made me lose my temper even more. Looking back, I was nearly twelve, and my hormones must have been all over the place. I was behaving like a normal adolescent, but in very abnormal circumstances. The backstreet abortion had really been the last straw, the final trigger, and I felt I could take no more . . . and yet the abuse continued relentlessly, just as before.

On one occasion, I felt so angry when I was being taunted that I put my fist through a kitchen window. The Stabards were very surprised by this, but they weren't concerned as to whether I had hurt myself, or whether they'd pushed me too far. Mr Stabard just said, 'Oh look, she's gone crazy again,' and I was humiliated even further, which made me feel even angrier. It was a bit like I imagine cock-fighting or dog-fighting to be like – you starve, abuse and chain up an animal and then let it loose on another unsuspecting opponent. I'd been starved, abused and chained for so long that I was easily goaded into flipping my lid – to my foster father's sadistic amusement.

I would no longer do what the Stabards wanted and they began to get scared of me. I was seriously out of control and began to challenge them back. I liked that feeling – that I could wield some power over them. I wanted to scare them, like they had scared me. I wanted to hurt them, like they had hurt me all my life. Smashing a window was very satisfying, just like smashing up the toys. It gave me a release, made me feel better and for a fraction of a second, I felt I had got my own back. But, as always, the Stabards had 'right' on their side and one night, after I lost my temper and started trashing things, they called an ambulance. When the paramedics arrived, I could see Mr Stabard talking to them outside in the front garden, pointing towards me back in the house. I was terrified, and I ran out to the garden to hide in 'Our Home'. Somehow they got there before me. Suddenly, there were two white men, coming towards me in green uniforms, and I was completely petrified. I started kicking out, and tried to bite them. I'd been pushed to the limit and was fighting for my life. If they called me 'crazy' all the time, I'd show them how crazy I could be. I was thrashing and trying to get away, when one of them came towards me with a syringe, then suddenly everything went dark.

12

Child Inmate

'Harmony's behaviour has been very disturbed and the staff have been unable to cope.' (Doctor's NHS notes)

When I came round I thought I had gone to hell. It was the complete opposite of the time when I took the pills and ended up in heaven. I found myself in a long white-walled ward with probably about forty beds in it. It was an adult ward and I was the only child. I couldn't believe what I saw around me, and for a while, I really had no idea where I was. There were people everywhere, just wandering around in their robes, half-naked, or crying, screaming or shouting. It was absolutely terrifying. There were a lot of old people there, who looked like skeletons. There was a man with his willy hanging out of old stripy pyjamas, talking to himself all the time. There were old ladies propped up in chairs, supposedly watching TV in a common room, but they were asleep and dribbling or talking to themselves. There were zombies everywhere – walking up and down the ward, in flapping, half-open gowns, or sitting in high-backed chairs, rocking backwards and forwards. These people were totally out of their minds. It was hell on earth.

Nobody spoke to me. Nobody explained anything. I was petrified. Eventually a nurse came up and told me I had been 'sectioned'. I didn't know what that meant. She explained that I couldn't go home because the hospital now had me under its control. It was like I had gone from one prison to another, just like that. Sectioned? I had never heard the word before. I was eleven going on twelve, and I was now imprisoned in this echoey, cold madhouse. I found out I was in a psychiatric hospital (which has since been closed down) built over a hundred years ago. It felt like it. It smelt like it too. The whole place stank of wee, of poo, of vomit and of sweat. People were just lying in bed groaning, crying out in pain. I'd never, ever seen anything like it in my life. I saw people in white coats and nurses in uniform holding people down on beds and injecting them, while the patient screamed and shouted swear words at the top of their voices. I saw three or four nurses wrestling a patient to the floor, and then dragging them along the floor and finally tying them up to a bed. I was in a nuthouse and I was terrified to death.

It was clear that the Stabards had sent me here to be punished even further. Yes, I'd broken the toys, and put my hand through a window, but was I really mad? I thought the Stabards' house was bad enough, but this was a hundred times worse. Were they teaching me yet another lesson about how evil I was? I had to be bad to be locked away here. People were out of their minds, and many patients had been there for years and years. Old hags with sticking-out white hair and no teeth came over and stared at me, drooling. I felt like an animal in the zoo they were taking a look at. Men came up and put their faces right up to mine, and grinned madly at me, with stinky breath and black teeth, which made me shriek with fear. I was not safe here; I was going to be hurt here as well, was all I could think.

When I went out to the bathroom, it was utterly disgusting. There was wee all over the floor, poo on the seat and brown fingermarks on the walls – it was more disgusting than anything I'd ever seen in my life. The bath was old and had black rings round the inside and someone had gone to the toilet in it. I felt sick just going in there. How could I be in here? How was I going to get out again? Would I be here for the rest of my life? Maybe the Stabards had made a deal that I would never, ever be let out again? At that point, even going back to the horrors of the shed and the box room felt preferable to being here.

I was in the mental hospital only a short time after the abortion had happened, so I felt I was somehow being punished even further – punished for being angry about being hurt and abused. None of it made any sense. However, nobody came to talk to me. Nobody asked me anything. Nurses would wander around, talking loudly to patients like they were the kids at my ESN school – as if they were simple or stupid. The nurses just seemed interested in dishing out pills to everyone, and keeping things to a very rigid routine. And that's where this place reminded me of the Stabards' house. It was very rigid, full of rules. You had to do what they wanted you to do, or you were punished in some way.

The food was also totally nauseating. It was just grey slop. There were lumps of cold potato, with hairs sticking out, and green and black 'eyes', which made me feel sick. Then there was the watery, grey mince which was inedible, even for me, who had eaten Winalot sandwiches and dog poo casserole before now. There was tasteless, overcooked cabbage, rubbery meat and solidified gravy. I couldn't bring myself to swallow most of it, and I had a really hardened stomach since I'd been starving most of my life.

The other thing that reminded me of life at the Stabards' was when they gave me tablets. The nurse came along and snapped at me, 'Take this.' She stood over me, stern-faced, while I had to swallow a load of little pills which made my mind go numb. They made me feel like someone had removed all of my emotions. Now I was like one of the zombies on the ward. I lay rigid in bed and stared at the ceiling, watching the hours go by slowly, while people shouted, screamed, cried, swore and wet the floor, all around me. The tablets numbed my thoughts, my feelings – even my taste. My tongue felt like a swollen slug. It was stuck to the roof of my mouth and I was terribly thirsty all the time. I couldn't get anyone's attention, and nobody spoke to me. The nurses weren't friendly like in the other hospital. There weren't any other children on the ward and I felt really very peculiar being the only one. There were quite a few other black people there though, which I found rather strange. Why were there so many locked up in here? Usually you didn't see so many black people in one place.

One day a doctor came, dressed in a smart, dark suit, surrounded by lots of nurses and other doctors in white coats. He looked like a very posh man and he stood way down at the end of my bed and stared at me for ages. One young doctor had a clipboard and was scribbling down something all the time the head doctor was there. The posh man just looked at the clipboard at the end of my bed, and talked to the nurses and the doctors, ignoring me. I couldn't hear what they were saying, and I just lay there, inert, in my hospital gown (which, embarrassingly, didn't do up at the back) while they talked to each other over my head.

Then the main doctor shouted at me from the end of the bed with his booming voice.

'So Harmony, how are we, today?'

I didn't know what to say. How was I? In this hellhole? What did he think I thought about this stinky, nasty place? I was scared I'd be very rude to him if I said anything at all. I didn't know how much I should say about the Stabards and what had been going on at home, or whether he meant how I was this minute. The drugs I was on were making my mind very fuzzy and I felt very confused. So I didn't say anything to him. I just lay there and pulled up the sheet over my face and hoped he'd go away. I could hear them talking to each other, so I peeked out again and saw the doctor with the clipboard writing something else down.

'You know, it won't get you anywhere being this angry,' boomed the big chief doctor to me.

He looked like a fierce headmaster looking down his nose at me, and I didn't like him one bit. What did he mean, it wouldn't get me anywhere? Did he think I was choosing to feel furious? He'd be angry if he'd been through what I'd been through. But I said nothing. I felt very intimidated by this man, and I didn't know what to say to him. All I could see was a lot of grown-ups staring at me with fierce faces, like angry masks. Nobody looked like they cared one jot about me – as usual.

'You know your foster parents care about you, don't you, Harmony?' said the doctor again, in front of everybody. 'I think you're being a bit ungrateful.'

Ungrateful! I would have got up and thrown something at the doctor if I hadn't felt like I was made of lead. All I did was turn on my side, away from his glare, and closed my eyes. I felt very tired and I didn't want to look at him and the whole staring gang any more. I missed Hope and Faith and I wished they were there with me. They'd understand. Even a glance or a twitch of a cheek would mean something between us. We could read each other like books. I knew every little mannerism of both of them, and they knew mine. With that man at the end of the bed, we would have exchanged a look and then we would have giggled quietly, and we would have understood that we all thought he was a complete idiot who understood nothing about the whole sordid situation. Then when we were in the woods, we would have acted out the whole scene again and then fallen apart, laughing helplessly at how ridiculously pompous he was.

Next morning the breakfast trolley, which was pushed around by two nurses, didn't stop at my bed. I was starving and breakfast was the only half-decent meal of the day – I could have some cereal and a glass of milk at least. I asked the nurse if she could give me some food, but she said no, because I was going down to surgery later. Surgery! I had just had 'surgery' at that big Victorian house and it was terrifying. The last thing I wanted was any more. Just as I was starting to get very upset another nurse came and injected me. After that I calmed down very quickly; I felt like someone had fed me a giant marshmallow. I couldn't speak or move or do anything.

Later these two men in white coats came and rolled me onto a stretcher and I was wheeled down to the surgery. I felt very lonely, but far away from my feelings, like I was watching myself being pushed along the corridor. Once I got there, I was lifted onto a bed – what must have been an operating table – and I saw that there was loads of medical equipment there. Someone in a green gown and mask came up and looked at me coldly. They picked up my wrist and looked at their watch, something medical people always seemed to do. I just stared at the blue eyes over the mask and I couldn't tell if it was a man or a woman, which seemed very strange. Then they were holding up a syringe. No-one said, 'Harmony we are going to do x or y to you,' they just did it, and I just lay there paralysed, unable to stop it all happening to me. I felt helpless, and I couldn't speak at all. I was totally in their hands.

Then I felt the needle go in – it was a sharp prick – and I fought to keep awake. I didn't want to go to sleep; maybe they were going to kill me, how did I know? I thought I was in a torture centre of some sort. Despite my struggles all went black, yet again.

When I came round my head hurt a lot. I felt like it had been punched in on both sides, and it was terribly painful. I couldn't remember anything either. I didn't know my name, or where I was, or how long I'd been there. My head was thumping and thudding. It felt like a ball that someone had sucked all the air out of, which was slowly filling up again with air. I felt so peculiar. I slept and slept and wasn't interested in anything. Next time I saw a nurse, and was awake enough to speak, I asked what the operation was. 'ECT,' was all she said. I didn't understand.

'What's ECT?' I asked.

'An operation on your head,' is all she said.

ECT. Electro-Convulsive Therapy. Thousands of volts pushed through my brain to give me a kind of fit, I found out much later. I was eleven, I had been sectioned and given ECT. I was 'crazy Harmony' who didn't need anything explaining to her. I was a mad, black girl, who was ungrateful, difficult and bad-tempered (as the Stabards told me over and over), and who ought to count her blessings (as the nurses and doctors told me over and over). I'd been taught all my life that other people could come and do what they liked to me. My body was to be abused, and now my brain could be too.

A few days later I woke up to find Mrs Stabard standing at the bottom of the bed. She had her navy coat on, and her usual shut-down expression. She was holding something and when I looked, it was a packet of crisps and a tube of sweets. I couldn't believe it. She had never given me anything like that before. What was she up to? She came and stood by the side of the bed and looked awkward. No kiss. No hello. No chitchat. I was furious and I didn't want to talk to her. So I blanked her. How could she put me in this mad place? It was her fault I was in this hellhole. She put the sweets and crisps on the side table and I brushed them off onto the floor. I didn't want them. It was too little, too late, and I was angry. How dare she pretend in front of the nurses and doctors that she usually gave me sweets and crisps? It was all a show, just like the last time, after I took the pills. In the hospital she pretended she cared, and then when we got home she didn't care at all. How dare she pretend she treats me well, when she actually lays us out for her husband to rape at night! I put my eyes down and refused to look at her. I did that a lot, and I knew she wouldn't like it. I wanted to shut her out; to teach her that she had hurt me.

'Harmony,' said Mrs Stabard, flatly. 'How are you?'

How am I? I couldn't bear to hear her voice, pretending that she cared about me. Suddenly, I felt this enormous surge of rage in me and I reached out and picked up the table on wheels that went over the bed, and I threw it at her. Mrs Stabard stepped sharply sideways, shocked, as the table went whizzing past and skidded across the ward, slamming into another bed on the other side. A couple of people screamed, but someone else cheered and for a moment I felt triumphant, until I saw the men thundering down the ward towards me. Mrs Stabard had retreated back now and was standing passively watching, saying nothing at all, as four hefty male staff held me down while one injected me. Everything disappeared down a black tunnel, yet again.

13

Getting Labelled

'Harmony is the only one who has presented any difficulties with her foster parents.' (GP's report)

I was in hospital for several weeks after that, although I really have no idea how many. Being trapped in hell, it all felt like it went on for weeks and weeks. I had no idea whether it was day or night, winter or summer, weekday or weekend, as the days all rolled into one great big blob of nothingness. The boring routine was the same every day, and I just hid in bed under the sheets, or lolled in a chair in a flimsy hospital dressing gown and watched all these people wandering about, half-dressed, moaning, throwing fits and shouting obscenities. I was eleven years old and locked up, against my will, with all these deeply disturbed adults. After the ECT I was being given loads of pills which made me feel very woozy, as if I was looking at life through a thick pane of glass. I felt very remote from my feelings, as if someone had switched off my emotions.

In all those weeks nobody really came and talked to me. The nurses would drift by, chatting to each other, eating our leftovers and shouting instructions to the patients – they always spoke to us like we were really thick. They would mainly give us pills, while the male nurses were always at the ready to wrestle somebody to the ground or tie them to a bed. The doctors would waft around every other day and the big chief doctor would come round once a week and boom at me from the end of my bed. I just ignored him now – I was too intimidated by him to know what to say. I just wanted to keep everybody out. I didn't want to look anyone in the eyes any more. I had stared into Mr Stabard's horrible cold blue eyes, bearing down on me at night, enough for a whole lifetime. His cold stare haunted me. At least here I was safe from him, for the moment. But this crazy prison, where I was locked in with all these mad people, well, it was just a different kind of hell on earth. I didn't know what I was doing there, or why I wasn't in a children's ward and I definitely felt being stuck in with all these crazy adults was part of my punishment. Perhaps everyone here believed I was evil and this was part of my 'purification'? Maybe the Stabards had convinced the big doctor that I was so bad that I had to have my head squashed in by electric volts and my emotions flattened by millions of pills, and then I'd be 'pure'? I still longed to be cured – to no longer be a naughty girl that had to be locked away.

Being in the hospital was like a game, in a way. Nobody ever sat down next to me, took my hand, and asked me what was wrong. Instead I spent my life double-guessing what it was they wanted me to say and then I'd try to give them what they wanted. In the Stabards' house, I always had to watch what I said. Any question or command always had a 'right' answer, and if I got it 'wrong', I would be punished. The horrors of the airing cupboard and the shed stayed with me, and had taught me to be very careful. So I'd learned not to take any question at face value, and to work out what the grown-ups wanted, and then to give it to them. I wanted to please people, even in this madhouse.

One day a nurse came along and stood by my bed. She

took my wrist and timed my pulse with her watch and put
a thermometer under my tongue. As she was doing all this,
which was part of the daily routine, she suddenly said, 'Do
you hear voices?'

I didn't know what she meant. Voices? There were voices
all around me shouting all the time. I didn't look up at her.
I'd learned that talking to people only led to me being hurt,
and I didn't want to let people in too close any more. I
said nothing, but tried to work out what she meant and
what answer she wanted. Anyway, why was she asking me
a question with a thermometer in my mouth? She wasn't
making it that easy to talk, was she?

'Harmony,' she asked again, more intently this time.
'Are you hearing voices . . . you know, in your head?'

In my head? I didn't know what she meant exactly. I
did think about Mr Stabard and all the horrible things he
called me and the nasty things he did to me. I 'heard' that
all the time – I had nightmares about it, and constant images
of his face in my head, if that's what she meant. I was
also thinking about Hope and Faith – I missed them and
worried about them all the time, and loved to remember
the things we said to each other, and the games we played
when we were at the woods. So I certainly 'heard' them
in my mind while I was sitting in this awful place hour
after hour, and wished they were with me. I'd always had a
strong imagination, probably because I'd had so little real
stimulation in the way of books and toys, so I relied on my
mind to keep me amused either for hours in the shed, or
now, in this brutal ward. So, in a way, I did 'hear voices'.

I shrugged. I didn't know what she wanted me to say.

'So you do? You do hear voices?'

She seemed pleased with my shrugging, so I shrugged
again. Then I nodded.

'Sort of'.

'Aha!' she said. She seemed very pleased now. I suppose I felt glad about her reaction, so I peeked sideways at her. She was smiling. I liked to please people; I was always looking for the love, care and attention that I'd never got. This nurse, whom I had got quite fond of during the weeks, patted my hand and said, 'OK, OK, we'll do something about it for you, Harmony.'

'Well, that was a result,' I thought. Somebody's going to do something about me at last. Whatever that something was. I had no idea what this conversation, if you could call it that, was all about, or where it would lead. But clearly something had happened, even though I wasn't sure what it was exactly.

Meanwhile, I had to concentrate on getting through the days. It was all I could do just to avoid stepping in the poo and wee in the bathroom, and to keep my head down when accosted by patients wandering the corridors. The food was disgusting still, but I got it down the best I could and mainly spent my time sleeping. That was the only thing that was good about being there: I slept and slept and slept. I felt tired all the time, as the medication made me feel like a robot, and I just snoozed my days through, the weeks ticking by as I moved towards my twelfth birthday.

The whole time I was in the hospital nobody visited much. Mrs Stabard came occasionally, but I always felt indignant with her shows of kindness, so it was never a good visit. I never saw Hope or Faith and I really missed them. I would lie on my bed trying to remember the beauty of Wildflower Woods, our private paradise on earth. I sometimes took myself on a mental holiday, imagining climbing out of the window, shinning down the trellis, and padding down the garden barefoot. I would eventually be up on the hill, wind in my face, stars and moon above, feeling free. I would breathe in deeply, just envisaging the indigo space of the starry sky with its friendly moon face. I would smile as I remembered our times running through the dead leaves in our trench area (which was an old Second World War shelter, I discovered later), or skidding down the chalk runs on our wet bin-bag liners. I hugged these memories to myself and then I'd come to, open my eyes, and see I was still in this nightmare – nothing had changed.

Eventually I was let out. As I was about to leave, the big chief doctor came round and told me I had a 'Diagnosis' – whatever that was – and they were going to give me some medicine to make me feel better. Diagnosis? Was that the same as 'sectioned?' As for medicine, I was sick of it. It just made me feel like the living dead. He told me, in his booming tones, that I would have to have an injection at the doctor's surgery once a month, but that my nice foster mother would take me there. He glared at me from the end of the bed.

'Now, Harmony, I'm expecting you to be a good girl and take your medicine, and behave better at home,' he commanded, in front of everybody.

I managed to peek up at his face, through my lashes. He was definitely like a strict schoolmaster. I was embarrassed, but I nodded. I knew they liked me to nod here.

'Good girl.'

And then he wafted away, surrounded by the doctors and nurses, like a giant gander with a loyal gaggle of geese.

Afterwards the nurse came along with a little silver tray and a syringe in it. She pulled the flowery curtains round my bed and asked me to roll on my side. I felt a sharp sting in my bottom – it really hurt.

'What's this for?' I managed to ask.

'Schizophrenia,' is all she answered.

'Skittywhat?'

But she was gone, and I had no-one else to ask.

The Stabards came and took me home and when I got there life continued just as before. Nothing changed. I don't know why I thought it would be different, but I did. I had been totally terrified by my trip to the hospital and the drugs also made me much more docile, so at first I actually felt relieved to go home.

For the first few weeks I just went back into the old routine. Almost immediately Mr Stabard started coming in to us in the box room at night again. I discovered that Faith had gone into hospital as her condition was worsening, so we'd actually both been in different hospitals at the same time. But Hope and I were back in the shed, back doing the chores, and back to being 'hurt' by him. I was also back at school. Nothing was said about me having been away and in fact I had missed nothing. I was back in the classroom with kids with loads of different disabilities and loads of other black children. Most of the kids there had had some kind of bad beginning in life. A lot of the kids had difficulty speaking or reading, so we did a lot of colouring in. We were back to bricks and blocks, and then more blocks and bricks for a change. We were given cards which we had to put into sequences according to colours and objects and it was all so incredibly boring and repetitive. I noticed the teachers just spoke to each other a lot of the time, and sort of ignored us kids, as if we weren't really worth bothering about. We did do gym, but the gym was really small and all we were allowed to do was throw a little soft ball at each other because it was thought we couldn't handle doing anything else. Since there was no running or swimming, or anything hard or stretching, I really missed my athletics badly.

I tried hard to calm down at school, because I didn't want to go back into the nasty hospital again. But I was very bored all the time and occasionally I'd even sneak a *Daily Mirror* into school to check I could still read – I was surprised I could and I would say to myself, 'I can't be that stupid after all, can I?' because I was able to make out stories still. After a while, I did make friends with one girl, Abigail Greer, who saved me from total isolation. She was an older black girl, the one who had told me about my monthly bleed being a 'period', which I wouldn't have known otherwise. She was beautiful and I would have done anything for her. She became very influential over me. I guess she could sense that I was very desperate and vulnerable, and needed someone to talk to. Of course, I never told her what was happening at the Stabards' – I don't think I had the words to explain any of it, and I didn't know whether it was 'normal' or not – but I became very attached to Abigail, and did all sorts of things for her. I would run and fetch for her like a pet dog, as I wanted her to like me. I was even becoming a slave to other children.

Meanwhile, back at the Stabards', I wanted them to understand that I was not going back to being the silent doormat that they could do what they wanted with all the time. Whereas at school I tried to behave, I began to find it hard to keep my cool at home. I did try, when I first came home from hospital, but when Mr Stabard came in at night and started the rape business all over again, I found it hard not to be angry. I found his behaviour at night even more disturbing now. After putting the light bulb in he would take my nightie off, and make me stand in the middle of the room and look me up and down. It was like he was assessing me. He seemed very interested in my breasts now, which sickened me. He was playing with them all the time, and even sucked on them, like a big baby, which embarrassed me terribly and made me want to throw up. I didn't know where to look or what to do when he did it; it seemed so very personal. He still brought the Sellotape quite often as he hated me looking back at him. My venom would show through my eyes. Drunk, shameless and feeling in complete control of us, he would still hurt me in front of Hope, and Faith too when she was there. Whilst I was in hospital the other two children, Raj and Prathi, had gone back to their own mother. I assumed that Mr Stabard's night visits had continued, just as always, while I'd been away – he wouldn't have wanted to deprive himself. Hope hadn't been to the woods without me though, as she felt it wasn't the same when I wasn't there and she was scared to go there on her own.

The Stabards were still watching *Roots* and kept up the weekly ritual of seeing it with their adult daughters, Petula and Jemima. They even brought the grandchildren round to watch with them all, so we'd have the whole family baying at us afterwards, like blood-thirsty hyenas, trying to intimidate and humiliate us. I absolutely hated these weekly sessions of being openly tormented, but the Stabards seemed to think they had a right to inflict it on us. We didn't spend quite so much time in the shed now, but instead, after the horrendous *Roots* routine, we were sent up to our dingy box room, with nothing at all to do.

Now I was officially crazy – or so everyone said – I felt I had a licence to do crazy things. I hated the way the medication made me feel, all woozy and woolly in the head, and I often fed my pills to the dog. The dog was a dopey old thing, and just slept all day once I'd fed her my tablets. I hated feeling so doped up all the time, so I felt justified. I didn't want to hurt the old thing, but I didn't want to take all the pills myself. Mrs Stabard also used my 'crazy' label as an excuse to get even more money. I noticed her filling in loads of forms all the time to social security claiming I had broken things and saying she had to replace them. This was a lie, but they got themselves money for new lamps, sheets, blankets and all sorts, because she claimed I was trashing the place all the time. I wasn't – at least not then – but it made me feel that I might as well have done.

One of the few positive things that came out of me going into the psychiatric hospital was that I was referred to a very nice doctor for individual sessions. I remember Mrs Stabard taking me there one morning, instead of going to school. We walked up a hill to the centre of town and then, to my amazement, I went in to see the doctor on my own. I was very scared of going in, but she was a really lovely woman, who sat at a low table with me, and put me at ease. She got me to draw a picture of 'my family'. I drew the house, and put Mrs Stabard and my two 'sisters' in the picture, but I wouldn't put in Mr Stabard anywhere. The doctor seemed quite concerned as to why I wouldn't draw him, but she was very nice about it to me, very warm and encouraging. I also drew the shed in the back garden, and called it 'Our Home'. The kind woman doctor kept asking me why I wouldn't put Mr Stabard in the picture and I didn't know what to say. I hated him and I didn't want him anywhere near me, so leaving him out of the picture seemed the best thing to do. I also made Mrs Stabard very small in the picture, actually smaller than me, and the doctor asked if she was another foster child. I said, no it was Mrs Stabard. She kept asking why she was so small, and again, I couldn't really answer. I just felt she was small because somehow she did nothing for us, but I couldn't explain that. I did all the work at home, so it seemed natural to make me bigger – or maybe I felt I carried all the responsibility for looking after the home, and my sisters, and being the focus of Mr Stabard's perverted attention.

I really liked talking to the doctor and I found doing the drawing very interesting, so I was pleased when she said, 'We'll do this again next week.' It was the very first time someone had really listened to me and asked probing questions, so I really looked forward to going again.

However, when next week came around I found that Mrs Stabard had written in and said we couldn't make the session. When I asked her if we were going she just shook her head. When I asked why, she just didn't answer. I felt terribly disappointed, like I was going to cry buckets, but I held the tears back. Later I felt anger, which added to the burning pile of resentment growing inside of me. They deliberately stopped me from going to see the nice lady doctor because they were terrified I might spill the beans. I was really sad not to see her again as she was the first person I felt who had taken any real interest in me. If the sessions had continued, I think, in time, I might have been able to describe what was really happening at 97 Forestlane Way– which is precisely why the Stabards made sure that my visits stopped. This one single act by the Stabards condemned me to at least another twelve years of mistreatment and abuse.

However, one day, soon after, something weird happened at school. The new headmaster, Mr Pringle, came into my unruly classroom and got down to my level and asked me to come with him immediately. I thought, 'Oh no, I'm in trouble again,' because I'd been losing my temper a lot lately. We walked down the corridor to his big office. When we got there he opened the door and imagine my surprise when I saw the room full of people, including a police officer in uniform. I shrank back against the door jamb, shaking, trying to hide, but Mr Pringle said gently, 'It's alright Harmony, just come on in', so I followed him gingerly, absolutely terrified, into the room.

14

Near Escape

'Harmony is lucky to have the Stabards as she is unattractive and inarticulate.' (Social worker's report)

I wanted the floor to open up and let me fall in and hide from all the adult eyes. I was absolutely terrified as Mr Pringle went and sat down in the big chair behind his desk. I stood to one side, trembling and feeling sick, trying to hide, and couldn't look at anyone in the room. I put my two fingers in my mouth for comfort. My heart was racing. The policeman sitting there in his smart black uniform was scaring me. What had happened? What had someone said? Was someone ill or dead? It raced through my mind that Hope had given the game away somehow while I was in hospital. Or maybe it was something completely different. Maybe Mr Stabard was dead in a car crash – I had wished it so many times, but now I didn't want it to be true. I had absolutely no idea what to do, or what to expect. I was so used to being excluded from everything in the world, I had no idea what to do when the world actually sat up and took an interest in me.

... *'Harmony, don't worry,' Mr Pringle says in a kind, gentle voice.*

He can see I'm shaking violently. I want to cry, but I bite my lip, as usual.

'*These people here just want to ask you a few questions.*'

My knees are wobbling uncontrollably so Mr Pringle stands up, gets a chair and puts it behind me. He then puts his hand on my shoulder and I plop down onto it. It's a relief to sit.

Then a man speaks from across the room. I hadn't really noticed him before. He's dark-haired, middle-aged, smartly-dressed and explains he works for the Social Services. The policeman's there because it's a criminal enquiry. At the word '*criminal*' my heart leaps nearly out of my mouth. Am I going to prison, finally? Mr Stabard has always threatened it. I look sharply at Mr Pringle who whispers, '*It's OK Harmony. It's OK. It's about Raj and Prathi.*'

I blink. Raj and Prathi? What does he know about them? Of course, they have gone home while I've been in hospital. They lived with us for nearly four years and I feel a bit sad at their going back, as I'd got fond of them, even though we'd all had to share our cramped space. I'd felt quite jealous of them taking up the beds in our box room, although sorry for Raj, who had been '*hurt*' a hell of a lot by Mr Stabard. I suddenly have flashes of Raj being forced to put his head down onto Mr Stabard's horrible stinking thing and I'm nearly sick on the carpet at the thought.

Mr Pringle starts to explain that Raj and Prathi went home to their family and told them some not very nice things were going on in 97 Forestlane Way. My heart is bumping so loud, I wonder if they can hear it. I keep my face straight. The children haven't slept since they'd got home, and are very distressed and confused by what has happened to them. I feel my eyes widening with fear as I listen. Oh my God, it was finally all going to come out. I feel a whole mixture of emotions rushing through me, although my head is still like porridge due to the pills I'm taking. Someone had finally come to rescue me, to rescue us! I wonder where Hope is and why she isn't here as she is still at the same school as me.

I think I might now be released – like the slaves in Roots *when they finally got freed – and it will all be sorted out, and I might go and live somewhere where people treat me nicely. And then it pops into my mind, quick as a flash, what Mr Stabard had always said – what he had said for twelve years over and over and over like a broken record – that if I tell, and am taken away, he'll have to kill himself. I will be responsible for his death. As much as I hated him, I don't want him to kill himself. I don't want that responsibility*

Given that I'm 'crazy', will anyone really believe me, anyway? What if I say something and the Stabards both deny it? Surely the authorities will believe them rather than me, a mere schoolgirl – and a dumb, naughty ESN schoolgirl at that. Anyway, I often have temper tantrums, which maybe they'll think would justify my mistreatment.

All this is racing through my mind as the man in the corner (who I don't like the look of) starts explaining something.

'I'm Mr Venetti,' he pipes up. 'I need to know if you've seen Mr Stabard do anything he shouldn't ... to Raj and Prathi.'

I sit riveted to the chair. I look down at my hands and start picking imaginary fluff off my dress. I always do this when I feel anxious; I pick, pick, pick while I think what to do. I bite my lip and shuffle on the chair. I can't look up, it's too scary.

'Harmony,' Mr Pringle's voice still sounds gentle, unlike the man from Social Services, who looks mean. 'Mr Venetti needs to know the truth, you know. You won't be in any trouble. Just tell us the truth. Tell us what you know.'

I look at Mr Pringle. He's quite a young man, with reddish hair and pink skin. He's got nice shining blue eyes and a warm smile. I think he's someone who actually likes children, even ESN ones. But what can I say? Where would I start?

'Do you think your foster parents have ever done anything

to harm Raj or Prathi?' asks Mr Venetti again, sounding a bit impatient. I don't like him one bit.

I think of Raj's head pressed on Mr Stabard's thing, and his crying afterwards and being sick. Eventually I nod. I can't look up, but I nod. My fingers are picking away at my skirt. The policeman is scribbling something down in his notebook. I feel very put on the spot. I suddenly think that I'll be locked up myself if I give anything more away, and I look up at the policeman in fear. Why are people always looking at me and writing things down?

'Raj and Prathi have said some pretty serious things, Harmony,' Mr Venetti says again, looking quite fierce. 'Do you think they are really telling the truth?'

I nod slowly again. I bite my lip.

'What do you think they have said?'

I can't look up. Finally I mumble that I think Mr Stabard hurt them at night. He liked to touch them and do things to them – and make them do things to him. And he would lock them in a shed in the garden and in a cupboard saying they're bad.

There's a shocked silence in the room. Mr Venetti clears his throat.

'And do you really honestly think these things are true?' He's glaring at me. I feel he's angry.

Pick, pick, pick at my dress with my fingers. Pick, pick, pick. I have to keep my emotions under control, but I'm shaking anyway. Even the pills aren't numbing me out enough not to feel really scared and tearful. I nod.

'You realise how serious this is, don't you, Harmony?' I see a glint in Mr Venetti's eye and I just want to run out the room. I put my two fingers in my mouth again to stop myself crying and pick at my dress rapidly with my other hand. I start rocking.

'Harmony, Harmony,' says Mr Pringle, gently, 'don't worry, we just need to know.' He pauses. 'Is it happening to you, too?'

I can't think, I can't breathe, I can't open my mouth. Pick, pick, pick, pick. What shall I say? If I say 'yes' then all hell will be let loose. If they don't believe me, I'll be sent back and be 'sectioned' again and have more ECT in that vile hospital. What if Mr Stabard hears and kills himself? Or kills Hope and Faith? Oh my God, I don't know what to say. Anyway, wasn't I crazy now? I'd been labelled a skittythingy, so who'll believe a mad girl? Oh God, what should I say?

'Harmony?'

I can't look up. My eyes are blurred, my mouth's dry. I don't know what to do. I want to cry, to run away, to leave this room with all these grown-ups. Why won't they leave me alone?

'Harmony, can you answer, please? We need to know.' *Mr Venetti sounds very sharp.*

I look up at Mr Pringle through my lashes. Then shake my head.

'No?'

'No.'

I look down. Pick, pick, pick.

'So you're saying that Mr Stabard has been hurting Raj and Prathi, but he hasn't hurt you, Hope or Faith or anyone else?'

I shake my head. Inside my head I'm screaming, 'Go on, tell him, go on, tell him — say it.' But I'm too scared. I'm too terrified to do it. I love Mrs Stabard, if the truth be told and I desperately want her to love me back. Even though she's cold to me, and does horrible things, like lay us out for him at night, I still forgive her somehow. She'll never forgive me if I say something. What if I leave home; where would I go then? I've always held out the hope that one day it would all be alright, and my foster mother would eventually love me. If I shop her husband she'll never talk to me again, that's for sure. And as for him, I hate him, but I also want his attention. Strange as it may seem, I was actually very attached to him, although I loathed what he did to me. Somehow I was used to it and it almost seemed a warped kind of relationship in a way. At least it was a relationship – without him, or them, I'd have nothing.

I was full of such a load of twisted emotions, that I couldn't make sense of it all. I didn't want Mr Stabard to kill himself and it was so drummed into me that he would do that, so I felt completely responsible at that moment for keeping him alive. Wouldn't I be truly evil if he died? And Mrs Stabard would hate me forever if I was the cause of him going away or dying. I was also afraid that I might get locked up again, and this time, in a real prison. How did I know whether these people in this room were being straight with me or not? I had learned not to believe what adults told me and I was really scared of people in authority.

'Are you absolutely sure he's never touched you in ways you don't like?' pipes up the policeman finally.

I look down.

'No, sir, he touches them, not us,' I hear my voice mumble.

'You are absolutely sure?'

I nod.

Mr Pringle turns to Mr Venetti and the policeman and they speak quietly for a moment. I don't listen. My heart's racing. Inside my head I'm thinking, 'Oh God, why did you say that? Why don't you tell them? Go on, tell them! Go on, this is your chance!' I look up at them, through my lashes, wanting them to ask me again, but they are talking seriously to each other. All the time my mind's racing and I'm panicking inside. I don't know what to say or how to go back on what I've just said. Part of me feels: well, at least I've helped Raj and Prathi. But part of me feels horribly loyal to the Stabards, like I won't be sent away from them now. I was scared I'd end up in an even worse situation, like in the hellish hospital. I couldn't tell on them, as absurd and as ridiculous as that might seem. I had a chance of escape and I couldn't take it. How mad was that? The minute the word 'no' was out of my mouth, I wanted to shout 'yes', but I couldn't. I was too scared. Something was stopping me, some invisible thread or cord that bound me to them. After all, I had been with them all my life, since I was three months old, and how was I to know that the whole world wasn't like it was at the Stabards'?

The meeting was suddenly over and I was taken back to class. Mr Pringle didn't say anything to me except a quick 'Well done.' I think he was disappointed in me or something. I sat the rest of the afternoon unable to think straight, just building blocks, one block on top of another, like a zombie. Then I'd knock them down angrily, as I kept thinking I'd missed my moment when I could have got out. I should've taken it, but I didn't. I regretted not taking it almost immediately. I'd been so scared by the situation with all the adults and the seriousness of the meeting. Maybe if one person had asked me face-to-face – like the nice lady doctor who'd got me to draw, or just Mr Pringle or the policeman – I might have said something. I didn't like the look of Mr Venetti, he'd made me feel scared, and I'd felt I couldn't say the truth to him at all. I didn't know why. The rest of the afternoon I felt atrocious.

When it was going-home-time I caught the minibus, just like always. Hope got on it. I didn't speak to her at first, and then I told her what had happened. Her eyes opened wide. 'Me too,' was all she said. We found out that she had also been interviewed that afternoon, by the same people, and she had said exactly the same thing. Hope had said it was Raj and Prathi, and not us who were being 'hurt' by Mr Stabard. We couldn't believe it. When put on the spot, she had felt she couldn't give the game away, either. And now she regretted it, like I did. We sat in total amazement as we drew up to the road near Forestlane Way. We had both had a near escape, but now we were going back to our hellhole as usual. Wasn't that a sign that I was truly mad? I could have got away, that very day, but I didn't. So didn't that mean that I deserved all I got? What a fool.

When Mrs Stabard opened the door to us, we knew we were in trouble straight away. She gave us her stern look, and then pointed down the hall, meaning we should go straight in. When we got to the lounge door I could hear voices. Mrs Stabard pushed us past the door and we went into the kitchen. We were just going out to the shed, very frightened, when the lounge door opened and suddenly, there was Mr Venetti, shaking hands with Mr Stabard. Mr Venetti? They seemed very friendly towards one another, like old pals. Mrs Stabard saw me looking and she shooed me out to the shed, along with Hope and we were quickly locked in.

Half an hour later the door was flung open by an absolutely livid Mr Stabard. He was blowing steam out of his ears. He grabbed me by the hair and started pulling me across the floor, and he proceeded to beat the shit out of me. He pummelled me and slapped my face and kicked me, and then he started on Hope. He gave us the worst beating I can ever remember having.

'But,' I kept saying, while he was hitting me, 'I didn't tell, I didn't.'

'You made up stories, porky pies– you're evil, you know that?'

He lay into me again, slapping, punching and kicking me into submission. He told us he was going to be charged for the other two, and if he went to prison, he'd kill himself and then it would be our fault – did we understand? But

I felt outraged, as I hadn't given the game away about us. Didn't he understand that at all? I couldn't say anything because he didn't give me a chance as he was so intent on slapping us into the far end of next week.

What I discovered a whole lot later was that Mr Venetti had worked with the Stabards when they volunteered as workers in the children's home that was eventually shut down after abuse allegations had been made about some of the workers there. Mr Venetti had been sacked in disgrace. It was a local children's home, but somehow Mr Venetti had got himself back into working with children again – God knows how. It meant that he had gone straight to Mr Stabard and had warned him about what was coming, and told him what we had said in our separate interviews. We had had our near escape – with the policeman and Mr Pringle there – and we had blown it due to some kind of warped loyalty. Meanwhile, Mr Venetti had protected Mr Stabard instead of us.

Perhaps unsurprisingly, Raj and Prathi's case against Mr Stabard was eventually dropped six months later due to insufficient evidence.

15

Angry Adolescent

'Mrs Stabard is to be congratulated on all the effort she makes for this very difficult, moody girl.' (Social Services' report)

I had missed my chance to escape, and now I was trapped yet again. I would never be free now. I was furious with myself for not getting out when I could, and furious with Hope for not speaking out either. I knew I couldn't really blame her for doing the same thing as me, but I wasn't feeling very rational about it all. I was also still furious with the Stabards for everything they demanded from me and did to us. I was resentful all the time, a boiling cauldron of rage that was simmering away, threatening to blow at any minute.

At first, after the whole psychiatric hospital episode, I tried hard to behave better. The pills dumbed me down and school was mind-numbing, too. I tried my best to keep calm. But the old regime continued, and Mr Stabard still came in at night, even though he was under investigation about Raj and Prathi. I guess the fact that we hadn't given the game away made him feel very secure with us: he had silenced us well and truly, as far as the authorities were concerned so he still felt safe doing what he liked with us. Once the case was dropped, he was obviously smug – he clearly believed somehow he'd never been in the wrong in the first place, and was a model foster parent.

So my life continued on its usual treadmill from the age of twelve through to about fourteen or fifteen. I would try to be calm, then I would have a volcanic blow-up after several weeks or months of trying to be 'good'. I would trash things badly, and the Stabards would either deal with it by locking me in the airing cupboard for days, or in the shed, or – if I got too violent, and I smashed up the toys, or pulled a knife on someone – an ambulance would be called and I'd be carted off to the madhouse for a few days or weeks. I was usually put on new pills, or bigger doses of the old pills, and I began to be injected with stronger anti-depressants and other things, like anti-psychotic drugs.

It was around this time that the doctors decided I was 'paranoid'; which meant I thought someone or something bad was out to get me all the time. In fact, it was true: someone bad was out to get me – and I lived with him. In a way, if felt like the authorities were also out to get me because apart from the one woman doctor who had tried to understand my story, nobody had ever yet asked me a single question about why I was so angry. The ambulance-to-hospital-and-increased-drug-regime felt like it was another 'out-to-get-me' experience. So I felt increasingly more paranoid, especially since I always ended up being sent back home to the 'saintly' Stabards, and reminded by everyone that the problem was all mine. It was all in my head, clearly, and they were not to blame. I had a crazy mind, so I should be grateful for all I had at home. To my mind, that was truly crazy.

Mr Stabard had retired by this time, as he was now in his mid-sixties, and he had become utterly obsessed with my body, particularly my breasts. He would hang around the house all day when I was home and up in the box room (we weren't always in the shed all day now we were bigger) and he would come in unannounced and just ogle my body. Typically, he would stand at the doorway and stare at me for a very long time. He was creepy in the extreme. It made me feel very self-conscious and awkward. I'd usually sit up on the bed, which made me feel less vulnerable than lying down. He'd shuffle in for a crafty peek, like the dirty old man that he really was.

... *'Take it off'*, *he barks.*

I ignore him, knowing what he wants, but willing him to go away. He takes a few more steps into the room towards me. I can smell his boozy breath on the air.

'Take it off. Your top. Take it off, show me.'

He stands a few feet away, his eyes glazed. I look at the ground or my knees, wanting him to disappear, feeling my cheeks flush with embarrassment. In the end, to get rid of him, I take my top off. He goes very quiet for a moment and I can hear his breathing getting heavier. He fumbles in his pocket, as if he's looking for something. I fight the desire to stand up and punch him or scream in his face – instead I start picking at my skirt with my fingers, trying to control my temper. I just want to shout, 'Go away you filthy old man,' or 'Leave me alone!' but I don't dare, as he'd punch and slap me into submission.

'Take your bra off.'

I take it off reluctantly, shivering. By then I've given up fighting him off and I just want it over with. I sit there, naked to the waist, in a freezing cold room, staring at the floor, and he stands there, inches away, licking his lips and drooling over my young girl's body. It feels disgusting. Like I'm a piece of meat on display in a butcher's shop window. Eventually, having had his fill, he goes away, only to come back later that night to start his sleazy ritual all over again.

After putting the light bulb in he starts the usual business, telling me to take my top off so he can see me. Then he touches me with his fat fingers while I just stand there passively, taking it. I feel so disgusted with myself, and ashamed with the other two watching. I have to cut myself off from my body and my feelings just to deal with it . . .

Mr Stabard usually seemed to favour me more than the others; perhaps because I was more physically developed than them at the time. The only relief for me was that it saved the other two from too much abuse, especially as Faith was very poorly now and didn't look like she was going to survive a whole lot longer. Since going to ESN school and starting her periods, Hope had become more rebellious than me, often challenging our foster father, which made him angry. Then he would punish us all, by withdrawing food or by locking us in the shed all weekend. I was in a difficult position, and often volunteered to do what he wanted just to save the other two from being hurt, and to save us from a more horrible punishment later. I hated him for putting me in this position and loathed him as he satisfied himself on my young flesh. But hating him did me no good at all and simply fuelled my mounting anger.

Even though I was angry all the time, and feeling increasingly rebellious by the minute, I still didn't dare to do things I'd been trained all my life not to. For instance, I would never have dared to go into the lounge and sit on the sofa and put my feet up. I still feared the Stabards enormously, especially as they were continuing to bring home the church people to exorcise us every few months. They still drummed it into the three of us that we were possessed by the devil and we had to be purified. I actually think they truly believed this, and it was sincerely part of their warped world view that black skin actually meant evil. We had been brainwashed so entirely to believe that we weren't worthy of sitting on the sofa and turning on the TV for ourselves, we simply would not have done it. It was unthinkable.

We did take the odd risk as we got older and more rebellious though. I do remember once or twice going into the beautiful bedroom next door to ours during the daytime and sitting on the beds. This felt incredibly naughty, like we were committing a major crime. Now we were in our early teens we wanted to look in the heart-shaped mirror above the dressing table and imagine ourselves living in this bedroom, like proper teenage girls. We'd all sneak in, hoping the coast was clear and they wouldn't hear us, and we'd pretend it was our room, and we'd lie on a bed each, with our hands under our heads for a few minutes, imagining we could sleep there. It felt fantastic. The soft duvets and springy mattresses, the carpet under our hardened feet, the flowery curtains and the pictures on the walls, all made us feel like princesses – for a few precious minutes anyway. Then, absolutely terrified of being caught in the act, we would rush back to our box room, close the door, and giggle at our wild adventure to the wonderland of the room next door. It was a small victory, but an important one, in the war against the tyranny of the Stabards.

We were genuinely defiant in other ways, too. Sometimes we stole things. We were still going to the woods, to save our sanity, but now we took food and even alcohol along. We would get into the larder and pour some gin or vodka into a plastic juice bottle and take it with us. This was particularly helpful in winter when it was cold, and was great if one of us was hurting badly after Mr Stabard's so-called 'purification' treatment. We would have little parties, and feel very naughty, but very excited, about our escapades.

We stole whatever we could get our hands on: bits of pork pie, slices of ham, cake and good old Winalot. We were growing girls and hungry all the time. We still had to eat the rubbishy leftovers out of dog bowls and were still occasionally chained to the door to watch the Stabards eating, if they were in the mood. Either way, we were constantly empty-bellied. We got better at slipping food into our mouths while preparing dinner. In our desperate bid to survive we felt we had to be as stealthy and as clever as we could. We had also learned from *Roots* how the slaves survived by learning to be manipulative and stealthy, hiding things, pinching things and using their wits to scavenge. I guess when you're desperate you'll do whatever you need to do to get through it all.

Something happened to Hope, during this time, that caused me a great deal of grief and created even more anger. The Stabards' grown-up children still visited regularly, and all were married themselves with children, so the Stabards now had eight grandchildren. Bernard was in his thirties and was a big strapping muscleman. His son, Kevin, was one of the children who had always hated us. He always used to shout 'wog' at us and taunt us when we'd been watching *Roots*. He'd been a ringleader in throwing food at us at the children's parties and always took pleasure in making us feel small. I don't know why he hated us so much; maybe he resented us being there, for taking up his grandparents' time and attention? I don't think he ever forgave me for trashing his toy train set, which I had done one Christmas, when I went berserk. Bernard never stopped him – I don't think he had ever forgiven us for upsetting his son either. Also, as Mr Stabard's son, he had absorbed his father's hatred of black people all his life, as had his two sisters.

Anyway, Hope and I were in the kitchen one afternoon when Bernard dropped something off for his parents. We shouldn't have been there, we should have either been in the shed, or in our room, but we'd tiptoed downstairs and were scavenging for something to eat. For some reason the Stabards were out somewhere – maybe doing some shopping for an hour. I was about fourteen at the time, which made Hope about twelve. Faith was in hospital, as usual. We never liked Bernard and were genuinely afraid of him as he was very burly and had his father's aggressive attitude, especially towards us as black girls.

... Hope and I are in the larder, just off the kitchen, rummaging quietly when he suddenly appears.

'What are you doing here?'

Bernard stands in the middle of the kitchen, hands on hips, looking very challenging. He knows full well we shouldn't be there, especially in the larder, because we always have to wait to be fed. We're not allowed to help ourselves to food. We freeze, hands behind our backs. We look at the floor.

'I said, niggers, what are you up to?'

He always uses terrible words to attack us. We're used to it, even though it hurts and makes me fume.

'Cookin' supper,' Hope says unconvincingly. There's no sign of steaming pots and pans. She always speaks for us first these days; she's now braver than me.

Bernard strides across the room and grabs Hope by the shoulder and spins her round. In her hand is a crust of bread and chunk of cheese. He spins me round, and I'm holding some apple pie.

'You greedy, thievin' little wogs.'

I feel a surge of fury, but bite my lip, too scared to move. Bernard grabs the food out of our hands and throws it in the waste bin in front of us. He's smirking, looking very pleased with himself.

'Caught you red-handed, haven't I?'

We both stand riveted to the spot. I hate this man, almost as much as I hate his father – he has the same menacing, cold stare. I want to slap him. Instead, I stare at him fiercely, trying to communicate my hatred with my eyes, but Hope is more courageous and confrontational. She's mouthy today.

'We can eat if we want to,' *she says boldly.*

Oh God. I clench my jaw at her defiance.

'You what?'

'We live here'.

Bernard puts his face right up to Hope's, snarling angrily now.

'What did you say, you little black bitch?'

I'm really scared now and get hold of her t-shirt and try to pull her backwards towards me, hoping to slide round the room and escape out to the hall. I can sense he's going to get very nasty and we just need to get out of there. Bernard has his nose right up to Hope's. She's looking down at the ground, trembling.

'I said, what did you fucking say, wog?' *he spits out at her.*

'We can eat if we want', *repeats Hope in a tiny voice.*

'Oh, you can, can you? We'll see about that'.

Hope darts a look of pure fear at Bernard.

'Don't tell', *she pleads, suddenly terrified.*

'Oh, "don't tell"', *he mimics nastily. Then he puts his face right up to hers, even closer.*

'How you gonna stop me, nigger?'

Hope's incensed at him using the 'n' word yet again. It always reminds us of the dreaded Roots. *So she raises her eyes and locks gaze with him defiantly. They stand, face-to-face, bound together in a staring match. I will her to look down, to move away, to stop. I think we might be able to end it there and then, but he has other ideas.*

'You owe me, bitch', *he hisses at her through clenched teeth. He really hates us with his father's venom – it must be in the blood.*

Without any warning, Bernard suddenly grabs Hope and throws her flat on her back on the tiled kitchen floor, which is, as usual, covered in dog pee and animal droppings. Hope lets out a shriek, and is winded, as her food goes flying but Bernard is suddenly on top of her, holding her down with his thighs straddling her, his knees pinning her to the floor, his hands pinning her arms above her head. I stand with my hands over my face, terrified, holding my breath. When I peek through my fingers, he has pulled up her skirt and got his thing out and is in her, just like that. On the hard, unwashed kitchen floor. Right there and then. Hope lays, with her legs open, looking sideways with no emotion on her face, and just lets him do what he wants. Years of training with Mr Stabard have taught her not to resist, but to go limp and blank it all out. Bernard moves in and out of her very fast, grunting and groaning, like a dog on heat, and then it's over. It's very quick. He springs back up off her, and I can see Hope, her legs spread uncomfortably, looking shocked. Bernard goes over and gets some kitchen roll paper. He zips himself up and hands Hope a couple of pieces of paper to wipe herself. She doesn't move, so he bends over and wipes her. I'm amazed. It's such a bizarrely tender gesture given that he's just raped her on the kitchen floor, in broad daylight – in front of me. Hope sits up and pulls her skirt down over her knees, a crushed look on her face. Suddenly Bernard bends over her and pulls her up to her feet by her arm. He half-hugs her – which is very odd too – almost to say sorry, for a moment. Then, without a word he rushes out the house. She stands there looking at the floor, totally numb and blank. She's no longer standing up for herself; she's been put in her place and tamed by yet another 'master'.

Horrified by what's happened to her, I go over, put my arm round her shoulders and steer her out of the kitchen. We go upstairs to the box room together in total silence, all ideas about food completely forgotten by now. Hope crawls into the top bunk (which is a treat as it's our favourite place, the safest place to sleep as 'he' can't climb up to it) and turns to the wall. I sit on the hated bottom bunk and wonder if I could just kill Bernard with a knife next time I see him. I imagine stabbing him in the chest with great pleasure. Maybe I could torture him or even cut his willy off? What right has he to come in and do that to my little sister? How dare he punish her like that, for taking food, which belongs to us anyway? Don't the Stabards claim money to feed us, then keep us starving most of the time? I hear Hope sobbing softly into her pillow, something she doesn't do very often these days. She used to cry more when she was little. I stand up and put my arm around her, but she shrugs me off. She's too upset for comfort.

'We'll go to Wildflower, tonight,' I whisper. 'I promise.'

She doesn't answer, just sniffs, and keeps her back to me, hunched round in a foetal position. I stroke her bony back gently, feeling terribly guilty that I didn't do anything to stop the bastard. How dare he! We were nothing to him. Just animals. Actually, beneath animals. Eventually, Hope lets me comfort her gently, at least for a while. As I stroke her hair, I keep telling myself that I could have hit him or pulled him off. I feel so angry with myself all over again, as if it's my fault that I let him rape her. I feel I should have done something to stop him, although what I could have done? I feel helpless, powerless and sickened to the core. What if he tells the Stabards we'd been out of bounds getting food – then there'll be even more hell to pay tomorrow. We certainly can't tell them what he's done – or anyone else for that matter. Mr Stabard does it all the time himself anyway, with his wife's blessing, so what will they care?

After this horrendous incident, Hope became even more rebellious and unruly at home. It was a major turning point in her life with the Stabards. Up until then I had been the one who gave them the most trouble. I seemed always to be the one carrying all the anger for the other foster kids. But this incident on the kitchen floor, the bald-faced crudeness of the attack, somehow tipped Hope over the edge. She began to talk back to the Stabards, which meant she got beaten more. She also started stealing things, and we joined in. It was only little things, like a few pence or some food, but it was a way of getting our own back. One thing we did quite often was to nick one of Mrs Stabard's Sunday brooches and hide it for a week or two under our wonky floorboard. It just gave us a hollow sort of pleasure to make her confused about where she had put something – she was now in her sixties and getting a bit more forgetful about things. It also meant going into her bedroom, which was a dare in itself, making us feel more powerful.

We also did something very naughty to Mr Stabard one Sunday. He had now lost most of his hair, although it was white for as long as I could remember. He bought a toupee (no doubt with our childcare money) and very proudly wore this to church on Sunday. One day Hope found an ant's nest at the bottom of the garden when we were cleaning out the aviary. She showed me, and almost without a word, we hatched a plan. The ant's nest found its way under Mr Stabard's toupee, and loads of ants settled in the false hair. The next Sunday he wore it to church. We watched in church as he started scratching his head, then his neck and his ears, during the service. We were nearly wetting ourselves as we saw him wriggling and scratching as the ants climbed down his neck. By halfway through he took the toupee off and we saw him turning it around in his hands and looking inside it, clearly puzzled. Then he half-jumped, half-shouted out, and we saw the wig go flying over the pew and land in the aisle. We nearly had a fit, and just managed to keep our composure, when he shot a fierce look over his shoulder at us. Luckily, we were mistresses of the straight face by then and we kept our eyes down, faces blank, although we could feel his eyes boring into us. All the way home he was fuming, and we knew that he was longing to lash out at us, but we shot in the house and out to the shed and leant against the door the minute we got back. I think he must have had too much to drink after church, since he fell asleep in the lounge, snoring loudly, and never came out to give us a walloping. We felt victorious: 'Operation Ants in the Pants' or rather, in the wig, had actually worked!

These minor victories meant an enormous amount as they were like little islands in a sea of almost unremitting misery. We almost never won, and so to win a tiny battle in the war that was life with the Stabards raised our confidence. Up until that point nearly all of our ire was focused on Mr Stabard. He was the target of our daily fury, and it was against him we fought the hardest. I still wanted Mrs Stabard's love, but I was never going to earn it, particularly as she was so remote and cold all the time, to us at least. One day the Social Services woman came for a routine visit, and I heard Mrs Stabard telling her that I was Mr Stabard's 'favourite' and that we had a 'special relationship'. She was making out that Mr Stabard was very nice to me, and gave me special treatment. I felt absolutely livid about this and later that day, when the social worker had gone, I threw all the washing and ironing on the floor and refused to clear it up. She was standing in the kitchen, pointing to the stuff on the floor and I was refusing to pick it up and sort it. It was a major stand-off. She then said if I continued to be bad like this she would call an ambulance and I would be taken away. This was used as the ultimate threat, as she knew how much I hated that hospital. I answered back, rudely, that if she did that then I would tell the hospital everything that was going on, and then she'd be sorry. They'd both be locked up in prison for ever until they rotted and died. I walked out of the room, triumphant. That would show them.

That night I was due for a bath; a rare treat. I only ever had baths about once every couple of months if I was lucky. Since the days of the chocolate treatment, I had felt scared of them. Now I always kept my clothes on in the water, for added protection. I was washing my feet, when I suddenly felt someone behind me and something went over my head. I was pulled under backwards and tried to gulp some air as I went down. I felt the water close over my head and I freaked out. Someone was dunking me under. My hands went up to my head and I worked out I was under a sheet or something, which was heavy with water, and that a pair of strong arms was holding me down. I fought wildly to sit up, entangled in the wet sheet, and kicked my legs, holding my breath and feeling like I might burst, before being pulled backwards and dunked under again. I was lashing out with my arms and legs, still holding my breath, but needing more air and desperately trying to get the sheet off my head.

Then someone shouted something from downstairs in the house – it sounded like Mr Stabard wanting something – and I realised with a total shock that it was Mrs Stabard doing this to me. It wasn't him. It was her! I was horrified and amazed. With an almighty push, I finally got myself upright and pulled off the sheet. As I desperately gulped in air I saw her back disappearing out the door, sleeves up, arms dripping wet. I just couldn't believe it was Mrs Stabard who had done this to me. She'd actually tried to drown me! I never knew she was that strong – or that angry with me. I couldn't believed she hated me enough to try and kill me; I was devastated. I loved her and wanted her to love me back. I sat under the dripping sheet, absolutely desolate and shivering with fear for some time after that, listening to the Stabards' voices downstairs and wondering if I would ever get out of their 'care' alive.

16

The First Cut

'*Harmony is of low average intelligence and appears emotionally immature, but copes fairly well with her foster home.*' (Social worker's notes)

It was after Mrs Stabard attacked me in the bath that I started running away. She'd never done anything so openly violent to me before and I felt totally betrayed. I had sort of got used to his mistreatment; but from her? Well, I was always holding out the hope that she would eventually love me one day. Now I began to realise that she hated me just as much as he did. Now I had nothing to lose; nothing to hold me back. I'd lost respect for her, which hurt a lot.

I was now nearly fifteen and one day after we'd had a massive argument I just slammed out the house and went where my feet took me. I felt very unsafe and I took off and just walked and walked and walked. I remember roaming the streets digging my fingers into my face, scratching and pinching my skin, and trying to hurt myself. I also slapped and punched myself, as I felt so agitated and trapped. People stared at me on the street and someone shouted out 'crazy' and spat at me, but I didn't care. After all, I was 'crazy Harmony' wasn't I?

I began to hurt myself whenever I felt I'd explode and needed a release. I'd get a vegetable peeler or a knife and I'd slice into my flesh. Usually I had a go at my arms. For a second, the act of slicing gave me a release; a real feeling of relaxation when the blood came. Then it would really hurt: a sharp, deep, nervy pain. I'd also take one of Mr Stabard's razor blades from the bathroom cupboard and slice myself with that too. I'd feel a fantastic release of all the pent-up anger when I cut myself – it was a strange sensation. If they hated my black flesh, then I did, too. I needed to dig into something, I needed to hurt myself, and once I cut, then it would release the tension. I didn't like the pain, but I used to be fascinated by watching the blood bubbling up and beginning to pour; I was almost mesmerised by it. I also burned myself on the legs with Mr Stabard's cigars. Sometimes the burns would go septic.

Hurting myself became a habit – an addiction. I think I was absolutely desperate and simply didn't know what else to do. If Mrs Stabard saw my cuts afterwards (which I often stuck a bit of toilet paper to, to stem the flow) she would say nothing. She'd just look briefly and turn away uninterested.

Hope was also getting desperate at this time. Faith was never there now. She was permanently in hospital and I don't think I really saw her again after I was fourteen or fifteen. I missed her a lot as she was a gentle soul, who loved the woods and somehow created a bridge between Hope and me when we weren't getting on. Meanwhile Hope and I were arguing a lot. I don't know if it was our age, or whether we were both so fed up with our lives that we didn't know who else to take things out on, but we argued constantly because we were caged up, and sometimes I felt totally infuriated with her. It wasn't her fault. She was more provocative than I was, and after the rape she began to go off the rails. I was worried she would get us into even more trouble, so I tried to quieten her down for all our sakes. I still carried the weight of being older sister, and now Mr Stabard only had the two of us to satisfy him, he used us both more frequently, which we hated. The neighbours complained because Hope and I would argue and shout, either in the box room, or in the cramped shed. We needed to let off steam and we would swear at the top of our voices – it was our kind of protest and I don't think we cared at all if anyone heard. We actually wanted to give the Stabards a hard time.

School was still frustrating, and I was bored out of my brain all the time. One day Mr Pringle called me into his office and I thought, 'Oh my God, I'm in trouble again.' The memory of that meeting with the policeman and the horrible Mr Venetti was still raw – the day I'd failed to take the chance to escape. That was something else I cut myself about. However, I was amazed when Mr Pringle said he had decided that I could try to do an exam at the local school if I wanted to. I was shocked; what did he mean? He explained that he thought I was good enough to try to do a CSE (Certificate in Education) in English at the comprehensive down the road. Instead of staring at the floor, as usual, I actually looked up at him, and saw he was smiling at me. I couldn't believe that somebody was saying that I was capable of doing something positive at last.

'I think you can do it, Harmony,' he said. 'I've noticed you wanting to read things and being bored in class.'

I couldn't help it, but I felt a huge grin spread on my face. Me, go to proper school, and read books, like the other 'normal' kids. I felt excited, but scared at the same time. Mr Pringle could see that I was nervous.

'Don't worry, they know that you're coming, and they'll settle you in,' he said. 'We'll take you there and back.'

I couldn't believe that someone was actually thinking about me and offering me something good for a change. It felt absolutely amazing to feel someone was on my side, for once.

True to his word, I did go to the school and studied alongside the other ordinary children in an annexe in the playground. I was taken there a couple of times a week. Mr Pringle kept saying to me, 'You're not stupid, Harmony, you're really not,' but I found it hard to accept. All my life I'd had it drummed into me that I was stupid, bad, crazy – you name it. I loved doing the reading – I drank in the books – but I have to admit that at first I was quite an unruly student. After so long messing about with building blocks, I found the whole experience of going to a proper school quite daunting. It took me a long time to get the hang of it. After all, going from primary school to the ESN school there had been no real discipline or order. We didn't really have to apply ourselves. Also, being on the pills all the time, my brain was fuzzy and I found it hard to concentrate at first. But I soon began to get the hang of it – even enjoy it – and I was pleased to be doing something constructive at last. As I began to settle down and I even learned to write essays. I felt huge pride in what I was doing although I never told the Stabards about it, of course.

I tried hard to behave better at school, and I especially tried to show Mr Pringle that I was worth his trust in me. So I made a big effort to be calmer at both schools I was now going to. I liked the annexe, I liked the lessons and I enjoyed the feeling that I was learning. I liked knowing things, and I felt less tired, less achy in the head, now that I was finally using my brain. I felt like my mind was being exercised at last, like a muscle, and I really liked it.

I began to have a feeling of pride in myself. The teacher at the comprehensive put me in for my CSE but tried to persuade me to go for my GCSE as well. I was terrified. Mr Henderson, the English teacher, kept saying, 'Harmony, you can do it, you know.' But I was scared. It felt like a step too far, too fast. He kept encouraging me, but I kept saying, 'No, I can't.' I said I needed more time, but I think I was scared to try and fail. I didn't take the opportunity when it was handed to me, and regretted it afterwards, but I had absolutely no support at home, and I guess it felt too much stress to deal with on top of the Stabards' regime. However, I gained a lot from the fact that two teachers actually thought I was worth investing in, and it did make a big difference to my self-esteem that they didn't think that I was totally worthless.

Back at the ESN school my friend Abigail Greer began to get me to do things for her which were against the rules. I think I was desperate for a friend at any price, and had made myself useful to her. She was older than me and was using me to do things like bringing in alcohol from Mr Stabard's huge supply, which I would sneak out in a juice bottle, just like I did when we went up to Wildflower Woods. I would also pretend I could buy her things from clothes catalogues that she brought in to school. I'd never seen anything like these things, but I would promise to get her stuff as a way of buying her friendship. I couldn't actually buy them and she'd get disappointed in me when I didn't come up with the goods (literally), saying I'd let her down badly. I'd feel terrible and would go home and hack at myself with a razor blade, feeling more useless than ever.

Abigail also wanted to introduce me to boys. When we went into town, or walked home together part of the way, she would stop and chat to boys and then start kissing them. I would stand behind her, watching, terrified. I didn't like all that, and it freaked me out. After all the years of Mr Stabard abusing me I wasn't in the least bit interested in boys. Sex just meant something horrible to deal with, something nasty, humiliating and painful. Emotionally, I was as naïve as a child. Also I had never been given any proper information about my body and how it worked, or about how babies were made, or about sexual hygiene, even though I had had my periods since I was nine, and had had an abortion at eleven years old. I had been abused sexually since infanthood, and yet knew nothing really about the birds and the bees, courtship, love or any of that stuff. So when Abigail was standing there snogging the boys, I wanted to get as far away as I possibly could. I didn't like it, it confused me, and I didn't want to be involved in any of all that. As far as I was concerned it just led to one thing – trouble.

Meanwhile, while I was trying to be a 'good girl' at school, I was being an increasingly 'bad girl' at home. All my frustrations came out there. I didn't respect Mrs Stabard any more – not after the bath episode – and I let her know it. My temper was really uncontrollable and any stresses about the exam I was taking, or about the trouble I was getting into with Abigail, would come out with me trashing furniture, throwing things and shouting. I think the drugs I was on actually made me more aggressive as well. It was strange, in that they shut me down and they also seemed to make me angrier, if that makes sense. I couldn't think straight, and I would lose my temper over the slightest things. I was taking loads of pills every day and the more pills I took the angrier I seemed to get. But I was numb at the same time; feeling heavy and dull, and yet furious, like there was an underground fire burning deep down, and I couldn't put it out. I was still going to the mental hospital, sometimes for check-ups and sometimes because I'd freaked out and the Stabards called in the paramedics to teach me yet another lesson.

Around this time there was a lot of discussion about what was going to happen to me next, which made me very insecure indeed. Hope was going off the rails now – she was out with boys a lot and had started drinking regularly. I could see things were going to get very difficult and the Stabards were saying they couldn't look after her much longer the way she was behaving. But they also discussed my future. They would never talk *to* me, but they would talk *about* me, when I was in the room, like I wasn't there. It was like, 'What shall we do with Harmony when she's sixteen?' Not, 'What would you like to do Harmony, when you're sixteen?' Apparently, at sixteen their official job of fostering me would come to an end and I was free to go.

I remember one of the social workers coming and there was a meeting in the lounge about me. I didn't get consulted, or invited in, but I listened at the door and heard them discussing my future. They never asked what I wanted. The Stabards never said, 'We'll support you going to college,' or asked, 'Is there a course you'd like to do?' Nothing like that. The attitude was: 'Dumb Harmony can't think for herself. She's crazy anyway, and there'd be no point in talking to her, so we'll make decisions for her, over her head.' I was an awkward teenager and nobody knew what to do with me. Least of all me.

I was coming up to finishing school and I managed to get through sitting my exams, which I actually enjoyed, even though I was nervous. And then two things happened, which triggered a lot of further upset. First of all, I had a huge bust-up with Abigail. I had tried to win her friendship by bringing her things, and pretending to buy her clothes but she finally got fed up with me and dropped me. I was devastated. The only friend I had ever made had dumped me, and I was back to being just lonely old 'crazy Harmony'.

Secondly, and even more devastatingly, Hope disappeared. She left after a huge row with Mr Stabard that started over the washing-up. After the kitchen floor attack she had really changed. She was bitter and angry all the time, even at me. Although she was only fourteen going on fifteen, she was much older than her years and furious, like me, about everything. When she finally blew her stack, refusing to do what Mr Stabard wanted, he hit her so hard that she decided to cut free. I had never thought that she would do that. We had been through so much together, and I hoped, against hope, that we would be together the rest of our lives – or at least keep in touch. She told me she couldn't take any more, but we'd said that so many times. Of course we often fell out – we argued, we squabbled, just like sisters do, and I felt jealous of her quite often because I thought she was prettier, thinner, and more confident. But, I loved her. She was my sister, my family, my world. One day after school she wasn't on the minibus. She just didn't come home that night, or any night after that. After a couple of days, Mr and Mrs Stabard called the authorities and there were meetings. They spoke to the school. I think, more than anything, Mr Stabard was terrified that she would tell on him. He certainly cared about himself more than her welfare. As far as I know she didn't blab. She just disappeared. Just like that. I don't think the police were ever involved – I think the Stabards were relieved she'd gone.

I was absolutely devastated she was gone and cried myself to sleep every night. Our little room was suddenly very empty. I also felt much more vulnerable to attack from Mr Stabard, as I was left to fend him off alone. I felt a mixture of anger at Hope, pain at her loss, and fear that he could really have me when he wanted me now.

Looking back, I think Hope blew a fuse, and just got on a normal bus and went to another town – probably with boys that she'd met and snogged after school. I think she'd had enough, and was so angry that she was even prepared to leave me. Her getting into alcohol and drugs had scared me as I felt she was going down a dark path and I couldn't save her. I heard years later that she had got heavily into drink, hard drugs, prostitution and had finally become homeless. I have no idea to this day whether she is dead or alive, as I never saw her, or heard from her, again.

With Hope gone, my world fell apart. I was utterly and completely devastated. I felt so terrified being left alone in the house with the Stabards, as Faith was now almost permanently sick in hospital. Mrs Stabard would say coldly that she wouldn't be coming back either – and good riddance. I mourned Hope daily. It was like I'd lost part of myself. It all got so much harder after she'd gone. Over the next months (probably to replace their lost income) the Stabards did have a few babies for short-term fostering for a while – and I would have to look after them in cots in my bedroom, of course – but the Stabards were now well into their sixties and not really up to it any more. Plus, I was an utter handful.

I actually didn't want to leave them. This may sound very strange, but with school coming to an end, and with Hope, Faith and Abigail gone, I felt extremely insecure.

I hated the Stabards, but I didn't know anything else. I wanted to get away, but I didn't know where to go.

I was now living alone in a terrible triangle with the Stabards. I slashed at myself and pinched my face and punched myself in desperation. One night I cut myself very deeply in my groin with a razor and bled so much that they eventually called an ambulance and I had to have stitches. At least I had a couple of days respite, with nice food and a comfy bed. However, it just confirmed to everyone how crazy I was. Back home and desperate I stayed awake at night, trying to puzzle out what I was going to do. Where was I going to go? Who would have me? What would happen? I was very afraid of the big wide world out there, as well as extremely afraid of the crazy world in here. I had no idea what on earth I was going to do next.

17

Bid for Freedom

'Mrs Stabard patiently cares for this difficult teenager well, despite being challenged daily . . . ' (Social worker's report)

The loss of Hope, Faith, and even Abigail left me unhinged. I hadn't expected my sisters to disappear like they did – so quickly and finally. Although Faith had been sick for so many years and I could see she was deteriorating, I didn't expect her just to disappear in a puff of smoke. The Stabards never included me in what was going on with her; I would never visit her in hospital and they didn't give us any information when she was away. Of course I loved her, and cared for her, but I wasn't given any chance to say my goodbyes. I couldn't ask any questions either, as they wouldn't be answered. I have no idea how things ended for her – she just went off the map. To this day I feel sick that I never saw her again. Was she alone at the end? Did she know I cared? I hope she did.

All this was coupled with the prospect of leaving school and with losing my one and only friend, Abigail. Leaving school was no big deal on the one hand, in that it had given me so very little in terms of skills and learning. In many ways it had undermined my confidence, rather than built it. But I did feel pleased that I had been chosen to study and take an exam, right at the end, and that did make me feel I wasn't entirely stupid. But I'd missed so many vital years of basic education by wasting my time playing with building blocks and colouring in. How would I ever catch up? So when I was leaving school I didn't feel confident at all.

My friendship with Abigail also seemed to set a pattern for what would happen in the years to come. The Stabards had taught me to be a slave, and I would take up a slavish position in all of my relationships from then on. I would always try and please people, to my own detriment, and then finally explode with anger once I felt I had been pushed too far. I didn't know what a healthy friendship was. I had such low self-esteem that I thought the only way someone would be friends with me would be if I tried to earn it – to please them, even if it meant putting myself at risk. I had learned to try and sacrifice myself for my sisters, and that pattern continued with all of my other relationships, well into adulthood.

What's more the Stabards were contemplating getting rid of me now. I could be thrown out at sixteen. The irony of this situation was that now I had the chance at freedom I didn't want to leave because I was frightened of the world out there. The mental hospital had made me terrified about what might lay outside. If it was all like that, then I would rather stay at the Stabards', unbearable as it might be there. It was a case of 'better the devil I knew'. At the same time, I regretted deeply the fact that I had not had the courage to leave when Raj and Prathi made their accusations and that I had failed to shop the Stabards. When their case failed – much to Mr Stabard's smug satisfaction – I then felt that my own cause was lost. If they couldn't prove a case against them, and they had a real mother and family fighting for them, then what chance did I have to convince anybody of the reality of life in 97 Forestlane Way?

It's hard to describe, but I felt totally stuck with the Stabards. It was like I couldn't leave and I couldn't stay. The alternatives seemed hopeless. I hated them, but I feared the unknown. They did not help me in any way try to work out what might be a good way to move forward. Neither did Social Services nor the mental hospital people when I came in contact with them. I felt stuck between a rock and a hard place, and that meant I stayed with what I knew for the time being, even though it was bad for me.

In the end the Stabards agreed to keep me on (I guess for more money) and we continued living our weird dysfunctional lives in a terrible triangle. Mr Stabard still visited me at night two or three times a week, and forced himself on me, Sellotaping my eyes shut; and Mrs Stabard still pretended she didn't know what was going on. They still shoved me in the shed, airing cupboard and box room, occasionally for punishment but I fought them more in our everyday life. I felt less powerful being on my own without Hope and Faith, as although we hadn't talked to each other about what was going on, we had always understood each other without words. Plus, our visits to Wildflower Woods had been the most magical, miraculous times and had really saved our sanity. Now that it was just me locked in with this strange couple who could do with me what they wanted, I felt I didn't even have the woods to escape to – it just wasn't the same experience without the other two. Without the release of being in the woods at night, my tempers got worse as I got more trapped and fearful.

When I left school at sixteen it was 1984, and Mr Stabard had been retired for some time. I would be up in the box room all day sometimes, wondering what the hell to do with myself, feeling utterly lonely and desolate, and then he'd appear in the doorway. He would never knock. He had no idea I might want privacy as a teenage girl, or might need some space for myself. There I was in the box room still, and he would ogle me, feeling himself through his trouser pocket and demanding to see or feel my breasts. I was just there, on demand, for him to play with – his property and sexual plaything.

One day, I'd simply had enough of all this and I had a terrible temper tantrum, trashed the kitchen, and stormed out the house to walk the streets, like I often did. I was fighting the urge to slash myself and instead was pinching and hitting myself. Then I spotted this big poster for the YTS – the Youth Training Scheme, which was a Government-funded training scheme for teenagers back then. All at once I thought, 'Oh, this might be an opportunity for me,' and decided to try and pursue it for myself. I felt lucky I could read at least, otherwise I would have missed it. I went home, determined things would now change.

Without mentioning it to the Stabards, who would have laughed and discouraged me, I ended up going to the Job Centre two weeks later. I sat for ages in what looked like a hospital waiting room after taking my ticket. When my number was called I spoke to a man through a window and he filled in forms. He asked me what I would like to do and I shrugged. I had no idea. He offered me a job of stuffing envelopes which sounded really boring, or catering, which sounded like yet more hard kitchen work. I ended up applying to work in a hospital.

What they offered me was a placement working in an old people's ward in a big local hospital. I think that by that time I felt like hospital was like another home. You got meals and a bed, and in the normal hospitals I'd been to so far, the staff could be nice and friendly, and the environment was clean and bright. The idea was welcoming to me, especially when they offered me a room with food and board, all paid. I thought it sounded a bit like heaven. At least I'd be getting away from Mr Stabard and would be able to sleep at night without being pounced on. However, I didn't tell them about my medication or past history at all, and I think the drugs I was on actually made me braver than if I hadn't been taking them. I was so numb I was more cavalier than I would have been if I'd really felt my fear.

So I said 'yes' without thinking at all what it meant for me. I had never lived anywhere on my own, or been away from the Stabards except when I was in hospital. I had no idea what it meant to be free. I was like a slave who was given their freedom at last, but had no idea how to use it – how to manage money, or buy my own food and clothes, or how to build relationships at work. These things are very complicated if you don't know about them and I threw myself into the unknown without having any idea what I was getting into. I guess I was very mixed-up at the time – still fuming about everything that had happened and was still happening – and I was so lonely without the other two girls, that I needed to make a move of some sort. I was also still doped up to the eyeballs, so I wasn't able to think very clearly about what I was doing. I was driven by a big feeling of 'I'll show you' which was mostly aimed at the Stabards, but maybe also at Hope, for leaving me in the lurch.

A few weeks later I was sent a letter which told me I had an appointment at the care home to meet the manager. Mrs Stabard opened the letter and read it, then handed it to me, looking annoyed.

'What's this?'

I looked at the letter and shrugged. I was excited and frightened, but I didn't want to show my feelings to Mrs Stabard. I knew she'd try to stop me.

'You won't last,' is all she said, turning away.

I felt like a balloon that'd been pricked.

'Yes, I will. I'm going to do it'.

'You won't last five minutes.'

I felt stung. She just wanted to keep me locked up here. I'd show her – I'd show them – that I could do something. I had to get out of there, I couldn't stand it any more. I thought of the comfort of the nice hospitals, of the cleanliness, the freedom.

'I'm going.'

Mrs Stabard turned and walked out the kitchen, and I felt really scared, but I also felt determined and thought: 'I'll do it for Hope, I'll do it for Faith – I've just got to try.'

I had a proper uniform, red and white checks and a paper hat. I was an auxiliary and I felt quite proud of myself. I had a real job. A proper role in life. I think inside of my head I had imagined the hospital would be nice and orderly, and I'd have my meals cooked for me, and would be able to get a good night's sleep when I needed one. However, reality hit once the ward sister handed me a long list of chores, a mop and a bucket and looked sternly at me. I thought, 'Here we go again. I came here to get away, but here I am doing the same thing as at home.' Then I ended up working on the grotty geriatric wards. I had no idea how to work with people, and I'd already spent my life cleaning up, cooking, and working hard.

However, I couldn't believe it when I was told to wash the old people. To wash them meant taking off their old clothes and pyjamas – some had soiled their beds – and to clean their private parts. After years of abuse I couldn't bear to touch them 'down there', not even the women. The men lay there, waiting for me to wash their bits, and I felt such hatred for them, I couldn't go near them. I knew it wasn't their fault that they were old and helpless, but the stench combined with my bad memories often meant I wanted to be sick.

The sister came up to me during the first week and said, 'Mr Brown says you haven't washed him.'

Without thinking I replied, 'How can he know I haven't washed him? He's blind!'

Only once I'd said it did I realise how stupid it was – I can even laugh at it now. The sister stared at me like I was a total idiot. I hated Mr Brown for telling on me because I felt I was now in my own little world in the hospital, and I could play at being an auxiliary. The truth was I wanted just to be in my little clean room, asleep in a nice cosy bed, being fed hot meals. I needed some nurturing, some respite from it all. Unfortunately, the sister didn't have the time or the inclination to train me up, and I have to say, I don't think I had the right attitude. I had no idea what was entailed in working in the outside world. In fact, I really just wanted to go to work for a bit of a rest from the horrible home I'd been forced to work in all my life.

While I was working at the hospital I found a guy called Johnny wandering around outside one day, and I brought him in. He stank of booze (worse than Mr Stabard even!) but I bought him some sandwiches and a drink from the automat, and even let him sleep on my floor. I felt really sorry for him as he had nowhere to stay. It was all very innocent: Johnny didn't touch me, just crashed out and snored. I got into trouble when it was discovered what I'd done. I had no idea what you did at work, or how normal people behaved, and I just thought the poor bloke was in need and that I should help him. Needless to say, I got the sack, and six weeks later was returned to the Stabards with my tail between my legs. I just felt stupid all over again. Stupid, crazy Harmony had messed it all up. I'd tried to escape and had fallen at the first hurdle.

Boy, were they smug! When I told my foster parents I'd lost my job I got a load of 'I told you so's. Worse than that, the day I got home Mr Stabard was waiting for me. Mrs Stabard was out somewhere or other. When I came back in the door, after my six weeks trying to do the job, he didn't say hello, but he just grabbed me by the hair, dragged me up the stairs backwards and beat me so hard that he broke the little finger on my right hand. He swore at me, kicked me in the stomach and thumped me until I was beaten to a pulp. My finger was agony, hanging limply at an odd angle. He also raped me on the landing floor – right there and then on the spot – and then threw me in the airing cupboard for two days. What really terrified me, was him saying that I'd have to start at Stage One all over again, in order to be purified. What a welcome home.

18

Wilderness Years

'Hopefully Harmony will be able to live with her foster family until she is discharged from care ... her security is being threatened by efforts made by Social Services to revitalize the links with her family of origin ... ' (Social worker's report)

I was back in the fold. I was back in the horrendous, punitive regime. I was back to Stage One of my purification programme, which meant being locked in the shed, shoved in the airing cupboard and enduring degrading drunken night visits from Mr Stabard at least twice a week, sometimes more. My foray out into the world was ridiculed; they laughed at me for being so gullible. My foster parents didn't offer me any guidance, they just poked fun and riled me, and then punished me for getting wound up. Meanwhile, my heart was broken, as I missed Hope and Faith so badly. My dear sisters were gone, and I was left to deal with the madness of my hidden hell all on my own.

I was desperate for friendship, but I had no idea how to make friends. I had only attached myself to Abigail in a slave-like worshipping way, or to waifs and strays – like Johnny in the hospital, to whom I gave a floor for a few nights. I had no idea how to talk to people, or exchange information, or how to build a friendship based on mutual respect, care, trust and even love.

I wasn't the faintest bit interested in 'boyfriends' either, in the way that Abigail or Hope had been. I wasn't keen on kissing boys, or flirting or doing any of that 'normal' teenage stuff. Perhaps I felt that anything to do with sex would lead to more unnecessary pain and trouble. Dabbling with boyfriends would open not just a can of worms, but a whole barrel-load. After all, how could I explain my physical experiences with Mr Stabard which had been going on for as long as I could remember? What boy would understand that? I had never had any innocent pecks on the cheeks, or casual flirtations, or first kisses. And I felt I never would have. Indeed, Mr Stabard had never kissed me, or shown me any tenderness or love. The kind of perverted act I was subjected to by him was the opposite of loving, tender sex. I was wary of getting entangled with anybody, in any way, that would lead to something that intimate. How would I ever trust anyone? Any physical touch would make me feel explosive rage. I think the feelings involved would have been too enormous to deal with and I already felt out of my depth, so I avoided them – telling myself that I was fat and unattractive anyway. I had been called ugly for so long that my self-esteem was at rock bottom, and I never expected any boy my age to find me attractive. Boys, sex and attraction was a minefield, and I had no idea how to cross it.

Thus, for the next two to three years, from leaving school at sixteen up until I was almost nineteen, I was in a kind of wilderness at the Stabards'. I did try to make one male friend after Hope left, someone I met at the ESN school and had quite liked, Mohammed. He had a very difficult background, with a lone, alcoholic mother who brought home violent boyfriends who beat him up and abused him. I felt I really had something in common with him. Perhaps I felt sorry for him too. He was another waif and stray I could help. I think it made me feel more powerful to help someone else. I wasn't interested in him sexually at all, although I think he was quite interested in me. It was rather like we were two lost souls trying to find our way in a tough, hostile world.

I bumped into Mohammed in town one day and we chatted for some time. We struck up a sort of friendship and, naively, I just hoped for a Valentine's card from him or something like that. Basically I wanted the status of a boy in my life without all the physical and emotional complications. That sounds silly, but I thought if I was nice to him he would be my Valentine, and then I would be a normal teenage girl, and an attractive one to boot. Sadly my innocent little plan didn't work out. One night Mohammed arrived at my front door in a real state and the Stabards actually took him in. He was homeless, after a big bust-up with his mum and her nasty, violent boyfriend, so he came to the Stabards for refuge. I didn't know what to do with him, but the Stabards contacted Social Services and I think they came to an arrangement (I guess they got money, as usual) to look after him for a while.

Mohammed was put in the box room with me – where else? We slept in separate bunks, like brother and sister, but sadly he soon was sucked into the madness of the Stabards' regime. One night I woke up and found Mr Stabard 'hurting' Mohammed in the same way he had hurt Raj. Mr Stabard was drunk as usual, and had Mohammed down on his knees, head at crotch height, pushing his mouth onto his foul thing. It was disgusting. Even though Mohammed was sixteen he was overpowered by Mr Stabard and forced to undergo his own so-called purification treatment. I was horrified. I hadn't really wanted him to come and stay in the first place, and now he was being pulled into the

Stabards' sick world. So I did something really silly after that – or perhaps just very desperate. A few days later I took twenty pounds out of Mr Stabard's wallet and then made out Mohammed had stolen it – which outraged Mr Stabard and confused Mohammed. He was duly shipped back to his abusive mother. It was the only thing I could think of doing to get him out of there. It was typical of me that I would try to protect someone else at my own expense – that's what I'd always done. It was more painful for me to live with someone else being 'hurt' by Mr Stabard, than to have to deal with it myself. It was similar to when I used to say to Mr Stabard, 'Take me, take me instead of them,' to save Hope and Faith from his torture. I guess it made me feel better about myself to shoulder the responsibility. My logic was that my friend's drunk mother and violent boyfriend couldn't be as bad as Mr Stabard.

I felt hugely guilty for not warning Mohammed about what he might be getting into at my house. I never spoke about what was going on at home. He had no idea what he was doing when he knocked the front door and asked the nice Christian people for help. I felt a responsibility to get him out of there, even if it meant framing him for something he didn't do. Needless to say, I never got my Valentine's card; and that was the end of that sorry relationship. Mohammed said nothing about what had happened to him either, as far as I know. Anyway, who would have believed him? He was just another unwanted, damaged kid who nobody liked much, who had nowhere to belong – just like me – and who had found himself falling into the nasty clutches of Mr Stabard.

Meanwhile, the Stabards continued to discuss what to do with me (over my head, of course) as I was clearly getting 'troublesome' to them. I wondered, at one point, if they would adopt me. I didn't like them, but I didn't know where else to go. I was very anxious to belong somewhere, even if that somewhere was vile. They made it absolutely clear to me that they didn't want to adopt me, and actually that they couldn't 'afford' to do it – a joke, considering that all their foster children had brought them riches far outweighing their expenditure on them. Deeply rejected, my temper tantrums continued to escalate wildly. Maybe the Stabards feared I would go on trashing the place and, as they got older, would start to fight back against them? Maybe I was too much for them to deal with long-term? Whatever, it was clear that saying they couldn't afford me was really just a feeble excuse – and despite everything, it really hurt.

My foster parents' rejection of me made me even more insecure – and angry. Why didn't they want to adopt me? What was wrong with me? If they had had me all those years as a house slave and sex slave, why wasn't I good enough to adopt? Their rejection led me to think more about where I had come from in the first place. Now that I was a teenager I began to wonder about my own mother, and my own 'roots'. I was longing to know more about my family of origin, but absolutely terrified to ask about them. Who would I ask? How would I go about finding out more about them? I couldn't ask the Stabards, who would never have told me the truth anyway, and would have just said something insulting about them. I did eventually have a chance to ask about my birth mother when a social worker visited the house for a regular check-up. I wrote them a little note in secret and asked for help to find her.

I think some enquiries were made on my behalf and I was told on a later visit, in a fairly off-hand way, that the trail to my mother had run cold. She was somewhere in London, but no-one knew where exactly. However, she'd had more kids after Hope, a couple of boys. So I had two half brothers? Wow. They couldn't tell me anything more than that. It was a real shock to think my own mother was still alive, still walking the streets, breathing, eating, living a life, just a couple of hours away from me. Did she ever think of me? Did·she ever wonder about that little baby that she seemed to give up so easily? It made me even more upset to think about being so totally rejected by my own mother. If she hadn't given me up, I wouldn't have ended up at the Stabards' and had to endure sixteen years of hell. I was furious at her for giving me up, and furious at the Stabards – it was all so unfair and confusing. Why was my life like this?

When I felt very aggrieved and things got too much, I would go on a rampage. I would smash things up and the Stabards would do their usual dialling of 999 to get me taken back into psychiatric hospital. I began to feel like I was living in a world of revolving doors. I would be at home, taking it all on the chin, until it got too much, and then I would explode and would be turfed out of the house and off to hospital. There I would be drugged up or given ECT, and left to stew on a mixed adult ward full of very distressed people, until I had calmed down. In the ward nobody would talk to me – my drugs would just be altered or increased, and I'd lie in bed like a zombie, watching the clock, until it was time to leave. Then I'd be back out, back to the house and shed and the Stabards' abusive regime, and I'd be docile for a while, until the anger built up to unbearable rage and boiled over again. Round and round and in and out, I'd go. No wonder I was confused and anxious all the time.

Meanwhile, in my calmer periods, I tried a few more jobs caring for older people. I went back to the Job Centre every so often and sat in the soulless waiting room, took a ticket, talked to a bored counter clerk, who usually frowned at my file. I was inevitably sent to one old peoples' home after another. I didn't want to work with old people, but they kept sending me to those places, probably because it was what I did first time around on the YTS scheme. Each time I came up against the same problem. I would be asked to do some very personal hygiene things, and I just couldn't. I think the years of being pounced on by Mr Stabard had put me off getting too close to old people for life. Plus, the lack of privacy I had experienced made me very loath to touch someone else 'down there'. I just couldn't do it, and each time I would return to the Stabards' to face a beating, humiliation and, of course, further purification.

Then, after one of his particularly violent and humiliating I'll-teach-you-a-lesson-you-ungrateful-black-bitch sessions (conducted on the landing floor after being pulled upstairs by my hair by an irate Mr Stabard on my return from yet another failed job), something happened. It was something that would escalate my problems with the Stabards in a way I couldn't imagine as I starved and sobbed quietly in the airing cupboard for two days after the brutal rape. It was something that was going to change my life forever, and which would, in the short term at least, send me down into further depths of pain, confusion and despair – the like of which I had never experienced before.

19

Baby Blues

'It'll be very sad to see the cycle of deprivation repeat itself once again.' (NHS psychiatric notes: Dr Brown)

Mrs Stabard had the weirdest habit. If she wanted to know whether I had a period or not she would come up to the box room and pull my knickers down to have a look inside of them. She'd done this for as long as I could remember, so I was used to this indignity. She wouldn't say a word, she'd just point to me to yank my trousers down or dress up, pull down my knickers and peer into them. Or she'd just say 'show me' and I knew what she meant. If there was any blood she would give me a sanitary towel, just like that, without a word. I was used to her doing this strange degrading ritual, and thought nothing of it. I didn't really pay much attention when she started doing it quite a lot. She was always monitoring me anyway, always watching me with her dead eyes and following me around the house. Now I was on my own with the Stabards, I became very aware of how much she was interested in the condition of my knickers. She seemed desperate to know if there was any blood and when there wasn't she seemed very grumpy about it. I had no idea why – not at first, anyway.

One day – I must have been eighteen at this time – Mrs Stabard came into the box room early in the morning again and pointed for me to follow her. We went to the toilet together and she made me wee onto a white stick which had a little plastic window on one side. She stood behind the toilet door as I did it and said, 'Don't look, pass it to me.' I had no idea what it was for, but she took the stick away and didn't speak to me again that day. I was used to her quirky ways and I didn't really think much of it. I certainly was never included in any discussion about anything, so I forgot all about the bizarre incident. However, a few days later the three of us – we made the oddest triangle between us – went to the doctor's surgery together. Mrs Stabard told me beforehand what I had to say. She told me I had to say I'd found out that I was 'pregnant' – although I wasn't entirely sure what 'pregnant' meant exactly – and that I had to say that a boy I knew had done something bad to me. Because of that, I was to say that I didn't want him involved in the whole business. When I got to the doctor's, I was very apprehensive. Once we went in to see him, Mrs Stabard did most of the talking for me, saying I had been raped – I jumped when I heard the word – and that the boy was no good, but that I would keep the baby and the Stabards would look after it. When I heard her say 'the baby' I totally freaked. What baby? What had any of this got to do with having a baby?

Meanwhile, the doctor asked me to lie on his couch, behind some curtains, and he felt my belly. I didn't understand at all what was going on. He asked me to do a urine test, which I was very used to, as I always had urine infections. He tested the urine with another stick and wrote some things down and all the time my head was buzzing with fear and confusion. All the while, Mrs Stabard was talking to him about me over my head, as usual, like it was the most natural thing in the world. There was a total assumption that I would keep 'the baby', and there was no suggestion that it would be got rid of, like before. I was so shocked, and remember getting off the couch, feeling my legs trembling like jellies under me. What on earth was happening to me? What did it all mean? Would they take me to the horrible woman in the big house again?

After that, I felt sick in the mornings. It was a nausea that was similar to when Mr Stabard 'hurt' me, as I often felt sick afterwards. I felt very woozy, odd and hungry all the time. I noticed my body was changing too. My breasts got bigger – which fascinated him no end – and I got larger all over. I didn't want to get bigger as I already felt I had a weight problem and I didn't want to put on any more pounds. I was never sent to a class to understand what was happening to me, so I was full of fear and ignorance. It was like I was just a body, carrying Mr Stabard's baby, and it had nothing to do with me.

I must have found out I was pregnant just before Christmas time 1987, just as I turned nineteen, and by the New Year I felt something moving around inside of me. I totally freaked out. I had no idea what was going on and I really thought that the devil had grown in my belly, because I had been so bad. I made a link between what Mr Stabard had done to me (because I was evil) and the lump that was growing (which must be evil too). It sounds crazy, but I was terrified of what was growing in there, and simply wanted it all to be gone. I was so scared that I ran away one day. I ran and ran and then, when I was out of breath, I walked the streets of my market town with its leafy lanes for a very long time, feeling totally desolate and alone. When I returned in the evening Mr Stabard was waiting for me. As ever, he had drunk a lot. He grabbed me the minute I came in the door and started slapping and hitting me round the head. He didn't kick or punch me in the stomach like he usually did, but he slapped and hit me on the arms, legs and back.

The next day, when I saw the midwife at the clinic, she asked what my bruises were and how I'd got them, as I had loads by then. I looked like a black and blue punch-bag. Before I could breathe in or think what to say, I heard Mrs Stabard pipe up, 'Oh, that's Harmony's ex-boyfriend. He turned up and she let him in, so he hurt her once again.' The midwife nodded and tutted and wrote it all down and I just sat there thinking, 'This is crazy.' I wondered who was crazier, me, the Stabards, or the midwife – why did everyone believe my foster parents when they lied all the time? The midwife spoke to Mrs Stabard about putting me in a 'safe house' whatever that was, but Mrs Stabard assured her that it wouldn't be necessary as they were there for me. I was sitting there thinking, 'Yes, please. Please take me to a safe house – anywhere away from these dangerous people.'

I still didn't really know what exactly was moving around inside of me. I had no idea a baby moved as it grew, so I sincerely thought I had a devil inside every time I felt a kick. I had been so brainwashed over the years to think the worst thing possible about myself, so how could I have something inside of me that was actually good? People kept saying I was 'pregnant' but I didn't really understand what that word meant. At night I would lie awake, willing the devil inside of me to stop moving; I thought if it was still, I would be less evil. I would lie there, in the middle of the night, watching my stomach moving, like a possessed thing, and think something grotesque would burst out of it any minute – a bit like in the film *Alien,* which I saw a lot later. I thought whatever was inside would just break its way out of me, rip me apart, but I had no idea exactly what it was. It was evil and terrible, that's all I knew.

The Stabards had their grand plan and I was part of it – but definitely not in on it. I heard little bits and pieces of conversation if I listened at the lounge door, and I could tell that Mrs Stabard was quite excited. It was like I was carrying a baby for her – like I was a body for her husband to use to have a baby with – so I, as a person, counted for nothing. I was an envelope carrying some kind of package for her. Meanwhile, her husband carried on coming into my room to look at me all the time. He was very fascinated by my breasts which were now very large, and my belly, and he didn't leave me alone. He kept on pestering me at night, and wanting to do what he always did, and I didn't want him to, but I couldn't stop him. I felt so ashamed, with the devil inside of me, like I'd broken all the rules. I kept very quiet about what was happening to me, and hid away in their house. I didn't tell anyone that I was pregnant; not that there was anyone really to tell. I felt very lonely at this time and really missed having Hope to talk to. I wished she had been there – not that we spoke about things in depth, but because we would have gone out to the woods and laughed, or a look would have passed between us, and I would have known that she understood how I felt about the whole thing.

I was on medication throughout the pregnancy, and still feeling very angry. But the worst thing was being completely unprepared for what was going on. I didn't read any books about pregnancy or go to any classes. Nobody told me what to expect, or how to handle it all. I had no idea what happened to get the baby out – I was terrified of the whole experience. I hated my body, in all its largeness and unpredictability: I hated what was happening to me. I hated not understanding what was going on inside of me. I also hated it being part of *him*.

I ended up going into hospital because I had what they called 'pre-eclampsia'. I didn't know what that was, but I didn't feel very well at all. I felt dizzy and strange as if my whole body had been taken over, and the devil had got a grip on me, from the inside out. Then the pain started. This was now in August 1988. It was hot, and I was terribly uncomfortable. Mrs Stabard was there the whole time. I didn't ask her to be there, she just was there, like a big blob on a chair, watching me coldly. She wasn't interested in me at all, she just seemed very fixated on what was going to come out of my body. The pain was absolutely agonising, like nothing I'd experienced before in my life, and I was petrified. It went on and on and on, and eventually the baby was ripped out of what felt like my bottom and the doctor said I had to have stitches. I didn't know where the stitches were or what they did, I just knew that everything hurt too much and that I was exhausted. I fell asleep immediately afterward and when I came round, there was Mrs Stabard holding the baby and cooing over it. I couldn't get my head round it. After all that, there was now a baby in the world torn from my body, but somehow it still wasn't mine. Mrs Stabard took charge of the situation from the start, and tried to control every single thing that happened.

From the word go she accused me of not 'bonding' with the baby. Bonding? I didn't know what bonding meant! No mother had every loved me or held me in her arms. I'd never been nurtured and shown care and attention, so how was I supposed to know what to pass on to a newborn? I felt completely at sea and didn't trust the two people who were supposedly looking after me and my baby. All I knew was I felt tearful and exhausted. What on earth had happened to me? How was I going to be responsible for another human being when I had so little control over my own life? When I did get my hands on the baby, I looked down at this little perfect being, and it filled me with terror. It was completely dependent on me to look after it. How was I going to do that? I had no idea. I had no money, no training, no job, no security, no proper family behind me. The Stabards didn't want to adopt me. No-one had spoken to me about what was supposed to happen once the baby came out. How was I supposed to look after it? There was an assumption I'd just know what to do, but I had absolutely no idea.

Holding that little bundle in my arms I felt nothing but fear and resentment. How dare this little being come into the world and make me responsible for her? I'd had to protect Hope and Faith all my life. I'd always had to put others first, and look after everyone else's needs. And now I had a baby to look after twenty-four hours a day on top of dealing with everything else. Would I never be free? For years I'd protected my sisters as much as I could, and now I had to start again with this one. It all felt too much to bear.

Somehow a decision was made that right from the start the baby would be bottle-fed. I had milk in my breasts from day one, and as they ballooned bigger and bigger they hurt like hell. Nobody asked me if I wanted to breastfeed my baby. I didn't know how to or what was involved, but when the nurse came in she would hand Mrs Stabard a bottle, not me, and she would pick up the baby and feed her. It felt like Mrs Stabard had told the nurses that she was going to have the baby and I didn't want her. But that had never been discussed – not with me, anyway. I did feel very confused about the baby, as I didn't understand what I was getting into when I was pregnant, so once she was there, I was definitely overwhelmed. However, she was mine, not Mrs Stabard's, and I felt very mixed-up about who was doing what.

The more Mrs Stabard fussed over her, fed her, and cooed at her, the less connected I felt with my daughter. I didn't feel like she was mine to pick up or cuddle, or mine to feed. Nobody said to me, 'Harmony, you hold the baby this way, or you feed her that way.' I just sat there, watching Mrs Stabard do everything, feeling like I had nothing to do with the whole situation. I just felt exhausted and very out of it.

At the beginning it was as if Mrs Stabard did everything she could to keep us apart. She didn't want me to bond with the baby, whom I called Anna Bella, after one of the dolls I wished I'd been able to play with when I was a child. However, there were moments when I peered at Anna Bella, especially when she was asleep, when I was overwhelmed by the beauty of her little face and eyelashes. I couldn't believe that this gorgeous little thing had been tucked away inside of me all that time, rather than the devil. But my overriding emotion at that time was one of utter helplessness. I was full of mixed emotions, and unable to think straight. I think I was having a big dose of 'baby blues' and felt very detached from Anna Bella. I couldn't tell anyone how I felt because I was afraid the Stabards would snatch her away if I did, or the doctor would put me back in a mental hospital.

Once we were back at the house Mrs Stabard would not let me take Anna Bella for walks in the pram. Instead she would take her out and push her, like she was her own mother. My foster mother played silly games with Social Services and myself, pretending somehow that the baby was hers, but expecting me to do most of the care behind the scenes. Mrs Stabard wanted the nice bits – the cuddles and the feeds – but she didn't want to change her nappy or be woken up at night. I had to do that, in my usual servant role. Then when we went to register the baby's name, Mrs Stabard came with me and insisted Anna Bella's surname was Stabard-Brookes and not just my surname, Brookes. I didn't want this to happen, but Mrs Stabard insisted, and took over filling in the form. This made me even more confused. Whose baby was she? When I'd asked them to adopt me, they had said no. But now I had a child, they wanted to put their name on it, like it was theirs. It was clear: they didn't want me, but they did want the baby.

Gradually I began to twig that Mrs Stabard saw the baby as hers, since it was her husband's – albeit with me. She couldn't talk about it openly, or acknowledge it to anyone, as it was a twisted situation, but that was the truth. She saw me as a surrogate mother for 'their' baby, as if I was just a vehicle to provide them with another one of their own children. I didn't count as a person in my own right.

I have to be honest and say I didn't know what to think about the baby. I hadn't been prepared for her in the least, and now here she was, needing my attention all the time, being very vulnerable and crying, sleeping, pooing and feeding round the clock. Was this now the end of my youth? Was I ready to be a mother? Did I have what it took? Or was Mrs Stabard going to take her over from me and be her real mum? Would I be relieved if she did, or would I resist? When Anna Bella cried in the day Mrs Stabard would be there before I had time to cross the room, picking her up, and making me feel inadequate. Although I had looked after kids all my life when Mrs Stabard dumped them on me, I was not ready for the responsibility of motherhood myself. I was too young, too inexperienced. I needed help to be a good mother, but I didn't want help from the Stabards, who I thought were terrible parents. After all, look how they'd treated me and my sisters!

While I'd been in hospital having the baby they had taken the bunk bed down so there was just one bed in my room now, with a Moses basket for Anna Bella. Once we were back home Mr Stabard started coming in to me at night, just like before, as if nothing had changed. Even though I had been through childbirth, had stitches and had a new baby to look after, he would still come in drunk and expect to do his usual stuff with her in the room. I felt sickened by him. My breasts were still hard with milk for the baby, and he would suck them, drinking her milk. I hated him for that. He obviously didn't care that I was sore and exhausted, he just took what he wanted and rolled out the room. And then the baby would start crying, and I'd get no sleep at all.

But then one thing really started worrying me, making me extremely anxious. Mr Stabard started getting very interested in the baby. He wanted to be there when I changed her nappy and would stand there, staring at her for a long time, with his cold blue eyes, and I'd feel very strange. I didn't trust him at all, and I felt he was getting far too keen on her. I didn't know how to keep her safe from him. I didn't want him touching her, and yet he would stand over the basket, swaying slightly, licking his lips and drinking in her naked little body. It made me shudder to think what he was working up to. He kept saying, 'Let me hold the baby,' or 'Leave her with me,' but I wouldn't.

Then one evening I went to the toilet and when I came back into the box room I found him holding Anna Bella and trying to take her nappy off, for no reason. I grabbed her, which made her cry with shock, and lashed out at him. I felt like a tigress protecting her cub. How dare he touch her! He was revolting and I didn't want him anywhere near her. I told him to get out and shouted at him, and he slapped my face hard, cutting it with his signet ring. Next day I went to the doctor myself with Anna Bella, showed him the cut on my face and said my boyfriend had come round and had beaten me up – I don't know why I was still protecting the Stabards, but I guess I felt too scared of them to tell the truth. The doctor referred me straight away to a local women's refuge.

That very night we moved in. Anna Bella was just three months old. It was a dark, bitter, November night and I felt lonely and terrified taking my little bundle in her navy carrycot with me to a secret address. As I settled into our new room I felt like the most unprepared and inexperienced mother of a young baby that had ever been on earth – and I'm sure that it showed.

20

Turbulent Times

'Mum has rejected child – says she reminds her of the girl's father who had promised to marry her after the birth but now refuses to do so . . . ' (Women's refuge worker's notes)

Despite my best efforts I wasn't a 'natural' mother. I had no idea what I was doing. I felt awkward and scared, cack-handed and naïve. I resented the baby, especially as every time I looked at her, I saw *him. His face.* She looked the spitting image of Mr Stabard, and I hated the fact that she was the result of one of his horrible night attacks. How could I feel anything else? Even so, I felt protective of her. She was just a little baby, after all. There were moments when I looked at her and my heart would melt, and I would see her little fingers and toes, and just want to put my arm round her. It was all very confusing.

However, the refuge was warm, clean and friendly. I was in a room with bunk beds and for a moment I was filled with fear that it would be the same regime as at home. Here I was watched all the time, just like I was at home, but in a different way. At least at the refuge I could go and sit in the lounge or go to the kitchen (they weren't out of bounds like at the Stabard's), but there always seemed to be someone there with a clipboard making notes about what I was doing. I had made a story up which I was sticking to. Mrs Stabard had started it all off with the tale she'd told at the doctor's originally about the violent boyfriend who raped me. Not knowing what else to do, I continued the myth of the boyfriend, knowing all the time that the very person we were both talking about was the man who was supposed to be my foster father and Mrs Stabard's own husband. That seemed very weird, but the doctor, the hospital staff, and the refuge people had 'bought' the story, so I continued to sell it.

The truth was that I felt so confused I didn't know which way was up. I had not set out to be a mother at eighteen, but now I was one I had to deal with it. I certainly had never wanted a baby with my foster father, but he had raped me so many times I'd lost count – probably thousands of times. And as I had been having periods for nine years now it was not surprising that eventually something happened. But now the outcome of the abuse would be with me for the rest of my life. How on earth was I going to deal with that? The baby tied me to him for ever, which is precisely why Mrs Stabard was trying to get in the way and take over. She wanted to prove to everyone that I was a stupid, crazy girl who hadn't bonded with her child. Well, in a way she was right, because I hadn't really bonded as yet, and I was feeling very powerless about how to look after this little thing that was now solely in my hands. I couldn't even look after myself properly, let alone a new baby.

Because Mrs Stabard had done so much for Anna Bella, I wasn't very skilled at things once I got to the refuge. They soon noticed. For instance, when I went to make a cup of coffee I carried the baby under my arm like a rugby ball, while I poured hot water into my mug. They were horrified and sat me down and told me I was doing it all wrong. I was upset; I'd actually put her under my arm to protect her. But they had to teach me how to hold the baby, to cradle her in my arms properly, and then how to put her down and go and make my tea. I felt very defensive and embarrassed, worried that people were always having a go at me and making out I was stupid; or else making notes about my every move. However, they obviously had a point and I had to learn the hard way how to do things the right way.

I also hadn't been making Anna Bella's bottles up – Mrs Stabard had been doing that. She made me feel like I couldn't begin to get it right, so I had left it to her. When I made up Anna Bella's feeds at the refuge I don't think I did it right, so she started to lose weight. The refuge got worried, and the baby was put on a 'failure to thrive' list, which meant she was in danger. Again, I felt terrible. I was trying to do my best for the poor little thing, but I was probably inept at making her feeds and forgot what to do a lot of the time. I was also still on about thirty tablets a day of different anti-depressant and anti-psychotic drugs. These made me very numb and forgetful. I think they also made it hard for me to be emotionally aware as it felt like I was trapped in a sort of rubber suit all the time, removed from the world. I'm not sure whether Anna Bella's failure to thrive was due to my not paying her enough attention, and not being able to respond to her needs, or whether, with so little experience of maternal care, I wasn't able to make her feel really loved and secure.

I just didn't 'read' my daughter's needs and demands very well. I think I also still had the 'baby blues' during the three or four months I was in the refuge, which nobody really picked up on, because I was already thought of as being 'depressed'. My depression was really anger at my situation and if I wasn't a model mother sometimes it was because I couldn't bear all the responsibility. I'd been looking after children for most of my life, and now I had to look after one that had been thrust upon me. To make matters worse, some days she didn't really feel like mine, as she was the product of something so painful. So in those early days it was hard not to reject her – at least at first.

Yet, despite all this jumble of terribly mixed-up and painful feelings, a new emotion started to emerge gradually. I found myself feeling very tender towards my daughter. I began to look at her, and see a little sweet face, with gorgeous fingers and toes. I began to want to hold her close, to rock her and protect her. These feelings came and went, alongside the other feelings of annoyance and frustration, anger and resentment. I didn't want any harm to come to her – not a jot – but I didn't know if I wanted to have her with me for the rest of my life. At the same time, Mrs Stabard started putting pressure on me to come home. She wanted us both back, she said, when in fact, she just wanted the baby back and me to do the work. She would call and beg me down the phone: 'Please come home, we need to see the baby.' I was very confused as to what to do. Part of me was pleased to be wanted, even though I knew it was just for the baby. I was stupidly tempted.

However, I did learn some things from the refuge. Although it was very tough going to be totally responsible for the baby all the time, and to have to hold my own amongst total strangers, I did begin to learn more about the world. I watched other mothers with their babies and learned from them. There were a lot of mixed race and black women with terrible life stories, so I didn't feel entirely alone in that respect. I didn't talk about my history, as I didn't have the words yet. I didn't know where to start and I didn't think anyone would believe me anyway. I also didn't really trust anyone enough to tell them the truth. It was such a messy tale. Where would I begin if I tried to tell where my baby had really come from? I carried the shame for us all, somehow. If I finally spoke out, would I be blamed and shamed?

Meanwhile Mr Stabard was sending me messages, through Mrs Stabard, that if I didn't bring Anna Bella home soon he would cause me big trouble. He knew how to pull my strings, even at a distance, and after four months we went back to the Stabards' house. Again, I could have broken free at this point, I could have disappeared from the refuge to somewhere else, far away, and never gone back, but I couldn't imagine doing it then. It's hard to explain what a hold the Stabards had over my mind. The brainwashing I had had for years left me feeling completely in their power. When Mr Stabard threatened me I felt like I had to comply with what he wanted without question. I imagined he could come and get me from the refuge or steal away the baby, who I was beginning to really bond with, so I felt it was better to go there myself.

What a huge mistake I made. The minute I got back Mr Stabard was more interested in Anna Bella than ever. He was no longer so bothered about me which was a relief at first. But he was showing a very unhealthy interest in his daughter. She had by now been put on a Child Protection Register because of her failure to thrive. She still wasn't putting on a huge amount of weight, although she was improving slowly. However, once I was back home with Anna Bella, Mr Stabard started leering at her in her cot, and hanging about telling me to take her nappy off. He wanted to see her naked all the time. I just wanted to protect her. I was frightened I would lose her, frightened he would do something to her and the way he kept hanging over the cot, drooling over her, kept stirring up terrible memories in me.

It felt like everything was coming to the boil. Mr Stabard's constant pawing at the baby made me feel so angry that I thought was going to burst. I had to keep the lid on my temper, otherwise I would lose Anna Bella, and so I began to feel suicidal, like I just wanted to smash myself into pieces. I struggled against these feelings as I knew I couldn't do anything to myself and keep the baby. However, a month after I returned to the Stabards I took an overdose – only a small one, about fifteen paracetamol, but enough to get me back into hospital. It was a desperate cry for help, the only one I knew how to make. They recommended I saw a psychiatrist and I found myself getting sucked back into the mental health system. I badly wanted to keep out of it, for Anna Bella's sake, but just after the overdose they took her into care for a few weeks while I recovered. I think they thought the Stabards were too old to look after a baby on their own as they were in their late sixties now, and I was unbelievably relieved.

However, once I was back home with them after a few weeks away, and yet again, reunited with Anna Bella, Mr Stabard started hanging around all over again. It wasn't me he was interested in at all now; it was the baby, in a way that made me both sick and furious. One afternoon, in the Spring of 1989, he came up to the box room and was hanging over the cot, looking down at Anna Bella. I was waiting for the health visitor to come for a check-up. The baby was beginning to put some weight on and he kept asking, 'Are you going to change her nappy?' I just knew he wanted to see her naked body, he wanted to look at her 'down there' and I feared I knew exactly what he had in mind. I didn't trust him one bit having seen him with so many children over the years. I remembered the chocolate business starting as far back as I could remember. I had flashbacks of those early days in the shed, or in the bath when the water turned red, when he would shove the chocolate into me and push it in and out brutally until I was ripped and bleeding. I remembered the creepy bouncing games on his lap, and the hard object underneath. I could feel all those times he put his fingers in me and hurt me hard.

I looked at my baby and I saw red. I launched myself at him. I thumped him and kicked him and scratched his face. I screamed at him to leave her alone. I said, 'I'm gonna tell everybody what you've been doing to me here. I know what you want to do to her, and I'm not going to let you. Y'hear?'

It was like a major panic attack, like I had looked over a cliff and seen how far down it was and realised I didn't want to fall. I knew what he would do to her, because that's what he did with young children, and now perhaps even his own. I picked her up and held her protectively in my arms shouting out at him, 'You're not having her, you're not having her.' I didn't want him anywhere near her. I felt sick, I needed him to get away immediately, so I pushed and kicked him out of the room and barricaded myself in. I could be very violent when unleashed. I was hysterical. I pushed all the furniture I could against the door. I had to protect the baby against him – against him doing to her what he had done to me all my life. I knew I hadn't been the mother I was supposed to be, and I wasn't really good enough for Anna Bella, but the one thing I knew I had to do was protect her from all the horror of the pain, degradation and humiliation I'd been through in my childhood. I didn't want her to be brainwashed into thinking she was evil, or that she had to be 'purified'. I couldn't bear the idea of her going through all the terror of the constant raping that I had been through. It was a nightmare and I was trying to protect her from becoming another of Mr Stabard's helpless victims.

The next thing I knew, the door was being banged on and a man's loud voice was shouting: 'Open up, Police.' I was absolutely terrified. I went over to the window where I could see a light flashing in the road and there was a police car and an ambulance outside, and there were paramedics and police talking to the Stabards. Mr Stabard was talking and pointing up to the box room, shaking his head, and I could imagine all the lies that he was telling. He was pointing to his face and I imagined him showing his scratches and saying I was 'crazy' and that I had launched myself at him in an 'unprovoked attack'. My place, as always, was in the wrong. Where else? I was mad and bad.

Again I heard a knock at the door.

'Harmony, open up.' It was a softer voice this time. A woman. Not Mrs Stabard. I waited.

'Harmony, you need to let me in. Is the baby OK?'

I looked down at Anna Bella. I was holding her tight in my arms and she looked a little scared, or was I imagining it? I thought, 'What shall I do, what's for the best?' The voice came again.

'Harmony, listen, we can talk about it . . . just open the door.'

I was eventually persuaded to open the door. I didn't want to hurt the baby. Reluctantly, I pulled the furniture away from the door with one hand, bit by bit, holding Anna Bella carefully to me in the crook of my other arm. I didn't want to let her go. He might get his filthy mitts on her if I left her for so much as a second. I opened the door just a crack, very carefully, and there was a policewoman and a woman paramedic. As the door opened, it was pulled open wide as the policewoman was talking at me. Although I couldn't really understand what she was saying a paramedic stepped forward and took the baby out of my arms. Meanwhile another got behind me and I felt the inevitable sting in my behind. The next thing I knew: nothingness.

21

The Truth Will Out

'I have confirmed that Harmony suffers from a mental disorder which renders her unfit to have the care of the child'
(Social worker's notes)

When I came round in the hospital I was very confused. At first I couldn't work out where I was, or what had happened. My first thought was for the baby – where was she? A panic gripped my heart and I looked around me, at my single bed, at the psychiatric patients wandering around and pulling their hair, or lying in their own beds, moaning and groaning, and couldn't imagine what had happened to her. What had they done with her? My baby! Where is my baby? I tried to get out of bed, but my legs were like rubber, my head hurt and I felt very woozy and sick. I fell back on the pillows, distraught. What on earth had happened to me? And then I remembered the whole dreadful scene with the paramedics and the police – but Anna Bella had been with me then . . . and the paramedic had taken her away from me. So where was she?

Eventually a nurse wafted by and I tried to grab her attention, but failed. Then another came and took my pulse and temperature. I demanded to know where my baby was, but the nurse just said she was safe and resting. I was very confused. I lay back for a moment, staring at the ceiling, but then I was gripped by panic. Was she back with the Stabards? If she was, how could she be safe? I called out for the nurse and tried to get her to tell me where my baby was – and I realised she must be back with them.

. . . I know exactly what he will be doing. He will be creeping in . . . pulling down the blanket and taking off her nappy . . . and . . . I just want to scream, to shout, to cry, to get someone to understand what we are dealing with here. The nurse stands over me and, with a cool expression, makes me take my tablets. There's about thirty of them, and I swallow them down, shaking all the while. At this very moment, he might be touching her, hurting her, and I'm stuck in this bed, unable to protect her. My job, as her mother, is to protect her. I have to look after her, I don't want the same things to happen to her that have happened to me all my life, and that happened to every other black child that has got within inches of Mr Stabard. But how can I get someone to understand?

When the nurse is gone I make a plan. No-one realises that I am always making plans. I have to double-think everyone all the time. If I think they want something from me, I give it to them, then they will take me seriously. For instance, when the nurse comes up and says, 'Do you hear voices, dear?' I say, 'Yeah, I do. I hear voices.' I think she means, in my head, when no-one's talking. But the thing is, I don't hear voices. I just say I do, and then the nurse looks pleased. She goes away and comes back with an injection, or more pills, and I sort of feel I am playing the 'pleasing people' game.

What I do see, however is his face. I see his cold blue eyes, staring at me with hatred and lust. All the time. I see his face bending over me, his boozy breath stinking as he grunts and satisfies himself, without any concern for me. That's what

I hear, what I see, what I smell, all the time. When I close my eyes, trying to sleep, his face is there. Sometimes I wake up with a start in my crisp hospital bed and I feel shock and terror. I think I see his face and it is inches from mine, sweating, panting, and staring down at me, hurting me with his 'thing' like he always does. He shoves it into me and rapes me until he has his fill. I am just a lump of flesh to him, a hole to fill, and he has his way with me and then goes off, not even interested if I am well or ill, awake or asleep, hurting or happy or anything at all. I am just a woman's body with holes in for him to have what he wants. And all the time he is hating me. All the time he loathes my black flesh, he hates my eyes and Sellotapes them down, and can't get enough of my hated black breasts. These are the pictures in my head. I can 'hear' his voice telling me I'm pure evil, a black bitch or an ugly 'wog'. That's what I can hear. Is this what the staff want to hear about?

As I lie in the hospital, fretting for my baby, I make a plan. I have to get them to understand how desperate I am. I don't want to go back to the Stabards, but I also don't want to stay here, in this mental hospital. I want my baby back and I need to show them how upset and hurt I am. When nobody is looking I manage to get some tablets. I have a little money in my bag and I put on my dressing gown and I go down the corridor. Nobody sees me. I have my slippers on, and my dressing gown, and I pad to the lift. I press the button to call it, looking down at the floor. Nurses go past looking at their papers; an orderly goes past pushing a mop. I am a young black woman in dressing gown and slippers and nobody pays me any attention. When I get to the bottom, I follow signs to reception, then I go through the big doors and I see there is a newsagents just outside. I go in, still in my dressing gown and slippers and buy some aspirin. The shop keeper looks at me oddly, but gives me the pills anyway. He's used to mental patients, I guess. I then retrace my steps and am soon back in my bed. I take the pills slowly, one by one, with water until the packet is empty.

Later I come round, feeling very ill. I am on a drip. I have a sore throat. A nurse comes up and looks at the drip and twiddles with it. She then looks at me, a bit sternly.

'OK?'

I don't reply. I gesture that my throat is sore.

'We had to pump your stomach. How d'you get them?'

I don't answer. She moves away. I close my eyes. Plan didn't work too well. I sort of imagined they would come running and then I would be able to explain – you see you have left my baby with a man who has raped me since I was a baby. That's why I'm here ... being told I'm a mad woman who hears voices. In fact, it's not only me who's been abused, but it's countless kids like me. There's my two sisters – one has probably died now, and the other, well, she's gone off the rails and onto drink and drugs and boys. Anyway, there's been loads of other kids who could tell you about my foster father. He likes having sex with kids, you see. And I'm worried he's going to start on my daughter. By the way, did you realise my daughter is his, too? No, it's not the product of me and some boy I picked up, as it says in my notes. No, it's actually the product of a rape, by my wonderful foster father.

All this is going through my head. These are the 'voices'. The truth. How can I say it? Who will listen to me? Who will believe me? I take an overdose – as I have done several times, and as I will go on to do many more times – because I want someone to listen. But, I am sorry to say, it has the opposite effect. Instead, the drugs are increased. And I'm given ECT which eliminates my mind, my memory. And so I am back to square one. Another square one ... another purification of sorts ...

A month after the overdose I was reunited with Anna Bella and put in a mother and baby unit at a local general hospital to be observed. Someone was always watching me. Another person with a clipboard making notes. I spent a lot of time trying to work out if he had done something to the baby yet. Some days I would look at her and feel detached, remote and angry. Her little face would remind me of his, and I wouldn't want to look at her. Then I would think, 'That's not fair. She's my baby – it's not her fault they made me have her.' Then I would remember to pick her up, and give her a cuddle. That's what mummies are supposed to do, aren't they? I would stroke her hair, and make sure she was washed, and feed her a bottle. I would enjoy that, so would she.

Sometimes I would look at her, and wonder what on earth I was going to do with this little bundle. I could hardly look after myself, let alone another human being. How was I going to cope with motherhood? How was I going to protect her?

And then, against my will, I was sent back to the Stabards, with loads of pills and instructions to be grateful that I had a home with good foster parents, and that I had to learn to control my temper. I was clearly just someone who heard voices and had a bad temper. The new medication made me feel paralysed, like I was frozen, and couldn't move my face or body. Taking it meant walking around, feeling like a zombie. Back at the Stabards' I was fearful and tense.

Meanwhile Mrs Stabard kept trying to take over the baby again. I would have just got used to looking after her on my own, and would be beginning to feel more comfortable about the whole thing, and then she'd swipe the baby away and feed her, or take her out in the pram without telling me. And then I'd come into the box room and find her husband hovering over the cot, lifting the blanket and peering at Anna Bella with that leering, drooling look I knew only too well. Then I'd want to kill him – I'd rush in and shove him out the way, and grab her out of the cot and she would cry, startled awake by my fear. He would sneer at me and give me a look that said, 'I'll get her, you just wait, black bitch.' I'd just hold her close, feeling desperate, not knowing how on earth I was going to get through all of this and get her away from these people.

One night I got scared of what he might do to her, and me. I was lying awake in the box room, and she was in her cot. I must have nodded off, and came to with him swaying over the cot. I jumped out of bed and shouted at him to get away. I was terrified. He tried to grab me then, and I managed to fight him off. It was terrible, a real tussle in the middle of the night, with the baby screaming in the background. She must have been about six months then. I got dressed, grabbed her, and before I left the house, I took a load of pills. It was all I could think of to do in my warped, fearful way of thinking. Then we went out into the night. I pushed her in her buggy, and as I walked along in the early hours of the morning, I've never felt more desperate. I wanted to just fall down and sleep forever, but I kept pushing the buggy until she calmed down. I walked into the centre of town – it must have been about three in the morning – and a police car drew up alongside us. They asked me what I was doing, and I said I was taking the baby for a walk . . . but that I'd taken some tablets.

They put us both in the car and took us back to the local general hospital. I had my stomach pumped yet again and we were back in a mother and baby unit. The social worker was sitting there when I came round, with the curtains closed round the bed. She asked me, in a kind voice, why I was taking my baby for a walk in the middle of the night having downed a load of tablets. Didn't I know how dangerous it was, putting us both at risk? While she was talking she put her hand over mine. I looked at her face – it was kind, she looked nice – and I finally found the words:

'He hurts me.'

She looked at me and didn't say anything at first. She squeezed my hand.

'What do you mean?'

'I've got to protect her, from him.'

She looked worried then and leant forward towards me.

'Does he do something he shouldn't?'

I nodded. Hot tears started scalding down my cheeks. I couldn't stop them. I nodded and sobbed. I'd held it back for so long, now I couldn't keep it in any more.

'I don't want something to happen to Anna Bella.'

The social worker wrote something down.

'Can you take her into care?'

She looked up at me, surprised.

'Why Harmony?'

I couldn't explain that I didn't feel confident enough to look after her myself, or able to protect her from him, and at the same time, I knew I didn't want her to be at the Stabards'. I was in such a state I didn't know what was possible and what wasn't.

I felt relieved that the truth was finally out, but scared about what would happen as a consequence. I remembered the horrible Mr Venetti and the beating after the Raj and Prathi meeting. If Mr Stabard knew I'd told on him, he'd kill me. As it was, nobody did anything. Amazingly, although this social worker told me she believed me, nothing was done. I didn't know if I was relieved or not. Sometimes I wanted him punished, other times I was relieved that nothing had got worse. I felt alone in the world and scared about what would happen if it all came out in the open. I was confused that the police didn't arrest him, and that no-one asked me to do anything, and the hospital and Social Services just kept sending me back to the Stabards, like before.

It was 1989 when I finally spoke up about the Stabards but absolutely nothing was done about it. It was written down on my record – as I have read it since – but nothing was set in motion to change anything. He wasn't arrested or questioned. In fact, he was soon to be given an award by the local authority for Thirty Years of Service as a Foster Father. He was in all the papers, receiving his award, smiling at the camera. He was clapped on the back and people toasted him with wine and beer, and said what a great job the Stabards had done for all those poor disadvantaged, black children that nobody else wanted. He was praised at the church, he was cheered at the British Legion. And meanwhile, I was bouncing in and out of mental hospital, swallowing pills, and trying desperately to keep my daughter out of his clutches. I had begun to tell the truth about Mr Stabard, but still no-one believed me. And even if they did, no-one did anything – which then made me think, 'What was the point of saying anything, when we're still going to be sent back to live with them?'

A pattern emerged during the first year of Anna Bella's life. I would go back to the Stabards and he would be sniffing around the baby, so I would do something desperate, like take an overdose, and then the Stabards would call the police and I'd be sectioned, and Anna Bella would be left behind with them. Of course this would make me even more desperate and likely to do something self-destructive. Sometimes Anna Bella would be taken into another foster home for a while, which would make me feel relieved, but I would miss her so much I would ask for her back.

I was caught in a terrible trap. Everybody seemed to think I was 'crazy' and that I was a threat to the Stabards, the baby and myself. I think I was behaving crazily, too, as I didn't know what else to do. Every time I tried to get some attention – the only way I knew how – the Stabards would call the police and I'd end up back inside hospital. Everyone would look at me and say I was an unfit mother, that I was paranoid and schizo. This exactly echoed what the Stabards had said to me all of my life about being evil. I felt everyone thought I was the problem, and absolutely no-one understood why I had the difficulties I did. I had no power, no voice and nobody was listening to me. I would see the psychiatrist, usually a man in a suit or a white coat, who would come round and ask me things. He would never say, 'Tell me what it's like at home?' Rather, it was all about whether I heard voices or not. I wanted to scream at him, 'You don't understand what's happened to me,' but where would I start?

After a few months the council finally offered me a flat in the town and I moved in with Anna Bella. At first it was great. We were in our own little place and I began to learn how to look after my daughter properly. I was beginning to feel very fond of her, and loved to hold her and watch her smile and respond to things. I wasn't always a good mother though. I was forgetful sometimes as the drugs made me very slow in my responses. Sometimes I put her on the bed and she rolled off, and once I put her in a bath for a few seconds when it was too hot. I didn't mean to, but I did make mistakes. If the social worker saw it, or heard about it, there would be a flurry of people coming round and observing me, asking me questions and telling me off. They always wrote on their clipboards. I had to go to a day centre, so they could watch me and make sure I learned to do things properly.

All that was fine, as I knew I needed to learn how to be a good mother, and I wanted to be one. But no-one had told me that they had given Mr Stabard a key to our flat, since somehow they believed that he still had some connection with me despite my telling of his abuse. One night, I woke up to find him standing in our bedroom, leaning over the bed where I was sleeping with Anna Bella next to me. I screamed out. The baby woke up and started screaming too. He'd let himself in while we were asleep, he tried to grasp the baby and grab at my breasts and I had to kick and punch him off. He eventually left, swearing at me and saying he'd kill me.

I was shaking like a leaf, and no longer felt safe in the flat. In the end I took some tablets to try to calm myself down, put Anna Bella in the pushchair and started walking round the town – again in the early hours of the morning. I just wanted the tablets to numb me out, to blank out the panic and the fear. I went to a park I knew and sat on the bench. It was pitch black and I could see the stars and the moon which were calming. Somehow it reminded me of Wildflower Woods, of being in the soft embrace of nature. I felt safer, more serene, when I was surrounded by trees and grass. I sat on the bench; it was cold, but I didn't care. I could breathe out here. Our little safe haven of a flat was no longer safe, as Mr Stabard had access to it. He could let himself in and do things to us, at any time – and I could do absolutely nothing about it. He could rape and kill us and no-one would even know.

It came to me, in a flash, that I would never be free of the Stabards. As I sat on the bench, in the cold and the dark, hearing the wind whispering in the trees above and watching Anna Bella sleep, all snuggled up in her buggy, I realised I would never be able to get free of this man who had ruined my life. The only thing I could do was save my daughter's life. Somehow, I had to keep her free of him. It didn't matter what happened to me now. But it did matter what happened to her. I had to keep him off her, even if I had to use desperate measures to do that. When a policeman eventually found us, I was nearly unconscious, but she was fast asleep and we were taken into the local hospital. I told them I had felt like hitting the baby and so she was taken into care. It was the only way I could protect her – tell them the lies that they could understand. No-one was doing anything at all to help when I told them the truth – so lying was my only real option. In a mad world, I clearly had to do mad things in order for us to survive.

22

Sucked into the System

'*Harmony now clearly likes her daughter and is physically close to her. Anna Bella likes to snuggle into Harmony when she is tired or upset and will always look to check that Harmony is close by. She recognises her voice and footsteps and will giggle and coo freely at Harmony. There is good eye contact, Harmony will smile and talk and responds to her demands, comes prepared with nappies and clothes and takes pride in her achievements and appearance.*' (Social worker's report)

I was my own worst enemy. My strategy for getting people to take me seriously was to act out against my own best interests. I often felt so frustrated, so pent-up with fury and powerlessness, that I felt I had to do desperate things to get people to take me at my word. I didn't feel like I had ever been listened to properly. Instead I had been labelled 'crazy', and that was how people saw me. That and all those other nasty words: ugly, fat, stupid, wog. Now I had begun to admit to one social worker a little bit about what was happening at home, I started having horrific nightmares and flashbacks all the time. It was like opening Pandora's box – everything was beginning to fly out. I kept seeing Mr Stabard's face all the time; that horrible, overbearing, staring face coming at me in the dark. It was like he was a Bogey Man and he half-scared me to death. I couldn't bear to have the light off at night. I was like a child myself.

However, after a year of bouncing in and out of hospital, back to the Stabards, out to a flat, back to a hospital, then to new accommodation or a women's refuge, I had begun to bond with my daughter. I'd made some terrible mistakes in the first few months, and had battled with all sorts of emotions. Becoming a mother was a steep learning curve for me, but by the time Anna Bella was nearing her first birthday I was much more comfortable in my new role. I still had many obstacles to overcome. I had no job, no money, and was very dependent on others. I had very few skills, apart from the obvious ones of cooking and cleaning, as I used to do for the Stabards. My education was limited and I had no idea what I could do in the world. I also had had so little exposure to normal life that I found it difficult to imagine how I would make my way in the world, earning a living, running a flat, making friends, having a social life or (God forbid) a sex life. I was dependent on doctors, hospitals and social workers and was living on handouts. I had no idea what it would be like to be truly independent and able to make choices for myself and my lovely daughter.

What happened during this first year of Anna Bella's life was that I would become depressed and suicidal every time I went back to the Stabards or had any contact with them. Then, when I was alone, I would be anxious that he might find us and break in, like he had done to my safe haven flat. Or days would go by and I wouldn't see anyone other than the baby and I would begin to feel claustrophobic. I wasn't coping very well, but I also didn't really trust anyone, and I was very isolated.

I missed my sisters very much at this time, and wished they had been there to share the baby with me. We would have had fun going out to the woods together, and I would have loved to have had some of our riotous birthday celebrations and dances under the moon, with Anna Bella and her two 'aunties'. Hope and Faith were the only two people in the whole world who, I felt, understood me in any way at all. Only they had been through the Stabard life – if you could call it that – and only they would understand what hell on earth it had been. They understood what had made me like I was – no-one else did.

I was unprepared for life and when I panicked I would want Social Services to take the baby and put her with a proper family. Then I would worry – what if they were just like the Stabards? Could I trust that any foster parents actually treat children well? After all, the council had just rewarded the Stabards with a huge prize despite all the pain they had subjected their foster children to. Then I would fear the social workers would trick me, and send Anna Bella back to the Stabards, despite me asking them not to. It was a terrifying time. I must have seemed mad to those in authority as I changed my mind a lot. I just didn't know what was right, or what I should do, or which way to turn. I wanted a kind parent or nice understanding person to tell me, 'Harmony, do this, then it will all be fine,' – just like the good fairy in the Cinderella story. I needed someone to guide me, to help us. Only I didn't know if I could trust anyone; or even if anyone in the world was actually trustworthy.

The other thing, which didn't do me any favours, was that I had become quite addicted to hospital. Not to the horrible mental hospital – which I never, ever liked – but to going to the ordinary local hospital, where they had nice clean sheets, and they cooked your food and took the worry off my shoulders. It was like I was looking for a good family to look after me. I developed a terrible habit of taking overdoses as a way of trying to get into hospital for a respite from either the Stabards (when we ended up back there) or from struggling on on my own in a soulless flat.

I'm not proud of owning up to this part, but I also think I got hooked on the idea of taking tablets; particularly as they numbed out all feelings for a while. It was a relief to take them, perhaps in the same way as an alcoholic feels relief when they get drunk and go into oblivion. When I took an overdose, it was a desperate cry for help. I seldom took enough for it to be potentially fatal, although I did once or twice, when I really meant it. Mostly I was saying to the authorities, 'Help, I can't cope. I need someone to listen to me.' It was the only way I could find of trying to get some attention for our plight.

Of course taking pills backfired – badly. There was a social worker in the council who decided to campaign to totally relieve me of my role as Anna Bella's mother. To be fair to this woman, Margaret Vallelly, she was doing what she thought was best. She was new to my case and when she saw my notes, and met me, she obviously thought she had to protect the child first and foremost. *From me.* I must have seemed like someone completely out of control and she didn't like me at all. I didn't like her either. She always looked at me like I was something the dog brought in, and she clearly didn't think I was a capable mother. I was so bombed out on my prescribed drugs that I must have seemed a bit slow and zombie-like.

However, I did love my daughter, and by the time she was a year old, I was beginning to get real enjoyment out of being with her. Every day she was doing new things and I felt proud. She had finally put on enough weight, and was sitting up, then crawling and was now trying to stand up. I was amazed to see how she was becoming a real little character, and she also looked very lovely, with deep brown chocolate eyes, and a sweet little face. She had dark curls and was becoming a toddler in front of my eyes; a real little girl with her own personality. I felt I had got past the shock of the beginning of her life and that we were now moving forward together.

By the time Anna Bella was nearing three years of age, two major things were happening. First, Margaret Vallelly, had decided she would end the situation for good by insisting that Anna Bella be adopted. Secondly, I was assigned a new psychiatrist, a woman who had come from outside the area to a new post, who had a completely different view of my case. These two things happening at the same time would set things on a collision course, as the social worker would want to take Anna Bella away from me, while the psychiatrist felt she should stay with me.

Meanwhile, I was being sucked further and further into the system, and the future for my daughter and myself was being decided by people who still knew nothing about the truth of the situation. Worse, in the case of the social worker, she was not interested in what had happened to me – after all, there were already notes on file about my accusations of abuse, which had sat there for three years without anyone doing anything about them. Margaret Vallelly was only interested in the child. In her view, I was a bad, mad mother and my daughter would be much happier with a steady, happy home elsewhere. She may never have said this to me directly, but everything she did, from the minute she came into the job in 1991, was focused on taking my daughter away from me.

Meanwhile, something extraordinary was happening

with the new psychiatrist, Jacqueline Brown. When I first met her, I was struck by the fact that she was very different from all the others. She was a woman in her late twenties (most of the others had been men in their fifties or older) and she was quite stern and brisk in her manner. Dr Brown was straight-talking and straight-dealing and she didn't beat around the bush. She told me, in no uncertain terms, that I had to stop messing about with overdoses. It was like she sussed me out straight away, which was quite unnerving. I think she could see that there was something going on that was making me take the pills as a cry for help – although I wasn't telling her (or anyone else) why I was doing it all the time. She was very straight with me, and told me I had to shape up. If I wanted to keep my daughter, I had to play ball with her. At first, I was furious. Here was another person telling me what to do. How dare she! I felt – wrongly, as it turned out – that she didn't understand what was going on with me.

In actual fact, Dr Brown turned out to be my biggest ally and my greatest saviour. She looked through all of my case notes afresh and she began to notice things which no-one else had noticed. She saw something obvious which everyone else had studiously ignored. Dr Brown noticed that I had spoken about abuse three years earlier to a social worker – and yet I was being sent back to the very same foster father who I said had abused me. Why was that? Why indeed? Dr Brown began to ask difficult questions and told me I had to think about coming off my medication to help my case.

She explained that if I wanted to keep my daughter, and not let her be adopted, then I would have to prove that I could look after her well. To do that I would have to stop taking overdoses and I would have to get off my drugs. Dr Brown said she thought the drugs weren't really helping me at all. In fact, she thought they were making me worse. Too right! All they did was make my mind feel like porridge which had been left out to go soggy in the rain. Why on earth was she the first person – the only person – to question my treatment?

However, the path was not a clear one, and it was going to be long and winding. It was not like I could do what she wanted overnight. I was too set in my cycle of reacting and overreacting, and it would take me a very long time to be able to trust her enough to take her sound advice. This is where I was my own worst enemy.

Meanwhile, I got a letter telling me that the council was now vigorously pursuing a 'freeing order' which would leave the path clear for them to get my daughter adopted. It was almost as if at the very moment when I was beginning to straighten up, with someone fighting on my side, the council was pressing ahead to snatch my daughter away. I couldn't believe it and it sent me into a tailspin. I decided I wanted to fight, with Dr Brown's help, but what I didn't realise, or calculate well enough, was how much power the authorities would have when they set their minds on doing something like taking a child away from its mother – especially if they deemed her both bad and mad. I also didn't realise how difficult it would be for me to clean up my act. Each shock wave about imminent adoption would throw me into a panic, which in turn made me want to overdose as a desperate act of protest. I felt like I was being sucked further into the system with every day that passed.

23

The Milky Way Kid

'Harmony has negative feelings about herself being black. She is also aware of her daughter being with foster carers who are white, and the possibility of repeating her own experiences and feelings in that situation . . . ' (Social worker's report)

While all this was going on – the tussles over whether I should keep Anna Bella, or whether she should be adopted; the wrangles as to where I should live and with whom; the battles between how Social Services saw me (bad and mad) and the way the psychiatrist did (hurt and self-harming) – something else incredible happened. I'd made a vow to Dr Brown that I would try to work at the things I needed to in order to convince the authorities that I could keep my child. This meant stopping the self-harming, including the repeated overdoses, and not running away. Usually if the pressure got too much, I would find myself hopping on a bus with Anna Bella in tow, and trying to start a new life somewhere else, only to come back again when the going got tough. I was all over the place. I guess I had learned to climb out the window and escape to the woods to free myself from unbearable pressures as a child, and the pattern of wanting to escape and running away continued into adulthood. Anyway, Dr Brown kept telling me I had to put roots down, to stay in one place and work things out, like a grown-up, and I realised that the word 'roots' had obvious, painful resonances – quite aside from the TV show.

Ever since I could remember I had been ridiculed and harassed for being black. I remembered the kids at school throwing all the usual rude words at me and saying horrible things like, 'Why hasn't your mum licked your lips and stuck you on the window while she does the shopping?' I would come away feeling so upset and I hated my lips for years because they were bigger than the other kids'. Although, I was black on the outside, I knew nothing at all about my family, my place of origin, or my culture. All I knew was that my mother was in London somewhere and didn't want to know me. I remember some black children I met calling me a 'milky way': chocolate on the outside and white on the inside. After all, I'd been brought up (if you could call it that) by the Stabards, who, in skin colour at least, were whiter than white. They hated black people and I took in that hatred through my black pores, and hated myself too. I was the ultimate 'milky way kid': I didn't fit with white kids because of my colour, nor with black kids, because of my lack of belonging, and lack of culture. I didn't know how to be around black people, as I didn't 'feel' black at all. But I didn't feel white either, so I didn't belong in either community.

Dr Brown tried to help me further by getting Social Services to assign a specialist Afro-Caribbean worker to me and I was encouraged to go to a local black day centre, where I learned about Caribbean cookery, songs and crafts and met other black people. I found it very difficult to fit in, especially at first. I was absolutely terrified. I wasn't very good at making eye contact, as I had spent the past five years or more avoiding people's gazes. However, now

I had a child, I knew I had to find out something about my heritage, as I didn't want to pass on to Anna Bella my sense of being totally rootless.

Anyway, one day at the day centre I was learning how to cook a traditional dish of rice and peas. An older woman was explaining to me what to do, and I was actually enjoying myself. I had always been forced to do the cooking and I was very at home in a kitchen, although I'd only made the usual white, English dishes like fry-ups and roast dinners up until then. I was enjoying learning about spices and stuff when a woman walked into the kitchen area and she stood there for a moment and stared at me. I thought, 'Oh God, why is she looking at me like that,' as I could feel her full gaze stuck like a magnet on me. But I wouldn't look up. I carried on chopping, feeling shy. However, when she didn't move, I peeked up through my lashes and my heart nearly stopped. She looked like someone I knew very well. She looked like me!

The woman came over and stood next to me. She was in her thirties and nicely dressed. I carried on chopping but my heart was racing, my mouth was dry and I thought I was going to faint.

'Who's your family?' she asked, straight out, just like that.

Family was a sore point with me, obviously. So I said nothing, and just kept chopping as much as I could. I wouldn't look at her, I wanted her to go away.

'I said, who's your family, girl?' She was insistent. The woman was about ten years older than me, but her face was so similar to mine that it was uncanny. For answer I just shrugged, and took the onions over to the pan on the stove. She eventually gave up and went away, sucking air through her teeth and shaking her head.

From then on I tried to avoid her. I went to the day

centre once or twice a week and I'd been beginning to enjoy it. Gus, my social worker, encouraged me to go, but I was scared of seeing the woman again, so I stopped going for a while. Gus came round to where I was living and tried to talk me into going back. After his visit it began to play on my mind that I didn't know who my family was, and that I felt so out of place wherever I was. I got very desperate and scared so after a sleepless night I ended up taking yet another overdose.

Whenever the pressure got too great and I got too wound up I found myself reaching for a bottle of paracetamol or anti-depressants and taking them. I had the baby with me, and I felt very bad about doing it, but I also felt if I ended up in hospital at least they could look after her properly while I tried to sort myself out. At least she wasn't at Mr Stabard's. It was like a major panic attack and in my twisted logic going to hospital was a way of trying to hold everything together. I knew that Dr Brown would be disappointed in me, but I just couldn't do everything she wanted as fast as she wanted me to. Meanwhile, I knew, in the back of my mind, that if I did this many more times then Social Services would win the argument saying that I was a lousy mother. If it was up to them, they would let the Stabards win. So it was the rock and hard place again, and I was in the middle of it, in no-woman's land.

Once more I ended up in the local hospital, with Anna Bella at my side. Those days in hospital always helped me get some perspective. It was something about the clean white sheets, the regular meals and a sense of routine and orderliness that made me feel calmer. Also in the normal hospitals the nurses were kind and helpful, and not as punitive as they seemed to be in the mental hospital.

Anyway, I was told to go down and have some blood taken one morning, to check me for anaemia as I was tired all the time, and I suddenly bumped straight into the same woman I had met in the day centre. I nearly dropped dead with shock. I couldn't escape her at all. Was she following me? It turned out she was a nurse herself, and worked in the hospital. That's why I had met her at the day centre where she helped out. I was completely taken aback, however, when she suddenly asked me if I would like to come home to her house some time for dinner. Come back for dinner? No-one had ever asked me to do such a thing. Not in the whole of my life. I didn't know what to say.

We stood in the corridor, me in my dressing gown, she in her nurse's uniform, and I felt some sort of strange affinity with her. We really did look alike. It was uncanny. 'Sure,' I said, not really thinking what I was saying. 'That would be nice.' I was in the hospital for a few weeks then, in a mother and baby unit, and a few days later a nurse told me that it had all been arranged that I would go and have dinner at the woman's house. Her name was Andrea. I was used to people organising things over my head and I thought no more about it. A few weeks later Andrea arrived at my bedside one evening and told me I was to come home with her. So I dressed and left the hospital, and Anna Bella and I went in Andrea's car to a council estate in a part of the town I didn't know. When I got there a good-looking black man in his sixties opened the door and I couldn't bring myself to look him in the eye, not at first, although I glanced up for a quick peek. He let us into the house and when we got to the living room, we all sat down.

Andrea said, 'Harmony, this is my father – Jeremiah, this is Harmony.'

She introduced me as her friend, although I hardly knew her. Then two other women came in, and Andrea explained one was Rina, her sister, the other was Veronica, her step-mother. They all said hello. Jeremiah smiled at me warmly, helping me relax. I still didn't really understand why they were doing this for me, as I'd never been invited to anyone's house for dinner before. I had no friends.

It was only then, when I looked at Jeremiah properly, my heart nearly leapt out of my mouth yet again. He looked the spitting image of Andrea, which meant he looked very like me. Jeremiah (or Jem) was very handsome and thick set. He was well-dressed and had an imposing nature. He made me feel he was definitely the head of the family and he had quite a charming personality. I sat there, not knowing what to say. Anna Bella was playing with a soft toy I'd brought with us, and we all watched her. It was all so awkward, as I really didn't know how to conduct myself in this kind of situation, so I just focused on her. I'd never been into a black person's home before either, so I felt like a real fish out of water. I must have behaved very oddly, but I didn't know what else to do.

That first night they had prepared a large white fish for dinner: a traditional dish from their island back home. It came in on a big platter and Andrea placed it proudly in the middle of the table. It was made with peppers, chillies and garlic, and was very spicy. However, when I had a portion on my plate, I had no idea how to eat it. I didn't know how to debone a fish as I'd only ever had fish fingers, fish and chips or tinned tuna, that kind of thing. I was struggling to deal with the fish, sweating away and shaking, and the whole family watched and started teasing me. It was a nightmare. There was the older man, Jem, and his wife, Veronica, and Andrea and her sister, Rina. They all sat and laughed as I struggled away. I thought, how mean is this? and I put my knife and fork down and gave up. I wanted to run out of there and decided I would never ever visit again. I was so sensitive to whatever anyone said to me, and had such thin skin, that I was quiet for the rest of the visit.

Back in hospital next day I decided I didn't like those black people very much as they had given me such a hard time. Andrea popped in to see me a few days later and told me I shouldn't mind her family and how they teased people. She told me I was too sensitive. I said I wasn't used to being with people much and hadn't been out to dinner before – and she looked really shocked. She tried to make friends with me, but I was a bit wary and pushed her away. She invited me to come again, and I said 'maybe' and we left it at that. But further shocks were to come.

One day, a few weeks afterwards, I had a surprise visit in the hospital from Rina. She came into the ward, spoke to the nurse, and then came over to me. She also looked very like Andrea, which meant she reminded me of me, as well. I was unnerved by her, and I didn't like her as much as I liked Andrea; she seemed to be a tougher cookie altogether. Rina stood by the bedside for a moment. She seemed to be thinking hard. I was sitting in a chair, and Anna Bella was next to me. We were in a small room, with the door open onto the ward. She looked awkward and I wondered what she wanted, but I kept looking down at the floor, fearing what was going to happen. Rina suddenly went over and closed the door, clearly fearful of being overheard.

'I have something to tell you', is how she started in a hoarse whisper.

I didn't respond. I sort of braced myself, as I didn't know what was coming next.

'I'm your sister, your half-sister, anyway and the man you went to see, at our house, is your dad.'

I couldn't compute it.

'What?'

'I said, I'm your sister. And he's your dad.'

I looked up at her finally and stared. The resemblance was uncanny.

'What about Andrea?'

'She's your sister, too. But she doesn't know,' said Rina, mysteriously.

'What do you mean, she doesn't know?'

'Only I know the story,' explained Rina, 'and she doesn't know you're one of us.'

One of us? What did she mean, 'one of us'? It was all happening too fast, I couldn't understand what she was saying to me at all. I felt sick and numb, and I started shaking. I had a thousand questions I wanted to ask, but couldn't bring myself to ask any of them. I'd spent the whole of my life with no family. I was now twenty-four and for the first time ever someone was saying I was 'one of us'. What on earth did she mean? What was I to make of it all?

I sat, shell-shocked. Rina went on to say that I had to take a vow of silence. I must not tell anybody, especially Andrea, until the rest of the family was told. Rest of the family? What did she mean? How many were there? I asked her and she said there were six brothers and sisters, all grown-up; all living around the town, or some in other big cities in the UK. Every so often they got together as a whole group especially at Christmas. Veronica was my father's second wife. His first wife was still in the Caribbean, where he'd left her when they split up. My mother was in London still, apparently, and had nothing to do with him. I then found out that she had been only fourteen, at the time, and that my illegitimate birth had caused a huge stir in the black community. But also I was not to mention anything about my prostitute, underage mother as my father refused to talk about it. She was a taboo subject – and therefore, so was I. However, I did discover from Rina that day that my mother's mother, my maternal grandmother, was still living in the area and always had been since I'd been born.

What? I had a grandmother living nearby, who had never contacted me for nearly a quarter of a century? Rina sat next to me and told me all of this with a deadpan face. I'm not sure at all why she told me. Maybe she needed to get it off her chest. But she warned me, several times, that I had to keep it a secret. I must not talk to my father, Jem, about what I knew, or Andrea. My shameful existence was not openly known in the family. The kids had known their father had a bit of a reputation with the ladies, and that his nickname in the Caribbean in the Sixties had been 'jerk-off Jeremiah'. Indeed that reputation had followed him to the Mother Country, where his wild ways continued. I had no idea how Rina knew all this and I didn't have the presence of mind to ask. I was totally dumbfounded.

Rina explained that they were a fairly happy family but that they couldn't just take me in, just like that. So I had to be careful. She was telling me this because she felt sorry for me. She said she could see I felt awkward and isolated, and that I had clearly not enjoyed the visit for dinner (she was right there). In a way she wanted to say sorry for all the ribbing I had had – that was just their way. They were a big family and they always teased each other. That certainly felt better. She was obviously trying to take my feelings into account, something which didn't happen very often. In fact, this felt like a first. However, Rina warned me, several times, that I had to keep all of this new knowledge to myself. Even if I saw Andrea in the hospital, I had to carry on acting as if I knew nothing. Of course, I agreed with her and said, 'Yes, I'll keep it to myself.' I wasn't someone who blurted things out and I'd spent years not telling people things.

Once Rina was gone home, I sat and stared at the wall for half an hour, then cuddled Anna Bella while she played with a dolly, and thought to myself over and over, 'I'm not alone, I'm not alone. This is amazing.' I tried to remember what they all looked like, and especially what 'my father' had looked like. I couldn't really picture them, and I suddenly had the urge to rush round there and jump into their arms. I knew I shouldn't, but the urge was upon me – I would belong somewhere at last. I had a father! He was alive and well and only a short distance away – finally I had someone I was related to.

I was discharged from hospital shortly after this visit from Rina. I was living in horrible digs but I went back and tried to make the best of it with Anna Bella. I was due to go back to the Stabards', which I was resisting. Dr Brown had warned me not to attempt any more overdoses as Margaret Vallelly from Social Services was working hard on my case. Dr Brown told me she felt I was getting much better at mothering my daughter, but that I still had to try even harder to make things work for us both long-term.

It was then that I made my big mistake – possibly the biggest mistake I've ever made. I found it impossible to sit on the news of having found my father's side of my family. The fact that all this time they had been so near, literally a few streets away, and were living a reasonably civilised life, having dinner round a dining room table, chatting and laughing with each other, was too much to bear. I wanted to know my father, I wanted to hug my sisters and brothers, I wanted to be taken into the fold, to be loved and cared for. I wanted to belong. It was utterly naïve, but my impetuous nature led me to retrace my steps to Jem's front door as soon as I possibly could. I foolishly ignored Rina's warning.

As I stood on the doorstep that Autumn evening, the thought in my head was: 'I don't have to be alone any more.' I knew Rina had warned me to say nothing, to wait until she had told everyone in the family and they were prepared to welcome me in. But I couldn't wait for that. I had waited too long already. My daughter and I were outcasts, we were 'milky ways'. I couldn't let the Stabards take Anna Bella again, but at the same time the council was trying to give her to a completely new family far away. I wanted to keep her with me forever, and in my naïveté, I thought, 'If I find my own family they will protect me. They won't let the authorities take my little girl away.' When the door opened, there was Andrea. I think she lived there with Jem and Veronica, and Rina lived nearby with her own family. Lacking all social skills, I foolishly stammered out my news on the doorstep, without any preparation at all.

'Hi,' I said to Andrea, 'I'm your sister.'

Her face went from a cautious smile to looking like absolute thunder.

'What the hell do you mean, Harmony?'

I thought she was going to hit me for a minute, she looked so angry. I then blurted out everything that Rina had told me, there and then on the doorstep. Andrea looked perplexed, then really furious. She didn't know what to do or what to say. Neither did I. We stared at each other for a moment and I could see she was struggling with this totally unwelcome news. I could see instantly that I'd messed everything up, so I turned and walked heavily down the garden path, trying to get away from there as fast as I possibly could. All I could hear was the door slamming very firmly behind me as tears stung my eyes.

24

Sad Farewells

'Harmony has a history of depressive illness and deliberate self-harm ... at least partly as a result of adverse experiences in her foster home' (Psychiatric report by Dr Brown)

What an absolutely huge mistake I had made. I felt like such a crazy fool. They were all right, obviously. I had not been able to hold back, or to wait, just when I needed to, and now I had ruined everything. I think I had felt so desperate all my life to belong somewhere that when there was a glimmer of possibility, I just leaped at it. I couldn't wait. I was also not very skilled with people at that time, and I didn't really understand social niceties. I should have waited, patiently, until Rina came back and said, 'OK, I've talked to everyone, now you can come and join us.' Instead I rushed it and in doing so, I pushed them all away. I'd scared them off and this obviously made me feel even more distraught.

At the time I knew that the authorities were closing in on me and Anna Bella. I hadn't coped very well living alone, and had been in and out of hospital like a yo-yo. Every time something went wrong, I took an overdose, which made things worse. But I didn't understand at the time what else I could do. I had got into a downward spiral, and although Dr Brown kept warning me I had to resist acting that way, I didn't seem to be able to do what I needed to do. It was a bit like cutting myself – which I was still doing. When the urge to hurt myself was upon me, it was incredibly difficult to resist, because it gave me such a feeling of release. The way I managed all the masses of confused feelings that were roaring around inside of me was to cut myself, or run away, or open a bottle of pills. I needed some release and as I had no other outlet, it had to do. A couple of times I'd said 'I'm going to kill myself', which sounds incredibly self-indulgent, given that I had a child in tow. But I can't really convey how desperate and alone I felt all the time, like the walls of the world were closing in on me and I couldn't cope. Of course, I was very aware of my daughter's situation, but I also felt the enormous pressure of having to meet her needs every minute of every day. I had no partner to talk to, no family to back me up; everything came down to me, all the time. I missed my sisters terribly, and now I had found a family, and rushed at them, they had also rejected me. So I was back to where I started, or so it seemed.

By 1992, when Anna Bella was four and I was twenty-four, the council had followed Margaret Vallelly's lead and was pushing hard for a 'separation order' – in other words, they were trying hard to separate me from my daughter. My mental health record was being used against me all the time, even though Dr Brown was trying to support me, along with my social worker, Gus. Gus continued to try to put me in touch with my black roots, but I was wary. Most days Anna Bella and I tried to get to the day centre, just to give the day structure. I was also determined to learn some life skills, like being able to handle my own money and fill in forms. Meanwhile, I was terrified I might lose my daughter, and then I'd have nothing left to live for at all.

I knew that I had been labelled 'paranoid' many years ago and yet the Social Services people increased my paranoia all the time. I knew Margaret Vallelly was trying to get Anna Bella away from me – whenever I met her she was openly hostile – and I was constantly being scrutinised. There always seemed to be someone with a clipboard, scribbling down what I was doing right or more likely, what I was doing wrong. I remember Anna Bella fell over and grazed her knee, and I bent over and hugged her to me and looked at her knee. The social worker in the day centre told me I was smothering her, and she should learn to toughen up. She said, 'It's only a little graze, don't pick her up.' It was all very odd, because another time when Anna Bella had fallen over and cried, I was told to pick her up, and not ignore her! Clearly I couldn't get it right, and I knew they were writing down stuff about me and my parenting skills (or lack of them) all the time and discussing me behind my back. I might be paranoid, but I had something to be paranoid about. They were still talking about me, not to me, and they did want to take my daughter away. So I wasn't that crazy – I was right.

Even though Dr Brown would tell them that I was now well-bonded with Anna Bella, and my mothering skills were coming on, Social Services were determined to see me as a mad, bad mother. It was like a war and I had to keep fighting, but sometimes I would get so tired of fighting, that I would begin to flag. Mainly I was on my own in the fight, then someone like Gus would come on board and fight alongside me for a while, but then get tired and give up, or be moved on, and I would be on my own again.

Another example of how they tried to make out I was not functioning was the mind games they would play on me to test me out – which I know sounds a bit paranoid, but I really think it is true. For instance, if I had a meeting with a social worker at ten in the morning, I would get there at ten, but they would call my mobile, at nine thirty, saying that I was late. I felt they were trying to trip me up, and trick me, and it would all go down on my record. If I said I thought the meeting was at ten, like we agreed, they always looked at me like, 'Well, she's mad, what does she know? She would get the time wrong.' If I spoke up for myself, and argued with them, I was being 'difficult' or 'stroppy', 'unco-operative' and even 'aggressive'. Social Services were against me every inch of the way. They were always saying I had 'low IQ' and 'poor mothering skills'. Even though they knew I was especially scared to go home to the Stabards', as I was scared for Anna Bella's safety there, they always supported the Stabards against me. After all, they had appointed the Stabards as foster parents in the first place, so they had to defend them, even though the abuse accusation had been made.

There was some discussion behind the scenes as to whether my new found black family would or could support me caring for Anna Bella. There was even a meeting between my father, Jem, (playing a model citizen) and a social worker, but it was deemed impossible. My maternal grandmother was even contacted, but she also refused to enter into any discussion about my daughter's future. So Social Services went back to the status quo, and saw the Stabards as the only possibility. Obviously, I wanted to do anything in my power to stop Mr Stabard doing to my daughter what he had done to me – so I protested as much as I could and Social Services said they'd continue to pursue legal adoption regardless as the only solution.

Eventually I was sent back to live with the Stabards, to my absolute horror. I hated it back there and was miserable being stuck in the dingy box room with Anna Bella, yet again. At least we weren't shoved in the shed together. Around this time Mr Stabard had to go away for a while and I was amazed how different things were. Mrs Stabard was remote as ever from me, but very friendly and sweet with Anna Bella, and we sort of rubbed along together without much friction. I became more stable with him far away, and was really enjoying motherhood a lot more. I particularly relaxed because I knew he wasn't going to appear at my bedside in the middle of the night, and I didn't have to keep watch over Anna Bella twenty-four hours a day. I could actually get some sleep, and my daughter could rest easy, and it was noted, even, reluctantly, by Social Services, that the stability of my situation had improved, and my mothering skills were better than ever.

I hoped and prayed to the stars and moon at night, out of my window, that he would never, ever come back. If things had continued like that, it might have been OK. But it wasn't meant to be, and after a few months Mr Stabard returned home, and my heart sank as I heard his hated voice once more in the hallway.

There was eventually a major crisis when Anna Bella was about four and a half. The authorities had never picked up that Mr Stabard had a drink problem, and if they noticed, they turned a blind eye. He was drunk again every night, and rolling into my room on a regular basis. I hardly slept, as I had to be vigilant all the time. He made it crystal clear to me that he wasn't interested in me any more, and that it was time for Anna Bella to take my place.

In fact, I had already noticed a disturbing change in her behaviour. I had a fear that something had already happened to her, somehow, as she began to scream when I used to change her nappy. She would let out this high-pitched shriek, and I had no idea why. Thinking about it, there were a couple of times Mrs Stabard had taken her out for a walk in the buggy, and I wondered if that had given him a chance to get his hands on her, in some way, when I was out of sight. I tried to protect her all the time, but he was very sneaky. He had never put Anna Bella in the shed, or bathed her – I had been very careful to keep her close to me – but there were odd times when he must have had access to her, when Mrs Stabard had charge of her without me around. I was terrified that something had already happened, especially when the screaming started like that.

She was now around the same age as I was when he started hurting me. I dreaded the thought of what he got up to when I wasn't there (such as when I was shut up in mental hospital). All I knew was he was utterly untrustworthy and unscrupulous and that he had no respect for anything or anyone – even his own flesh and blood. He just wanted to have what he wanted, when he wanted it, especially when he was drunk. He even drank first thing in the morning these days, so he was drunk much of the time. The man was a beast, and it made me so furious we were stuck there with him that I could hardly breathe when he was anywhere near us.

One night he staggered into our room, as usual, about two in the morning, while Anna Bella was fast asleep in the little child's bed they had got for her. She looked like a beautiful fallen angel, with long, dark curls spread out on her pillow. I must have dropped off, because I came to suddenly and found him swaying over her, pulling down her blanket. He was staring down intently at her, with his drooling, leering look, and I leapt out of bed and rushed over to him. I tried to pick her up, but he pushed me out the way, very hard. I knew he wanted her all to himself, to satisfy his sick urges. I wouldn't allow him to hurt my daughter the way he'd hurt me, so I grabbed some clothes and started to put them on, thinking we had to get out of there, fast. He was still focused on Anna Bella, who was awake now, and looked scared. Meanwhile, I was rushing round the room, trying to find her clothes, my bag and stuffing things in desperately, trying to get out of there. Mr Stabard, intent on having Anna Bella, stooped over the bed and started pulling her pyjamas down. I leapt on his back and pulled him off, and we tussled for a time. I was fierce and full of fury, and as I pushed past him I threw him against the wall, grabbed Anna Bella and my things and then made out of the room. He was slow on his feet, as he was really quite old now, and very drunk, and I made it down the stairs before he got to us. I carried on putting on my coat, as I lifted Anna Bella into her buggy, covered her up and rushed out the house.

Round the corner was a telephone box and I found some coins and phoned 999. I didn't know what else to do. I told them I was hitting my daughter, and that I might harm her. I said I couldn't cope with her and I might even kill her. I had no idea why I said that. I think it was the first thing that came into my mind. I was so scared of Mr Stabard and I knew that the authorities believed him over me, always, that the only thing I could possibly do was to sacrifice myself for her safety. I knew that if the police arrived and I said he was trying to hurt her, that they would recognise the address and my name, and remember all those times the Stabards had called the police to take me away to the mental hospital. They'd had me sectioned from that house, and I was labelled schizophrenic, psychotic, depressed and paranoid. Why would the police believe me now over them? In my twisted, panicky logic, it was the only thing I could think of to get Anna Bella away from Mr Stabard – which sadly meant getting her away from me, too.

Suddenly, I saw the police car and ambulance arriving, their lights flashing. It must have been about three in the morning by then. They took my little girl away, having checked her over for cuts and bruises, and I felt relieved she was going with the police to somewhere safe. I saw her little face disappear into a car and I felt terrified I might lose her, but I had to protect her. It was such a wrench to see her go, but I was more scared for her safety, in that moment, than anything else I could think of. I certainly didn't care about myself. I believed, in my heart, that the authorities would never take a baby away from its mother, especially if that mother was showing signs of progress. So I thought that she would be with me, soon after that.

How wrong I was. What I didn't really understand at that time was how far things were proceeding with Social Services and how successful the hostile Margaret Vallelly had been in turning things against me. Even though Dr Brown was writing positive things about me, Anna Bella was put out to a foster family – not the Stabards, thank God – and I felt reassured for a little while that I had done the right thing.

However, that night I went home, after the police had taken my daughter away, Mr Stabard came into my room – it must have now been about four in the morning – and he raped me with such violence, hatred and brutality, it is a wonder that I am alive still. He had drunk even more after the police had dealt with me, out on the street, and when I came back he slapped and punched me, knocking a tooth out. I was bleeding from the mouth and he was utterly furious with me. He couldn't have my child, so he took all of his anger out on me. He kicked me, kicked me in the face, punched and slapped me all over my body. After he raped me I was a bleeding, blubbering wreck, but I felt, at least for tonight, I had saved my daughter from the grasp of this totally perverted and sick man.

After this I took a major overdose and ended up again in hospital. I was at my wits' end, but at least I knew my daughter was away from the Stabards. I was terrified that despite everything I'd done to protect her he might have already found a way to hurt her, and was really frightened of how it might affect her. While I was in hospital, I found out to my horror that Anna Bella had now been sent to another city, far away. I was distraught. I thought she was going to be with a temporary foster family (hopefully a loving and kind one) and I would see her soon. I was told I would be able to visit her, yet every time there was a date set, somehow it would be cancelled, rearranged, and then cancelled again.

I thought it would be for a few days, a week, even weeks, but six whole months went by and I had not seen my daughter. All that time I was in mental hospital. I took repeated overdoses, as an act of desperation, trying to bring attention to my terrible situation. Unfortunately, my drugs were increased, although Dr Brown had been trying to get them down to a lower level. I had more ECT, and also I was sectioned for my 'own safety' as they told me. I just wanted to see my daughter. I missed her terribly. I was used to being with her every day and we had our little games and songs we played. I missed her sweet smile, her little voice, her enjoyment of everyday things. I loved her smell and having warm hugs with her. Now she was gone and I couldn't seem to find out how I could get her back. I felt utterly desperate. I was told I should get a solicitor, which I did, although I didn't know how to deal with any of the legal things. The social workers who tried to be on my side, like Gus, helped me do this, but we were up against the might of the system. Meanwhile, Dr Brown would keep telling me that if I wanted to get my daughter back I'd have to stop trying to hurt myself. I would try, but then the feelings would take me over and I would feel distraught and lonely and completely despairing, and I'd trot out of hospital and get myself some pills, and then wham, I was back at stage one, yet again.

I was eventually let out and rehoused in a flat in my town; but I couldn't settle down there. I was missing my daughter all the time. I wanted to know how I could get her back, how we could start again together. Life felt completely empty. I felt very suicidal all the time, and was fighting against the urge to slash myself and take an overdose. It was the only way I knew how to make myself heard. I was also very lonely in the flat, as I missed the company of being in hospital. Also, once Mr Stabard got news that I was out (they would always give the Stabards my address) he'd be around, ringing the doorbell, following me around. He would try his best to intimidate me, I guess, because he wanted to keep me quiet.

During the summer of 1992 I finally found out that new prospective parents had been found for Anna Bella in the far away city where she was being fostered, and that the council were finally getting her adopted, against my wishes. It was going to court to be finalised, even though Dr Brown wrote a powerful report supporting me as Anna Bella's mother. She thought I was making progress and it was the wrong time to take my child away. I think she knew it would destabilise me further, and I was really trying to get myself together at the time. However, even that couldn't stop the process Margaret Vallelly had started and I was going to be forced to give my daughter to complete strangers who lived hundreds of miles away.

On the morning of the court hearing I was getting ready to go, with a very heavy heart, when a nurse came in to me and told me there was some more bad news. She sat me down on a chair and told me Mrs Stabard was dead. I couldn't understand what they meant. Dead? The nurse nodded. Apparently, she had gone to stay with her eldest daughter and had had a pain in the leg. She had got out of bed and collapsed of a heart attack – it was a thrombosis, a blood clot which had stuck in her heart. I felt my own blood run cold and was very sad indeed. As much as Mrs Stabard had never loved me, I had always hoped she would and I actually cared for her very much. I loved her. I sat and the tears started coming and I felt absolutely desolate. This news pushed me to a new level of desperation and despair. Mrs Stabard was gone. Really gone. I couldn't take it in properly. Meanwhile, they wanted to take Anna Bella, that very day and she had become my only reason for living. She was now five, and we loved each other deeply. She was my little angel, my beauty, and the thing I got up for in the morning. All I had done was try to protect her from Mr Stabard and in the end, everything backfired on me.

In the end the council won their case and I didn't even get to court. And the course of both our lives – that of my dear daughter and I – were changed, forever.

I was soon taken to a 'Goodbye Meeting' where I was to see the new parents – a very nice, if strict, African couple – in the faraway city where Anna Bella now lived. It was heartbreaking and I could hardly breathe as I sat on a train (my first train journey ever) with a social worker. How could I say goodbye to my little angel? I loved her, I wanted to be with her, but all the forces were against us, and I was having to give her up. The social worker kept telling me that it was 'for her own good', and that I was being 'selfless and sensible', but my heart was breaking into little pieces the whole way there. How could anyone love my baby as much as I did? I had cared for her, looked after her, loved her, and I knew her so well – surely it was best for her to be with me, even though I had my own problems to overcome? Dr Brown thought I would manage, with the right support. But no-one was willing to give me a chance. That was how the system worked.

Once we arrived I sat in a cold waiting room for a long time, desperate to see my daughter. The social worker told me Anna Bella had now been told not to call me 'mummy' any more. She had to call me 'Harmony' instead. All these rules and regulations! I had a five-year-old whom I loved to pieces, and who loved me. I wanted to look after her – I just needed some support to do so. Then I was called into a room. It was a horrible, ugly, grey meeting room, with a table in the middle and chairs all round. There were five council workers already there, and then one came in carrying my beautiful girl in a new set of clothes I didn't recognise. I hadn't seen her for over six months and she'd already changed a lot. She put her little arms out to me, calling 'Mummeeee' and I put mine out to her, and we hugged, a long, sweet hug. But as soon as she did, and I could feel her clinging on, the social worker pulled her away. This was our 'goodbye'. Anna Bella looked distressed and I wanted to cry, but bit my lip.

The new parents were standing in the doorway, the black couple dressed very smartly in expensive clothes. I had been told by my social worker what I could say, and what I couldn't say. I had made a little photo album, but they wouldn't let me give it to Anna Bella because I wouldn't include a picture of the Stabards. I had to just give one small photo of me. That was all I was allowed. I could see that Anna Bella was confused and upset by everything that was going on. She looked at me for reassurance, and I smiled, and held my hand out to her. She held her hand out to me, but the social worker pulled her away and our fingers didn't touch again. I felt my heart rip further – I loved her to pieces, I loved her so much, and I could see her being carried across the room, and handed to the woman in the dark suit, who now held her firmly in her arms. The black adoptive parents nodded to me, serious-faced, but never smiled or spoke to me. And then they turned, and the whole party was gone.

My daughter was gone. I slumped onto a seat and tears streamed down my face. I was desolate. Empty. Afraid. The pain was so severe that I thought I'd stopped breathing. Those last little glimpses of her ringlets, her dewy, chocolaty eyes, her dimpled cheeks – that's all I would have to sustain me for the next fifteen years. Distraught I pulled out a crumpled photo from my pocket and stroked it. My own little Anna Bella. I clasped the photo to my heart which was breaking into a million shattered fragments. This event was simply the beginning of the end of my whole world.

25

Freefall

'*You have judged Harmony unfit to have care of her child, and I would confirm that her shortcomings in this respect are related to her mental health . . .* ' (Consultant psychiatrist's letter to social worker)

'*. . . I believe Harmony would grow into a good mother given the right level of support . . . she needs another chance to live in the community with her child . . .* ' (Dr Brown's report to social worker)

. . . Toy cars. That's what they look like. I look down and feel numb. The traffic is whizzing past on the dual carriageway below at sickening speed. It's going home time. I guess they're all going home. To families. To loved ones. Home.

Then it hits me again. I feel a pang and I decide to heave myself over. I have nowhere to go home to, nowhere to belong. In my right hand the photo is now crumpled. I daren't look. I've only just stopped crying and I don't want to start again.

With all my effort, all my attention focused on this moment, I try to pull myself up on to the top of the brick parapet. All I have to do is get to the top and drop. Simple as that. I'm a bit heavy for all this, although I used to be able to run. Can't run now, but I can drop. OK. One, two, three. Heave . . .

A strong hand lands firmly on my shoulder. Shit! It's a big, white hand against my black skin. Further up is a hairy arm

*in a white shirt belonging to a big man, who's looking at me
with what seems like concern. I've seen that look before. Shit. I
pull hard against his hand, but it holds fast.*

*'Wait a moment,' the man's voice says, urgently. 'Think
about it.'*

*I look away from his concerned face, down back over the
bridge to the road below. It's so inviting. So seductive, with
its hard, stinking endless drone beneath me. It's beckoning me
with its siren call – come on, jump. I can't look at the man. If I
do, I am done for. I've got this far.*

*I pull hard against the man, trying to wriggle from his iron
grasp and hoist myself up onto the parapet. Just a few inches
more and I'll be gone. I'm nearly there. I can let go. I'll be free.
I'll fly, like a bird in the sky. Get away you stupid, interfering
man. Leave me alone. Let me be.*

*But the hand is holding on firm. The voice is droning on
and on too.*

'You have something to live for.'

*Suddenly I am angry. Furious. Stupid bastard. What does
he know?*

'No, I don't,' I shout. 'No I don't – there's nothing left.'

*Everything I had has been taken from me. I've nothing left
to live for. At twenty-five I've had enough of this life.*

*Out of the corner of my eye I see some figures running from
the direction of the hospital. I struggle harder. The man is
holding on, still with an iron grip.*

*Suddenly, the photo in my hand drops to the pavement. Oh
God. I panic. I see a sweet little face, black curls, dark eyes. It's too
much. I try to snatch the photo back, but I'm pinioned. Bastards!*

*'Come on,' coaxes the man. 'Come down now. Nothing's that
bad, believe me.'*

*But it is. She's been taken. They fucking won. Suddenly, my
legs are jelly. There's another firm hand on the other shoulder.*

I turn and see a familiar face. 'Come on, Harmony,' says the male nurse firmly. 'Come on now.'

In answer, I struggle and fight. I put all my effort into trying to wrench free. As I wrestle, the two hands restraining me are strong and I feel their fingers digging into my arms.

'Let me go. Let me go!'

I've nowhere to go. Nowhere to belong. Nothing to live for. This is the end and I want it to come right now, hard and fast.

Moments later I feel a sharp prick in my buttock.

Darkness . . .

When I came round, the truth seeped into my mind and I wanted to push it away. I had lost her. They had won. There was nothing left to live for. It was over.

From that moment on my life became a blur. For months I tried seriously to kill myself. Too many times to count I'd sneak out of the ward and try to throw myself off the bridge again. I was told I'd traumatised the staff; I'm sorry about that, but my life was finished. I felt that I would be stuck in the mental health system for the rest of my days. The future stretched out before me like a meaningless mass. Other times I'd tiptoe out with money clutched in my hand and buy aspirins, paracetamol, anything I could get hold of, and take all of them at once. When I slipped into unconsciousness, I just felt relief. I wanted darkness now.

Then I'd be brought round, and it'd all begin again. The roundabout of rules: *Harmony do this, Harmony do that; Harmony behave; Harmony drink this, Harmony think that.* All that time I'd tried so hard with Anna Bella was for nothing. Now each time I was supposed to see her, the appointment was magically cancelled, or moved to another date and then cancelled again. When I was let out for a weekend to go to a flat that had been found for me, all I'd do was find old pills from ancient prescriptions and swallow as many as I could. I was self-destructive, I just didn't care any more, so I'd get sectioned 'for my own good'. Even Dr Brown had to section me a couple of times. I had to be controlled by the state because I was a risk to myself. I felt worthless. I didn't care.

In all this time I was never counselled, and I never had therapy. I was just given drugs and Electro-Convulsive Therapy to numb me and shut me down. No-one asked why I was so angry and self-destructive; and even if they had, I couldn't really have explained. It was too big a story and no-one ever believed me.

Even back then it crossed my mind to write a book. I started scribbling things down as far back as 1994. It felt good to get it down, but some things I just couldn't write yet. They were too dark and difficult to put into words. How do you put a lifetime of rape and slavery into a sentence?

Eventually Dr Brown told me that I was being my own worst enemy. What else could she do? I had given up. I was so defeated, and so angry in defeat. I wanted my daughter back and I appealed against the adoption, but the council fought me and I lost. When I asked to see my beloved daughter, I was blocked. The very fact that I was in a mental institution made me an 'unfit mother', but nobody ever asked why or how I got here in the first place. During all this, Dr Brown was the only one who really pursued my cause and tried to make sure I stayed in touch with my social workers. Dr Brown never gave up on me, but I gave up on her. It was part of the anger and powerlessness I felt inside.

Over a two year period, from the age of twenty-five to twenty-seven, I tried to challenge the adoption, and fought constantly to see my daughter. I was made to feel that I was a bad influence on her life and that I would only upset things. Anna Bella was getting further and further out of my reach, like she was on a raft, drifting out to open sea. I felt like I would never see her again, and it killed me inside.

Meanwhile, I was encouraged to take a case against my foster father. With the help of Dr Brown, my accusations were finally being taken seriously by at least a couple of people in the system. Although Social Services had known about it for years, Dr Brown was the only one moving things along, stirring things up. However, most of the time I was out of control and unable to cope with life. Unable to function, I was now completely in the hands of the mental health system, having given up the fight to improve my own life. For so long I had tried to get away, tried to survive, but I had reached a boiling over point, where I couldn't deal with all that had happened to me any more, and I just wanted to lie down and die. I felt broken down: broken on the wheel of my life.

During this period I had some occasional contact with my father's family. Although they were not very willing to help with the care of my daughter because of her mad mother, they were very concerned to hear about the case against my foster father. They were ashamed of me, of my very existence. I was told that my case was bringing too much disrepute on their family. Remember: my father, a pastor and a respectable married man, had me with a fourteen-year-old girl, who was a prostitute. I was the unwanted product of his bad behaviour. But now my mental condition, and the fallout of years of abuse at the hands of despicable, white foster parents, was too much for his reputation to bear, so he distanced himself, at the crucial moment, and I was abandoned yet again.

My maternal grandmother also distanced herself, despite Gus' efforts to try and bring us together. One day my grandmother came into the hospital to see me. I hadn't seen her before and didn't recognise her. She came to my bedside, a frail elderly lady dressed in her best clothes. She brought no flowers, no grapes, no words of comfort. Instead she leant over and said, straight into my face, just like Mr Stabard would do: 'They should've burned you at birth'.

Message delivered, she turned and walked out, leaving me utterly stunned.

At the time when I needed them the most, my natural family were all too ready to disown me as being far too much trouble to deal with. No-one ever asked themselves why I might have ended up in this isolated position in the first place. Was it my fault I was illegitimate or that the pastor could not control his urges with a child prostitute? Had my grandmother let her daughter keep me, I would have had a home. Or had my father brought me into his house, as surely he should have done as a religious man, I would have had somewhere. But both had turned their backs on me, and as a consequence I had the incredible bad luck to end up with the Stabards. Now I was a totally homeless person. Nowhere to go, nowhere to belong.

Eventually, sick to death with all of it and all of them, I ran away again. It felt like I was always on the run to somewhere, anywhere. When I was let out of hospital for a weekend, I just got on a bus, and went to another city, far away. I'd just choosen a name on the front of a bus – randomly, because I liked the sound of it – and went. It wouldn't be the city where my daughter was living, but anyway I'd decided to start again. I just wanted to get away from everything and everyone who knew me, who had labelled me, who hated me. However, I was not really equipped to live life independently, so I found things too hard and ended up attempting suicide again.

I was in and out of various mental institutions for a very long time, then on to another women's refuge and then a halfway-house for people who had nowhere to go. My life was in freefall, but I just didn't care. I didn't care about anything any more. Someone else was combing my beautiful daughter's hair, putting on her school dress for her and making her packed lunch for her. She was calling someone else 'Mummy' and giving them hugs and kisses. Someone else was watching her jump and play and smile. Every time her birthday came round, I'd light a candle, and buy her a present. I'd sing 'Happy Birthday to you' to an absent Anna Bella, my gorgeous little girl. But year after year the pain didn't go away. It deepened, like a hole in the ground, filling with rain.

I eventually get a letter from my social worker, Gus, to tell me he and Dr Brown were now helping to pursue the legal case that I wanted to take against Mr Stabard. Finally a case was launched against him, so I needed to make a statement to the police. I wondered if it was really worth it. Losing the adoption case had soured my taste for things legal. Did I have the energy to go back and talk to the police and find times, dates and places in my memory to set the record straight? It would also mean going back to the town I grew up in; that horrible place where they spat at me and called me ugly names. I didn't know if I could face going back, I hated the place so much. At least in my new home I could disappear, and there seemed to be many black people who were simply accepted as 'normal' human beings. However, I wanted Mr Stabard to be brought to book; I needed him to be punished and exposed for what he really was. I couldn't bear to think of him getting away with it all, and even worse, standing there, smiling smugly, holding his 'thirty years of service to fostering' award. It made me sick.

Mr Stabard was now in his seventies, and to my mind he was like one of those old prison guards in the Nazi era that people spend their lives tracking down and bringing to justice because he has got away with murder. I read in the paper that people say that war criminals like that are too old, and should be left to die in peace. But why should they? What peace did they give to innocent children, who were treated worse than animals purely because of their race? By now there were laws against racism, so why shouldn't I try to use them?

While I was debating all this with myself over and over, all I could feel was the unending ache in my guts at having lost my precious daughter. As every day went by I knew the memory of me must be fading for her; as her new life took over, and her new mummy and daddy took centre stage, I would eventually be just a vague memory from the past, a strange, shadowy person that she once knew, as if in a dream. I was to be that shameful thing that had to be hidden from sight, at all costs. Everybody told me so.

While all this turmoil was going on, I met a guy, Alan, in my new town. He was a drunk, and I felt sorry for him. We began a relationship of sorts where I'd live with him sometimes, when I wasn't back in hospital after overdoses or episodes of self-harm. I was twenty-six at the time, and at a real low point. I'd burn my arms with cigarettes and the pain would give me relief somehow. Alan would beat me when he was drunk – kick me in the belly with his boot, slap my face and call me 'bitch' – but I didn't care. He made me give him my money. I only lived on income support, but he'd come with me to the post office when I cashed it, take the money and drink it all away. With his help, I got into a terrible downward spiral. At another day care centre, I got another chance at knitting jumpers and cooking things, but since I wasn't doing it for my daughter it was hard to care. I became convinced that everyone I met didn't like me, and that they didn't really want me there. Mostly I just felt like I was going through the motions. All the time I was hoping there would be a call or a letter to say I could see my little girl, but it never came.

Then one day, I finally got a letter saying I needed to go back to my old town to talk about the court case against Mr Stabard. I thought hard about it. Was it worth it? It wouldn't bring my daughter back. Then I thought again about Hope and Faith; I remembered Raj, Prathi, and Mohammed and all the other children I'd known who'd been abused by Mr Stabard. He must have hurt hundreds of kids in his time as a foster parent and even before that, when he was working in the children's home with his nasty pal, Mr Venetti. I thought about the 'thirty years of service' for which he'd got his civic award. How many kids are walking around hooked on drink and drugs, or being used as prostitutes, or hurting themselves – or were simply dead, like I wanted to be – because of his wonderful foster-parenting skills? He had got away with it, and was still getting away with it, and it made my blood boil all over again.

So eventually, I gritted my teeth, and took a bus back. It was a long journey home. I left Alan, who shouted abuse and shook his fist at me as I went. I sat on the bus and looked out of the window at the people on the street, carrying shopping bags, pushing their kids in buggies. Is life like this for them? Do they all have their struggles, like me? I saw a mother pick up her child and kiss it and I wanted to cry. I bit my lip instead – no more tears. When I got to my town, I went to see the social worker who told me I had to see a solicitor. Gus arranged a flat for me in town to live in, but now Gus was leaving and another social worker, Ray, was taking over. The social workers are always leaving and moving on.

A few days later, I am awake late at night in my flat when the doorbell ring. I get up and push the button to hear who is down there at this time – it is about three in the morning. I hear a familiar slur, a drunken gravelly voice, and I know it is him. 'You fuckin' black bitch, you're not gonna beat me. Y'hear, y' bitch?'

I start shaking, hearing his voice. Somehow he's already tracked me down. Who's given him my address? It's a small town, so I guess he just asked around. There aren't many black people living here, so I still stand out uncomfortably in a crowd. Maybe Social Services told him, still believing that he's the model citizen and I am the sick one.

'Go away' I shout. 'Go away, leave me alone.'

He goes on to shout crude, revolting things down the intercom, telling me how he'll kill me, and smash my face in if I go any further with the case.

After that it goes quiet and it's obvious that he's staggered off. But my peace is shattered now I know he knows where I am.

Next day I phoned Ray, and eventually I was moved to another address. But it was all too much, and crushed and hopeless, I took another overdose, ended up in hospital, and the destructive cycle started again. Round and round I went, overdosing, trying to jump off bridges, feeling like there was nowhere to put myself in this world where everything, everywhere was full of pain. Where I have nowhere to belong.

Then I heard the news. Gus tried to break it to me gently. The case would be dropped, due to 'lack of evidence'. He told me they needed other foster children to come forward and corroborate my story. Mr Stabard got the last laugh. I'd let down Raj and Prathi and now it'd all come full circle – they'd let me down. If only I knew where Hope was. She'd be able to back up my story. But my two dear sisters, who went through it all with me, couldn't endure the pain in the end. One is dead, and nobody cares. The other has gone off the rails, and still no-one cares. We are just dispensable. We kids were thrown on the scrap heap and no-one seems to be able to do anything about it. No-one will ever know what our foster father got up to behind his white-painted front door and nice, neat front lounge. Mr Stabard has been let off; he won't face the music, or be brought to book. Where is the justice in that?

It was too much to bear and more overdoses followed, and more silent screams in the night where I'd rail against the moon. I was rescued over and over; a couple of times I nearly didn't come back at all.

Then I heard, through the grapevine, that my father was going back to the Caribbean. He was fed up with life in the UK. I don't blame him, but it meant another door had closed. Before he went he came to see me in hospital and asked me for help. He explained that there was a friend back home who needed an operation and he was trying to raise money. I was angry with him at first, because I felt abandoned, but he was so charming and nice – and after all, he had come to see me. Maybe he'd decided to like me after all? Maybe he'd changed his mind and I could be included in his family at last? You never know, people could change. My father handed me a piece of paper.

'Harmony, now you're one of the family, I wonder if you could help me?'

Jeremiah was very charming and I felt his warmth.

'I have a friend who is in big trouble, and I need to get him a loan. You know it would be doing God's work to help, and I'd be eternally grateful.'

He explained that I'd have to sign the form for a loan, but that he would be responsible for it. There was a line he had to sign, too, that had 'witness' written next to it.

I was deeply flattered that my father wanted me to help him. I wanted to be included and forgiven, and I hoped against hope that this was the start of a new phase with my birth family. He even hugged me when I signed, which made me feel very emotional. I signed it because I wanted to help my father; I was desperate for him to like me. It was a bit like wanting to get things for Abigail Greer; except that back then I'd let her down and lost her friendship. This time, I wouldn't let anyone down. After I signed the document, my father said he would come see me again soon. He never did. I didn't ever see him again.

A while later I get a letter saying I owed £10,000. I didn't understand. In a panic, I phoned my social worker and when we met I showed them the paper I signed, which I discovered, to my utter horror, was a loan for £10,000. Now I was liable for the debt. My father had used the money to travel back to the Caribbean and extend his house out there. How could he do that to me?

I was reeling from it all, and very confused. Then a few months later, Andrea and Rina turned up one day and asked me to sign similar papers. They looked pleased to see me and said they needed my help. I was amazed that they were being friendly after all that had happened, but I told them I didn't know if I should and explained about the first loan. Andrea told me she thought I was confused, and that her dad – our dad – was a fine man. I was nervous because of the way I blurted out family secrets to Andrea, and the way they'd reacted to me, and now I didn't want them to go away again. I was scared of signing, but when they explained that they were in trouble and that family should stick together I let myself be persuaded. I was naïve, desperate, alone, and unworldly so I signed the papers. A bit of me hoped that now I really would be included in their family. It was nice to feel they'd turned to me when they were in trouble. That's what people who belong to each other do for each other, surely?

To my total horror, I later found out that I had signed loan documents to the tune of £40,000 to fund their house improvements and furnishings. Following their father's example, my half-sisters had decided to use me as a signatory on debts that they, and I, could never repay. I was so scared of what I had done that I couldn't face it. When letters came, I put them in the bin without opening them. I was now over £50,000 in debt for loans that I never saw a penny of. To make matters worse, I now knew I wouldn't be getting any financial compensation for the years of mistreatment by the Stabards. I was not worldly or wise, or prepared for this kind of trouble. I kicked myself: how stupid could I be? The situation brought up all my feelings of self-loathing, and it was all I could do not to slash myself or take an overdose. But this time I resisted.

It was because I felt so completely at sea that I signed the documents in the first place. I had a kind of empty, nihilistic feeling that nothing mattered, so who cared if I scribbled something for someone? None of it felt real. But now I was in a real mess and felt like I had a noose around my neck that would take years to take off.

Of course, I didn't tell anyone about these financial troubles – not even Dr Brown – because I felt terribly ashamed of myself. I knew, deep down, that I was being taken for a ride. But the hope to be loved, the desire to belong to a family – to matter to someone – was so overwhelming that it led me to do things which went against my better judgement, and against my own welfare.

The time from when Anna Bella was taken away from me until I finally got free from the mental health system as a full-time patient spanned more than twelve wasted years. From the age of twenty-four to thirty-six I spent most of my time as an inpatient, going in and out of the system. I probably attempted suicide over a hundred times. I was sectioned endlessly; sometimes for months, sometimes for a whole year. Overall, I had probably twenty loads of ECT and enough pills to sink a battleship. I became dependent on the system, and on the system's view of me as bad and mad. I never really got over the loss of my darling daughter, or the mess that happened around the adoption. I still think, to this day, that it was badly handled and that the only lone voice in the wilderness was Dr Brown, who kept trying to explain to people that there was more to this case than met the eye.

All the time I was in and out of hospitals I also had Mr Stabard threatening me in person – tracking me down every time I moved, following me, harassing me whenever

I was let out into the community. This carried on until the day he died. He was terrified that I would tell on him, and, tragically, he was never brought to book. As far as I know he died peacefully in his bed, of old age. Certainly the community believed he was a stalwart citizen, and the church and Social Services upheld him as a solid family man and great foster parent, to the very end. Since every child harmed by him was either black or Asian their protests simply didn't seem to count. Enoch Powell was right. There were 'rivers of blood', but those rivers were made of the blood of the children who nobody loved and nobody thought had any rights – the black dispossessed, the kids who didn't belong, the lonely, scared and unloved kids who were just like me.

26

Somewhere to Belong

'Harmony shows no sign of mental illness ... her symptoms and behaviour are a result of adverse experiences in her foster home ... to this end, there are no doubts that Harmony has been sexually abused ...' (Dr Brown's report)

Schizophrenic. Psychotic. Depressive. Paranoid. How often did I hear those labels attached to me? I was bad, mad, crazy Harmony, always out of control. I was 'difficult', and I had temper tantrums, and that was proof enough for them.

I know now that I owe my life, and my gradual recovery, to the efforts of Dr Brown who completely re-examined all my case notes (and helped me get them from the NHS eventually) and who was the only psychiatrist out of the dozens that I saw over the years who finally twigged that my behaviour had something to do with the abuse I'd suffered as a child and the other terrible experiences I'd been through as an adult. She was a beacon, a leading light; the only one to believe me. It is to her that I owe everything now that my life is finally turning around.

Firstly, Dr Brown believed I was traumatised by the rape and inhuman, racist treatment I had experienced at the hands of the Stabards. Hence most of my 'symptoms', including the flashbacks where I'd 'hear voices', were down to me having an acute case of post-traumatic stress disorder. All of my erratic behaviour, my anger, my fear and accompanying symptoms were explainable. In Dr Brown's view, I was not mad, I was distressed; I was not bad, I was traumatised. With the rapes, beatings, racist humiliations, starvation and other obscene punishments being part of my daily life, why was Dr Brown the only psychiatrist to be able to see her way through the maze of other people's dismissive reports? Partly, it was because she came to my case with fresh, unbiased eyes. Partly, too, because she saw me as a human being − a woman struggling with a mountain of terrible feelings − rather than someone who was inherently crazy. Also, when Anna Bella was adopted, Dr Brown believed I was on the brink of becoming a good mother. She thought it was a tragedy that my child was snatched away just as I was beginning to improve under her guidance.

In the reams of notes about my case, Dr Brown is a lone voice, arguing against the accepted idea that I am just beyond help. She writes things like ' . . . I feel she might be able to cope with looking after her daughter provided there is appropriate back up,' but she also notes that the 'Social Services team is very hostile'. Most importantly, when Anna Bella is finally wrenched away from me, Dr Brown's notes make it clear that I am experiencing 'reactive depression', and I am 'bereaved, like any normal mother who has lost her child.' Of course it is not only my daughter that I have lost, but also my only little bit of family − my sisters, Hope and Faith; Mrs Stabard (whom I loved, regardless of her faults); and even the possibility of having a relationship with my birth families on both sides. There was clearly a lot to feel traumatised and bereaved about.

Dr Brown was brave enough to go against the grain. She was tough; she told me over and over to stop overdosing, and I often ran away, in protest. But when I came back and asked her to take me under her wing again, she generously agreed – if I would come off my medication. Unlike any other health practitioner that I met, she believed that the drugs were increasing my feelings of aggression and paranoia. She also thought that they were stopping me coping, rather than helping me to cope. Together, we worked on a long-term programme whereby I had to give up the drugs slowly (because there were lots of them, at high dosage), and eventually I learned to live with feeling my feelings properly again. It was as if I had been so drugged out for so long that I had no idea who I was really underneath it all. I had been so zombified that I had to learn to taste things again, to feel and touch and to start smelling and seeing the world as it really was. This was obviously a slow process, and I fell at many hurdles, but eventually I got there. After a long battle I finally ditched my medication in 2004, and was able to start taking charge of my life for the very first time for myself, with a newly clear head.

This meant that I was able to start slowly but surely moving myself into the community. After a period of being in a half-way house, I decided the best thing was to consider moving to another part of the country. Every time I saw people in my home town, like Andrea, Rina, or other members of my extended family, it was always very awkward. I even met my maternal grandmother by accident, and heard that other relatives knew who I was, but nobody wanted to know me. I was still paying off my debts all the time, but I learned not to take on any more loans for anybody and eventually I found a helpful solicitor who managed to shift the responsibility back onto the people who had tricked me into signing the documents in the first place. They are now having to pay the loans off for themselves.

The most important step in my move towards having my life back was when I had a brief relationship and got pregnant again – I decided to have the child. This time it was my decision, and nearly ten years ago I had a wonderful son, Jason. Again, I had to follow a steep learning curve in terms of being able to look after him properly, and cope with all the emotional and practical demands of life, but I was a bit better prepared this time. I was a lone parent, as his father was not really involved with me after his birth, but I was fine about that. I was not ready for a relationship either, so I decided I would make the best job of it that I could.

Since Jason's birth I have gained a lot of strength as a person; I think I needed to have someone to care for, to keep me carrying on through life. Isn't that what life is all about? Once I'd moved away, I kept in contact with Dr Brown, who was always encouraging and helpful. For the past five years now I have been learning to manage my own life, bringing up my son, and trying to live as normal a life as I possibly can. I kicked the habit of reaching for the pills when in despair, and I have tried hard to live an ordinary life of a mum who has to get her child to school on time and pay the bills. It's not been easy, and I have had many false starts, but I feel pride that I am going it alone at last. Everything is down to me, but I have so much joy and fun with my son, who is doing well at school, that I feel I am lucky to have been able to establish my own little family at last.

Every year I light a candle on Anna Bella's birthday, and tell Jason that somewhere he has a lovely sister who is simply gorgeous and that I hope someday we will all be together as a proper family. I have spent many long nights wondering if she is still with her adoptive parents, and whether she remembers me at all. I made many attempts to see her, but unfortunately the adoptive parents cut me off. Perhaps they feared what I might bring to their family life as a 'mad, bad, woman'. Oddly, about three years ago, I woke up in the night almost choking and feeling a great sense of fear that something had happened to my daughter. I was convinced that she had been hurt, but I had no way of checking at all, so I just had to try to forget about it as life went on.

From time to time I went back to my town of birth and bumped into people connected to my family of origin. I ended up being threatened and actually beaten up by one of my half-brothers. The old fear was still there: that I would bring disrepute on their family. I was literally run out of town. Nowadays I can understand that these people treated me like a scapegoat for their family's problems. It's difficult to forgive them, although I do try to. Although I had no control over the circumstances of my birth, they somehow held me responsible for it. I heard that my father had now married a new, much younger woman, and started a whole new family back home, abandoning Veronica in the UK – who died of a broken heart. Nothing new there then.

In my darkest hours, I continue to wish for a family, for a place to belong, for someone to love me and to have someone to love (apart from my gorgeous son, of course). I have not been able to form romantic relationships very easily, as I have felt it to be too painful to be vulnerable with someone else. I'm not sure if I know yet what healthy love is – let alone sex. However, I have begun to form friendships slowly with both men and women, and although it is a painful process for me, as I find it hard to trust and disclose things about myself, I am gradually learning how to do all those social things that I never got a chance to do earlier in life. Luckily, I have a wicked sense of humour and that gets me a long way. I recently joined an Afro-Caribbean society in the city where I am now living, something I would not have dared to venture into before. This time, it has proved to be a very welcoming and positive experience. Perhaps I am gradually beginning to feel that there is a place for me – and for us – after all? I have recently got myself my first proper job, working to support people who work in the mental health system. It's certainly something I know about and it turns out that I am doing well. And I am now saving up to buy a house, so I can provide a proper home for my son and me.

The reason for me finally writing this book is not only to put the record straight (I started it as far back as 1994), but also as a way of letting go of my extraordinary past. I hope by setting it down, I will be able to lay things to rest, and finally move on. I still have to live with the legacy of my childhood experience, but I don't want it to define me for the rest of my life. I want to help to change the world for the better, especially where the treatment of young people and black people is concerned. I want to help people shake off the negative labels that get attached to them, and which limit their lives in a negative way. It's time for us all to move on, isn't it?

However, my heart has still hankered after seeing my beautiful daughter again. I wondered whether to put my name or a letter on a national register and wait to see if she wanted to contact me. I have spent many hours wondering what to do, or whether I should try to let it go. Then someone told me about Facebook and as I can now use a computer, I found myself looking at it recently out of curiosity, and something impetuous made me type in my daughter's name. I've always remembered her adoptive name. There she was! To my absolute amazement her profile popped up. Suddenly, she was grinning back at me from the screen, now a fully grown, absolutely beautiful twenty-one-year-old. I burst into tears and kissed the screen. I touched her screen face with my fingers – she was alive and she looked well. What an amazing beauty she had grown into. My beautiful daughter. Still living, it seemed, in the city she had gone to over fifteen years ago.

I spent several days wondering what to do about it, wrestling with whether I was being selfish in wanting to contact her or not. What if her life was wonderful? What if everything was perfect and she didn't want to know about the sad old mum she'd left behind? What if she was happy and settled – what right did I have to disturb her life? Would she want to know me? Would she remember me? Would her parents be furious if I contacted her? And then I thought, she's twenty-one – an adult. She can decide for herself.

Gingerly, I typed a short message on her Facebook page. I thought, well, if I write something simple she can ignore it or delete it. My heart was in my mouth and I didn't sleep all night. Next day, there was a message saying, 'Hello, I've never forgotten you, Mum. I'd love to be in touch.' Tears trickled down my cheeks in an unstoppable flow, as I read about her life. I thought my heart would burst. I did a little dance round the living room. When my son came home from school, I showed him her picture. The similarity between them was obvious and he was thrilled.

After all, his family is very small indeed – just we two – so another addition would be great for him too.

My daughter and I exchanged many emails over the next few days and I discovered that the very night, three years ago, when I woke up feeling scared about her safety she had in fact been in a very serious car crash and had been in intensive care. She'd nearly died. Apparently she had called out for 'Mummy, Harmony Mummy' when she was fighting for her life. We had really bonded back then and I was heartened that, despite all the problems and the years in between, we still loved each other. A connection remained that was stronger than the prejudice that had torn us apart.

On my fortieth birthday I had a wonderful family dinner with my daughter, my son, and my four-year-old grandson, Thomas – a child she had herself at seventeen. We spent the evening laughing, telling stories, hugging, crying, holding hands, giggling and eating loads of lovely Chinese food. It was the most amazing birthday present for me: that magical evening with my new-found daughter and her son, my grandson.

I soon began to find out about Anna Bella's life as we exchanged emails and texts. She had had a good upbringing with the African couple who were very strict, but loving, and she had done well in school. She had been to university and was now earning well as a professional. I was amazed. She was a sweet, kind girl, although she said she hadn't had very good relationships with men and had left the father of her child. I felt bad hearing that, and wondered if I had contributed to that somehow. She noticed me look thoughtful.

'It's not your fault Mum,' she said, 'I'm grateful for the parents I had, but I'm also really proud to have you as my mum. It means so much to me to be here with you two. Don't worry, you're not to blame.'

We all laughed and relaxed. We had a lot of stories to exchange, and when she came to stay with my son and me for a weekend soon after my birthday I was amazed at how well we got on. She was a kind, gracious, intelligent girl and, despite my own pain of losing her for all those years, she had had a good childhood, totally unlike mine. That made me feel some of the pain had been worthwhile. I was only relieved that she had ended up with good people, who had clearly loved her and taken good care of her. Now we have a lot of catching up to do, and I have to take it one day at a time, as we learn to fit into each others' lives. Hopefully, we have a lifetime to do it in. Now I have my son, daughter and grandson in my life.

My own family at last.

Despite everything, I now know, deep down in my heart, that I finally have somewhere to belong.

AFTERWORD

The reason I felt compelled to write this book was to highlight the long-term effects of abuse on children, with the hope that in relating my own personal experiences I might help bring someone else's terrible suffering to an end.

We, as a society, have reacted against the threat of child abuse by putting up barriers between people. Today there are so many restrictions on closeness between children and adults that working with young people can feel like walking across a minefield. I find it devastating that a teacher is no longer allowed to cuddle a child in their care, even if they're hurt or upset. What are we saying to children when we make rules like this? Do we really believe that outlawing caring human contact will stop paedophiles from hurting children?

I know from bitter experience that this is not the case. The problem with this sort of legislation is that people come to believe that their children are protected; that the laws mean that nothing bad can happen to them. I believe that instead of relying too much on legislation we need to work together as a society to create a safe environment for our young people.

It breaks my heart to think that child abuse is still going on in the twenty-first century. Even with all the new technology and ways of communicating we've developed, children still aren't being heard. We have to learn to stop and listen to what our children say and see the way they behave, and not be too quick to label them as troublemakers, without finding out what might be causing their 'bad' behaviour. We must spend time with them – really get to know them – so if they are ever hurting or frightened, they'll know they have someone to talk to; someone they can trust; someone they know cares.

For years now our prisons, secure units, children's homes and psychiatric hospitals have been full of abused and confused people. This has got to stop before more troubled lives are wasted. By telling my story I want to open people's eyes to the suffering of thousands of angry young people who have slipped through the net.

We read in the papers every day about youngsters killing and being killed in our streets. These are often youths who don't know how to deal with their feelings of hostility and sense of being on the margins. Some end up in gangs, where they get a sense of respect and belonging – until someone crosses them, or else looks at them the 'wrong way'. All it takes is a tiny trigger for their insecurities to come flooding back, and then, in a moment of madness, lives are destroyed forever.

The newspapers are full of stories of tragic wastes like this. Now's the time for us to start asking difficult questions: Who loves these kids? What makes them go wrong? And how can we help them choose a different path?

I believe we all have a collective responsibility to provide more for all our young people – especially the angry confused ones. Yes, they desperately need youth centres, walk-in clinics, training and incentive programmes. But most of all they need someone to listen to them and take their problems seriously.

We all have a role to play in our society. We look at our children and we worry about the future, wondering if things will improve for their generation. It's up to all of us to make sure it does, and that no child ever has to suffer in silence. If children live in an atmosphere of praise, stability, love and understanding, they have the chance to grow up into successful adults who have a real feeling of esteem and self-worth. Sadly, without this start in life, they are much more likely to manifest feelings of anger, bitterness, resentment, and self-loathing.

We also need to extend the same concern and support towards adults who have been victims of childhood abuse in the past. We need to help them to take back control over their own lives. This means acknowledging that while their memories will always be there, we can try to take away their power to cast a shadow over their lives.

I spent so much of my life being angry – towards my foster parents, towards Social Services, but mostly towards myself. I found it hard letting people get close to me, and even when I did, I'd keep testing them to see if they really did care about me. It became a vicious circle where I'd push away anyone who was trying to help me. When I read reports of young people acting out, I understand what they're going through. Like me, they're just doing their best to survive any way they can.

The bottom line is that everyone needs someone – especially the so-called 'problem kids'. We are all a product of the environment we grew up in, and it's up to all of us to offer encouragement and a sympathetic ear to the next generation.

I hope that this book will make people sit up and think about the society we're living in, and their own relationship with their children. I also hope it might contribute to a change in 'the system' for the better. Most importantly, I hope it will offer comfort to victims of abuse and inspire others who may be suffering in silence to come forward and seek help.

Harmony Brookes
2009